OUR HORSES, OURSELVES:

DISCOVERING THE COMMON BODY

Meditations and Strategies for Deeper
Understanding and Enhanced Communication

Paula Josa-Jones
CMA, RSMET, SEP

Foreword by Linda Tellington-Jones

TRAFALGAR SQUARE
North Pomfret, Vermont

First published in 2017 by
Trafalgar Square Books
North Pomfret, Vermont 05053

Disclaimer of Liability
The author and publisher shall have neither liability nor responsibility to any person or entity with respect to any loss or damage caused or alleged to be caused directly or indirectly by the information contained in this book. While the book is as accurate as the author can make it, there may be errors, omissions, and inaccuracies.

Trafalgar Square Books encourages the use of approved safety helmets in all equestrian sports and activities.

Library of Congress Cataloging-in-Publication Data
Names: Josa-Jones, Paula, author.
Title: Our horses, ourselves : discovering the common body : meditations and
    strategies for deeper understanding and enhanced communication / Paula
    Josa-Jones.
Description: North Pomfret, Vermont : Trafalgar Square Books, 2017. |
    Includes bibliographical references and index.
Identifiers: LCCN 2015031435 | ISBN 9781570767524
Subjects: LCSH: Somesthesia. | Human-animal relationships. |
    Horses--Psychology.
Classification: LCC QP448 .J67 2017 | DDC 615.8/51581--dc23 LC record available at https://
lccn.loc.gov/2015031435

All photographs by Jeffrey Anderson except pp. 20, 22, 53, 55, 82, 90, 91, 98 bottom right, 113, 137, 138, 139, 140, 144, 145, 148, 150 bottom, 159, 160, 165, 178 bottom, 184, 185, 188, 197 top, 208, 209, 210, 218, 231 top, 235, 237, 239, 261 (Pam White), pp. 43, 193, 232, 253, 257 bottom (Paula Josa-Jones), pp. 59, 60 (Miha Fras with permission of Marion Laval-Jeantet), p. 63 (courtesy of John Killacky), p. 65 (Nelson Photography), p. 66 (Brad Pettengill), p. 68 (Jean Cross), p. 74 (Steve Hopkins), p. 78 (courtesy of Sheila Ryan), p. 98 bottom left (Susie Cushner; pottery by Joan Platt), p. 119 (Dragan Beljan: https://grabcad.com/library/cube-with-diagonals), p. 120 (Pietr Kers), p. 150 top (Susan Fieldsmith), pp. 163, 243 (courtesy of Ann Carlson), pp. 168, 257 top, 258, 259 (courtesy of Gillian Jagger),pp. 196, 199, 200 (Jon Katz), p. 197 bottom (Maria Wulf), p. 198 (Kim Gifford), pp. 217, 220, 221 (Henri Ton), p. 223 (Ward Ritter), p. 231 bottom (unknown artist), p. 266 (Franz Marc)

Book design by DOQ
Cover design by RM Didier
Typefaces: Bembo, Scala Sans Pro

Printed in China

10 9 8 7 6 5 4 3 2 1

For the horses and their humans

CONTENTS

FOREWORD

This year I will celebrate my eightieth birthday—an amazing number that doesn't intimidate me one bit! In fact, I am so, so looking forward to all the delightful ways I will get to honor the many truly special people and animals I have connected with, as well as all those I have yet to meet. After all, that is what my life has been about—meeting and connecting with others as I've traveled the world sharing the Tellington Method and all I believe it can do to help humans, horses, and other animals understand each other, and learn and grow together in good company.

When I first started this journey as a horsewoman, and later, when I wrote my bestselling book *Getting in TTouch*, it was unusual to be on the road many months of the year as I was, teaching at clinics and symposiums, and writing down methods for others to learn and use. Only a few of us did it regularly. Today it is far more common: we see so many trainers and new techniques, it can be hard to know where to look. And when you *do* think you know where to look, you might not know where to start. It is for this reason that Paula Josa-Jones's book is a breath of fresh air! It is all about where any one of us with a true desire to really *be* with horses, to partner with them in work, pleasure, or competition, should begin.

I know Paula as she has attended a number of my clinics over the years. She is a seeker of connection, like I am, and a true student of horsemanship in that she has an open mind and is extremely in tune to her own body—a result of her lifetime as a dancer, choreographer, and artist. Her background gives her a genuinely unique vantage point when it comes to the physical and emotional self we bring to our horses. And it is her intense investigation of movement and somatics—a field within bodywork and movement studies that emphasizes internal physical perception and experience—that has led her to discover new avenues of understanding: not only how to be when around and on horses, but how the horse-human relationship can profoundly affect us, change us, and help us be better partners, parents, workers, and friends. Through the many exercises in this book, Paula shows us how to explore our bodies and our minds in ways that may seem foreign at first, but I can tell you it's really worth staying with it. What you learn here can give you a foundation of self-knowledge and self-assurance that then provides the ultimate base for horsemanship *with heart*—something I strongly advocate in *all* my teachings.

What Paula has provided in this book is a wonderful complement to the Tellington Method components of TTouch bodywork, groundwork, and ridden work. The stories and philosophies she shares will open new pathways in your life with horses. The exercises will help you learn to know yourself better, inside and out, and with this new insight you will discover how to know your horse better, too.

I love, love, love this book, and believe it is a valuable asset to the world of riders. I hope you love it as much as I do!

Linda Tellington-Jones
Kailua-Kona, Hawaii

PREFACE

I believe that when you are ready, horses will find you. They can sense your need and they come. Their beauty, their power, their deep stillness can—some studies show—change the very molecular structure of who you are in an instant. I have felt this.

From an early age, my hunger for horses was obsessive—like smoke or thick lava seeping into everything; serial ambushes by passion and longing. *Black Beauty* destroyed me. I read Walter Farley until wild stallions ran through every moment, waking and sleeping, and when those books ran out, I looked for more. I yearned for their bodies, for the smell and touch of horses.

My early horse memories are like a series of dark snapshots. On my aunt and uncle's farm in Sioux Falls, South Dakota: *I am lifted onto the broad, thick-coated back of an old pinto pony.* I don't remember moving—just the thrill of sitting high up on a breathing being, and the smell of his damp, wooly coat. *I bend over a paint-by-number kit of a Palomino's head, filling in the neat little patches of blond, brown, and tan, my brush lingering around the lovely eye, parsing the mystery of this horse, number by number.* I was fearful, tentative, dreaming of dancing and riding, touching horses. *In the fall we go for a trail ride somewhere west of St. Paul at a ranch where tired horses with hard mouths and no hope wait, heads drooping, tied to posts, anonymous as porters.* In an old Super 8 film: *My mother, sister, and I stand at a fence. There are a dozen ponies, nuzzling us across the barbed wire.* I am startled to see my mother's hands trailing gently over their bodies. I had not remembered that she cared at all for horses.

In Hindu mythology, it is said that Uchchaihshravas, a seven-headed, winged, snow-white horse, was one of the fourteen precious jewels created when the "ocean of milk" was churned by Lord Vishnu and became the salty sea. By the time horses truly found me, I had been churned from milky youth to salty adulthood. I was ready for salvation.

We were living on Martha's Vineyard, off the coast of Massachusetts. I had begun to notice the horses—standing in fields, moving across the island land-scapes, their bodies like a moving bridge between the stillness of the rolling hills and the swirling ocean beyond. I saw barns, people riding, and soon found myself in a tack store, stroking the smoothness of a saddle, picking up brushes, halters, boots. Seeing and feeling the horses around me, I wasn't looking for an abstract or contemplative experience. I wanted to wrap my legs around a horse, stroke a horse, get dirty, get close and then closer still. I wanted to ride horses, but also to smell them, touch them, be changed by them, literally *moved* by them.

Author and horsewoman Mary Midkiff says, "We ride to find excitement and danger and power and freedom. We ride to explore the outside world and the one inside ourselves. We ride as a form of expression and communion and escape. We ride to enjoy their bodies."[1] Moving toward the horses, I knew that I wanted to discover their bodies and in the process find my own. Waking and dreaming, I felt the horses moving toward me. Then, one Sunday, I happened to drive by the Agricultural Hall in West Tisbury. In a big outdoor arena a carousel of little girls in velvet hats, snug navy jackets, and shiny boots went round and round and up and over jumps, each perched on an impossibly lovely pony. I stopped and watched, leaning against the fence in the shade at the far end of the arena, away from the crowd, which was good because then others could not see me start to shiver and then weep when the gorgeous curve of one mahogany bay's neck caught me by surprise, undoing me completely. Suddenly, I could feel myself arching backward into the deep, hungry waters of my childhood love for horses.

I asked a friend about riding lessons, and she said, "Go see Susan." Susan Fieldsmith was a wise woman with a backyard barn and a pretty little white horse named Tilly, among others. I watched amazed as Susan's daughter and her best friend, both thirteen, both named Mariah, mucked stalls, brushed their horses, tacked up, rode, cleaned bridles, bits, girths, saddles. They were sassy and easy the way thirteen-year-old girls can be when they are horse-crazy. I felt awkward and shy.

I began to take riding lessons. Because I had been dancing for so many years and my hip joints were badly worn, riding was hard and painful, but I persisted because it seemed that now I needed to smell and touch a horse every day. There was something so urgent and essential about the new rhythms: the rocking of the walk, the heart-pumping trot, and the rolling waves of the canter. On a horse I felt that my body was coming home...to something unfamiliar and yet deeply known. I had been called, and now I was being carried.

After these many years, on the days when I do not know what else to do, or when I have reached the end of a certain line of writing or dancing, I go to the horses. There is nothing like it. In their presence, I can breathe again. Sitting on the horse restores rhythm, balance, and steadiness to my body and my mind. But really the riding is secondary. I only need to be in their presence. They send their knowing deep into the cave of my body and find what is essential and true there. To them, my words are like rain or the chattering of the birds outside—it is not what they listen to. Instead, I can feel them reaching into me, winnowing the true from the false in the quake of my heart and the threads of my breath. They are "feel-seeing" me, and in that, they sift me free of the distraction that I carried there on my sleeves, in my hair, in the crevices of my busy mind. They tell me that quiet is best.

Here it is then. They have found me. I have found them. They teach me, every day, what it is to be still and to steady my heart. I have been etched and carved into wholeness by horses, one breath, one touch, one step, one ride, and one dance at a time.

Paula Josa-Jones

Our Horses, Ourselves

INTRODUCTION

One of my teachers, the horseman Mark Rashid, is a black belt Aikido master and guides his students from the perspective that riding, like Aikido, is hard because you have to change yourself, and that it works well *if you get yourself right*. This book is about this idea: how body-mind practices can help you *get yourself right*, so that when you are with your horse, you can listen to him and approach him from a place of generous and good intention, as well as an active awareness of what and how we are communicating from moment to moment.

Learning to connect with horses in this way teaches us how to develop our inner selves, become more comfortable in our own skin, be more trustworthy to ourselves and others, and gain greater skill, sensitivity, and resilience in social communication. With their help we can soften physical resistance and open wells of enthusiasm and creativity. Horses can help us learn that losing and finding balance is an integral part of life's dance. That we can, like surfers, find, lose, and re-find balance on the crests and troughs of even the biggest waves, the most turbulent emotional and physical waters. They can help us to release our fears, our hesitancy, and become comfortable "on the edge," where answers and inspiration arise spontaneously from an open, curious, and attentive mind and body.

Each of the meditations and strategies in this book—noted with a "Try This" throughout—is intended to nourish some aspect of *getting yourself right* and then *getting right with your horse*, because it is there, in that relationship, that we can find the means to overcome physical and emotional limitations. We can discover the horse as shelter, a place of refuge and support, as well as the gateway to regularly attaining pleasure and joy.

The stories and exercises in the pages ahead provide a means to better engaging the horse's cooperation. They introduce skills that, while centered in *your* body, can ultimately help the horse that avoids, tunes out, or refuses to connect. They hone a sense of when to move and when to wait, teaching you to be a better listener, and more creative and resourceful in your training and riding.

These meditations and strategies grew from many years of dancing, riding, teaching, and "working the clay" of my own body in partnership with my dancers and students and horses. They are not a checklist, but are meant to be consumed slowly, savored, and returned to as often as desired. What that means is that you may stay with one exercise for a day, a week, a month. They are about deepening feeling and expression in your body, helping you to create greater physical and emotional balance, thus opening new doors of communication with others, whether horse or human.

They will help to:

- Develop a consistent feeling of softness and connection in all aspects of your life and your horsemanship.

- Learn how to track your own body and increase its sensitivity, enjoyment, resilience, and wisdom.

- Build feelings of confidence, mindfulness, and a spirit of improvisation.

- Connect with your horse using bodily practices that are intuitive and playful, both on the ground and in the saddle.

- Create physical and emotional balance for both you and your horse.

Recently a friend introduced me to a book about the "wood wide web"—how trees are connected through the network of their roots, including the microscopic fungi that live on and around the roots in a symbiotic relationship with the trees. The roots and the fungi constitute a vast communication system that allows the trees to share resources and send one another information.

I believe that humans and horses are like that "wood wide web," profoundly interconnected, but that we often don't know that we are actually communicating or exchanging with each other. My hope is that by "waking up" the body and the mind we will begin to hear each other all the more clearly.

CHAPTER ONE

THE COMMON BODY:
SHARING BREATH, BODY, AND EARTH

A sky. A field. A hedge flagrant with gorse.
I'm trying to remember, as best I can,
if I'm a man dreaming I'm a plowhorse
or a great plowhorse dreaming I'm a man.

THE SENSUAL BODY

One morning after a swim, I sat at my breakfast and could not eat. I felt myself riveted in a river of sensations: the remnants of the water's touch, my deepened breathing, the resiliant stretch of muscle, bone, and fascia in the swimming strokes, the soft envelope of the water holding the equally soft envelope of my skin, my watery body indistinguishable from the surrounding water.

The *Common Body* means that the body and mind of the horse and the human are joined at the deepest levels: anatomically, energetically, psychically, spiritually, and emotionally. Understanding the Common Body begins with discovering our sensual selves in the way I did that morning: experiencing the rush of the blood, the liquid flow within and between the cells, the columns of bone, the rich thrust of muscle, the elastic connectivity of tendon and ligament. Beyond the anatomical dimension lies another world—a carnal linguistics related to sight, sound, touch, smell, taste, and movement. And still further within are the mystical depths of the body, explored and revealed by the writer, the dancer, and the artist. Realizing the Common Body means *listening* and *feeling into* these layers, to the subtle, hidden, and utterly unexpected bodily revelation that can go unnoticed in the rush and tumult of our normal, daily lives.

Jane Hirshfield is an equestrian, a practitioner of Zen meditation, and a prize-winning international poet, translator, and essayist. Her subject is often the horse, but in her poems, the horse often stands for aspects of our own human experience: what it means to be human, to live in a body, to be a feeling resident of the earth. When I asked her about the ways in which horses have taught her, she said: "To be fully truthful, horses have taught me as much about my body's awkwardness as about its sensuous capacities and depths—if there's a stiffness born of fear or simple inelasticity, if there's any lack of balance, if the mind's ideas or hopes interfere with the rhythms of what actually is, being with a horse amplifies that failure into awareness. Failure, of course, is a gift. Awareness that

Our Horses, Ourselves

Dancer Ingrid Schatz inviting "Pony" to join her in the dance.

something's not right is the only way we can know that something in us needs to change. And then, in those moments of perfect union, the rare times when a flow is continuous between horse and person, when there is no separation between horse and person, well that stays in a life, its remembering rings like a summoning bell. 'This is possible—how do I find it?'"

Hirshfield also finds that there is an extraordinary opportunity that comes in working with horses from the ground, and that the relationship of two beings with their feet on the earth is as revelatory as the one found in riding.

"There's the exhilaration of body language in liberty work, where the horse moves freely, and the person stays on the ground," she says. "It teaches the immaculate precision of movement among creatures who don't live in words, how fully movement is meaning. The smallest change of expression or eye focus, the dip of a shoulder, and a gallop turns into a sliding stop. Ears pinpricked, nostrils blowing, all that wind-energy comes stepping toward you, almost on toe tips, he's so ready to spring off again. But he does not. He comes, he stands, he dips his head toward the ground...and just as you've changed his energy, he changes yours. It's as if you shared a single circulation system of blood and nerves, the change of body and body is so intimately, immediately shared."

THE HUMAN AND THE HORSE

I have been a dancer, as well as a lover of horses, most of my life. Much of that time was, in a way, an out-of-body experience. Years of dance training meant pushing the body, often with very little awareness of what it was telling me about pain, limitation, and feeling. My body was first and foremost an instrument, and I expected it to work. When I found myself hungering to "dance" with horses—not just ride them but draw together my two great passions—it was then I discovered that it was the horses that brought me most deeply *into* my body. Horses have taught me many lessons, including how to feel my body in startling detail. They have helped me to notice my emotions, and become more aware, expressive, and focused in the present moment. That connection can give us a more embodied, intuitive, and heartful relationship with each other and ourselves. To be *embodied* means that we are experiencing our bodies in a feeling, conscious way—that we are listening to intelligence and insight that arise from the body itself, rather than from cognitive learning alone. We are *feeling into*, rather than only *thinking about*.

The Horse Connection

What is it about the horse? Why does he have such a magnetic appeal for millions of people? Horses are mythic, beautiful, and big. We revere them and we fear them. They are planted deep in our psyches—in a field, on film, in dreams—capturing the dancing light of our consciousness, memory, and imagination. Horses, like us, are playful, social, but unlike us, completely, utterly present. They are not distracted by the past or the future. They possess an intricate kinesthetic language that is revealed in their keen sense of touch, movement, and sensory perception. Among horses, signals get passed almost invisibly with movement, breath, and subtle shifts in energy. A twitch of an ear, a glance, a sudden start, or a deepening stillness, all travel in currents through the herd: "Look out!" "Better grass here." "Get away from my mare!" "Follow me." While we humans, too, live in "herds," we tend to think of and experience ourselves as individuals with independent lives essentially separate from one another. Because we are continually thinking, analyzing, second-guessing, making assumptions—much of which overrides our intuitive, bodily knowing—we are actually less adept at reading signals and decoding the subtleties of others' behavior and meaning.

To live fully *in* your body is to enter what poet James Wright calls "wild arenas we avoid." Horse trainer, philosopher, and writer Vicki Hearne says that most humans lack a clear vocabulary and syntax of the body—we don't understand its language fully or always communicate well with it. Learning about horses—their nature, their physicality, their ways of sensing and perceiving—can carry us into Wright's "wild arenas" and open us to a greater depth of somatic experiencing where we more fully inhabit every moment.

Congruent vs. Incongruent

Horses are profoundly attuned to humans, in part because we are predators. They are continually reading our behavior and intentions through the expression of our bodies and psyches. They can discern in us layers of feeling that we are not aware of. The predator is wily and subversive: he does not want others to know what he is planning. As prey animals, however, horses are, by necessity, keen observers and interpreters of their world. Reading their environment is key to their survival. They are wary, alert, and intuitive.

The prey animal is *congruent*, meaning that his inside feelings and intentions *match* his outside expressions and behaviors. His responses are *authentic* because he does not dissemble or have hidden motives. Humans—predators—are often *incongruent*: feeling one way and acting another, our bodies and behaviors mirroring our habits and unconscious thought patterns. These are felt by our horses, who in turn reflect these unexpressed, contradictory emotions back to us, mirroring what we might be feeling but perhaps are not showing or want to conceal.

For example, when you are riding a horse and *acting* brave but *feeling* fearful or anxious, the horse reflects your fear because that is what is "true" in that moment. His reaction shows you are out of sync, that your inner and outer expression is discordant. When you learn to pay attention to the horse's behaviors, you can become more aware of your emotional landscape and its relationship to what you are expressing outwardly. In this biofeedback, our horses provide us rich and fertile soil for observing and understanding ourselves, and unraveling the unconscious mysteries of our bodies and minds, showing us how *thoughts* become *things*. They offer us the opportunity to shift our minds and bodies away from what we fear and toward what we want to create in our lives.

Amadeo and Henry: Lessons in Congruence

My horse Amadeo has taught me a lot about congruence versus incongruence. For years, I could not figure out why he was so jumpy, fearful, and explosive when I rode him. I saw that my trainer had no such difficulties when she rode Amadeo—he was relaxed and quiet, easily moving through even the more upper level movements that I yearned to master. I had suffered a concussion from a fall several years before and often felt fragile and vulnerable with Amadeo. Eventually I understood that he was reflecting and embodying *my* emotions: I was acting calm on the outside, but inside I felt terrified that he would bolt or spook, and I would fall off and be hurt.

I saw the same thing with my friend Elsa. Her horse Henry was spooky and reactive when she brought him out of his stall to groom him and tack him up. While usually confident, Elsa became tentative and ungrounded as she moved around her horse. Her breathing was tight and irregular; her hands fluttered as she brushed Henry's body—and then his eyes widened with concern, his head

LETTING THE BREATH BREATHE ITSELF

🕐 10 MINUTES

PURPOSE: By inviting the various parts of the body to breathe—finding breath not just in the lungs, but at the cellular level—we encourage a more differentiated self-awareness of the local tissues of the body. Developing awareness of the sensation of the breath in the individual parts of our bodies supports a softness of the whole that transmits effortlessly to our horses, dissolving the separation between their bodies and ours, and connecting inner and outer awareness.

1. Close your eyes and bring your attention to your breathing with a soft, receptive mind.

2. Allow the breath to softly enter the body, then flow easily out. Be aware of the air outside your body entering with each inhale, and the air from inside your body becoming part of the atmosphere around you as you exhale. Feel this rhythm as a continual commingling of inner and outer. Let the breath *breathe itself*, without your needing to shape or change it in any way.

3. Open your eyes and continue to be conscious of your breathing while noticing what is around you.

came up, ears pricked forward. Henry was reading Elsa's physical language, and his nervous responses were directly related to her uncertain, quick, breathless movement. Slowing her touch, connecting her breathing down through her legs and feet, becoming aware of any tension in her body, and adding a quality of depth and feeling to her touches changed Henry's breathing in minutes. His body visibly relaxed as Elsa gained confidence and steadiness in her movements.

Learning to be congruent, like horses, makes us more trustworthy—to ourselves and to others—and more comfortable in our own skins. We become more attuned to the "currents" passing among us, more able to blend, empathize, and act with balance, sensitivity, and kindness. Each of the exercises in this book aims to support these ideals.

"In" vs. "Out"

Humans often struggle with how to have *inner awareness*—how to notice and feel what is happening in their bodies—while at the same time being aware of

4. Close your eyes again, maintaining awareness of what is around you and the sounds you hear.

5. Continue to slowly open and close your eyes, aware of the inner and outer dimensions of both your breathing and your vision. Can you sense both "in" and "out" at the same time?

6. Now feel the sensation of the breath *in your hands*; then the sensation of the breath *in your feet, your ankles and knees*. Simply focus your awareness on the presence of breath in these parts of the body. Move your awareness *inside your body* and to the feeling of the cells breathing themselves. Rest.

7. Breathe into the whole envelope of your skin, from the soles of your feet to the crown of your head. Feel your body as a long, soft column of breath. Imagine your breath moving through the pores of your skin.

8. Standing next to your horse, settle your hands on his neck or hip. Let the sensation of your hands "breathing" transmit to his body and the sensation of breath in that part of *his* body transmit back to you. Imagine going "under the tone" (not just the muscles, but the organs and other tissues) to find a quality of resting, where both of you let the breath *breathe itself*.

the outer world. Most of us feel that in order to go "inside" we must close our eyes or in some other way shut out the outside world. We feel that when we come "out" somehow, the "in" goes away.

Horses, however, are neither "in" nor "out." For them "inner" and "outer" are essentially inseparable. Because they are not distanced from their experience by *analytical* thinking and *verbal* language, their understanding is a seamless blending of the experience of *within* and *without*.

Humans can experience this confluence of inner and outer awareness in several ways. We can focus on sensation within the body as we maintain a sensory awareness of the sights, sounds, smells around us. We can follow the inflow and outflow of the breath. For many of us, however, this experience of focused awareness may disappear when we move into action.

According to Body-Mind Centering® (BMCSM) originator Bonnie Bainbridge Cohen, "Awareness is the motor act." What I believe she means is that we need awareness for movement to happen naturally; that it is actually *through the awareness* that we move. If you feel your leg, you can move it, but without awareness of the leg, it is a most difficult task. Awareness is *more* than noticing or thinking—it is a sensory, perceptual process that allows us to more fully experience our bodies and minds, and a necessary precursor to somatically conscious action.

According to BMC practiner Toni Smith, "The nervous system is organized as a 'sensory motor loop' in which information comes into the body-mind via the senses (the five senses plus vestibular). It is interpreted or perceived in the brain and then responses are 'motored out' via the nervous system. To develop awareness we have to be engaged in the act of 'seeking,' 'looking,' 'focusing,' or 'motoring out.' For example, if I want to *become aware* of my breath, I must consciously seek sensory information. I could focus on the rhythm of breathing, the sensation of air in the nose, the movement of the diaphragm, the expansion and diminishment of the lung tissue. I will not become aware of my respiration without the 'act of searching for sensation information.' Awareness does not happen automatically on its own. It is awarded or becomes known by those who look for it."

Bainbridge Cohen goes on to say that, "The more you awaken to the existence of yourself through breathing, the more you have accessible to then move."[2] She is not talking about just inhaling and exhaling, or about having to breathe. That kind of breathing is connected to the nervous system and can be activating, rather than settling. If a rider is worried about a competition, for example, her bodily tone (muscles, organs, fascia) will be high, and her breath may reflect that. In other words, the function and expression of our movement, as well as our experiencing of ourselves, is inextricably tied to our awareness, not just of the breath, but of all the parts of our bodies. We need self-awareness of every local tissue— including the musculoskeletal system and the organs, the fascia, the cells, and so on—and to bring that awareness to the corresponding part of the horse's body, and thus achieve the true connection with him that we desire. How do we gain this "local awareness"? Through touch, through movement, by listening to and observing our patterns, and by developing a moment-to-moment global and local awareness of our bodies.

As riders, we want the same degree of responsiveness and fluidity from our own bodies that we ask of our horses' bodies. Often though, we ride from our habits and imbalances, which means that local awareness has been lost. By inviting greater awareness into the parts, we can awaken the places that have "fallen asleep," and re-engage them in a more conscious way. In fact, as awareness touches these "frozen" or "lost" places—in our bodies and in the bodies of our horses—they will often *shift themselves*...we don't have to "think them back into alignment" or use effort to achieve easeful functioning.

Our Horses, Ourselves

CONNECTING

Phoebe Caldwell has worked for over 30 years as a practitioner with people whose severe learning disabilities are linked with behavioral distress. I discovered her in the course of working with my autistic godson, Jacob. His mother and I watched a video of Caldwell working with children and young adults using Intensive Interaction[3], her method of engaging and communicating with the autistic person's brain by using signals with which it is so familiar they do not trigger sensory distortions or sensitivities. In the film, Caldwell subtly reflects and responds to the movements and sounds that the autistic child is making.

Over a period of several minutes, we saw one child go from isolated, self-directed withdrawal or compulsive, repetitive, self-stimulating behaviors, to active, engaged, nonverbal connection with Caldwell. In her book, *From Isolation to Intimacy*, Caldwell states, "If I am to have any hope of meeting my partner, I need to learn to attend not only to his or her sensory experience, but also to how he or she receives my sensory messages. I do this by setting aside my own world and entering my partner's, to focus not just with my eyes or ears, how I feel or see or hear—but with all my senses."[4]

My first thought was how similar this is to the way I believe we can better understand and communicate with our horses.

Caldwell goes on to say that we must do this by sliding in "without causing a ripple, so that we do not trigger our partner's anxiety."[5] Reading that, I thought of Jane Goodall and the chimpanzees at Gombe; how she learned not just to imitate chimpanzee behavior, but also to slip seamlessly into their world of movement, sound, and sensing. And of Temple Grandin with her ability as an autistic person to understand that animals—particularly herbivores and prey animals—see the world in pictures, as she does.[6]

"The reason we've managed to live with animals all these years without noticing many of their special talents is simple," writes Grandin. "We can't see those talents. Normal people never have the special talents animals have; so normal people don't know what to look for. Normal people can stare straight at an animal doing something brilliant and have no idea what they're seeing. Animal genius is invisible to the naked eye."

To understand the Common Body—what we as animals share with horses, and with other beings—we need a clearer and richer sense of our own bodies, finding ways to be more multisensory and flexible in our perceptions, less habitual, more exploratory and improvisational. Since we cannot understand what we cannot see or what lies outside of our experience, we need, Caldwell says, a willingness and ability to shift from an "exterior conversation, which is rooted in what we perceive from our own sensory experience" to an "inward conversation of 'self with other,' the focus of which is shifted to an exploration of our partner's experience."[7] With our horses, that means stepping out of our habitual ways of

ENTERING THE RIVER

🕐 10 MINUTES

PURPOSE: Too often we walk our horses to the barn, the paddock, or the arena without consciously inviting them into that transition from one place to another. "Waking up" to connecting while simply walking with our horses is a way to create partnership by shifting our awareness to what Phoebe Caldwell calls an "inward conversation of self and other"—one that harmonizes body and mind of human and horse.

1. Take a walk with a friend, either human or another species.

2. As you walk, begin to feel the similarities between your gaits, the way your rhythms match and echo each other. Simply *feel* the movement of your body, rather than thinking about what you are doing.

3. Consciously shift your own rhythm and pace so that your walking begins to feel more and more aligned with that of your companion.

4. Let your partner's walk summon you into a rhythmic flow, as if you had placed the canoe of your body into the river of your friend's movement.

interpreting their behaviors and our rote responses and assumptions, to listen more deeply for what connects us and for what is being communicated.

With my godson, Jacob, that has meant setting aside any agenda or particular goal when I am with him. I begin with a feeling of openness and attentiveness to what he is doing: how he is using the space, how his body is moving, and how he is responding to me moment to moment. I feel my own breathing and the relative tension or relaxation in my body, and visualize *connecting my breathing to his*. That becomes a baseline for our time together. When he is agitated or I am uncertain what to do next, I return to feeling my breath and connecting to his.

It is the same with my horse Amadeo: as we walk from the barn to the arena, I tune in to our breathing, feeling the way my feet connect to the earth and a synchrony between our walking rhythms. I pay attention to the softness and invitation in my hand on the lead rope or reins. While riding, if I lose the feeling of softness and harmony we had on the ground, we stop and stand, quietly breathing together until I feel that we are once more connected. Then we begin again.

Our Horses, Ourselves

THE LANGUAGE OF THE SOMATIC SELF

What does it mean to be "in the body"? How do we go about becoming *embodied*—that is, fully experiencing the wisdom and expressive potential of our bodies? Why is it important and how can it help us with horses? How does it allow horses to help *us*?

For one thing, the body is a clear and immediate reflection of the mind. Dancer and movement educator Susan Aposhyan says, "By watching the movement of the body, we can see the movement of the mind."[8] Seishindo master Charlie Badenhop writes in *The Language of the Somatic Self*, "At every moment in time your subconscious mind speaks to you through your body, in a language that is as refined, systematic, and complete as your verbal language. Becoming fluent in somatic language can help you to think less, yet know more."

According to Badenhop, the language of the *somatic self* is both highly organized and graced with many fine nuances. "What has happened for most of us is that we have truly forgotten that there is a somatic-emotional experience on which we base our verbal language. Having forgotten this we think that our verbal language is our experience. But in actuality our verbal language is one step removed from our actual experience. It is an abstract description or labeling of our experience."[9]

Horseman and author Monty Roberts spent hours watching feral horses interact in the wild. He realized that horses "communicate extensively and almost entirely using body language: they do make noises but in the natural environment, silence is paramount, because no member of the herd wants to alert predators. The horse's highly developed senses of smell and eyesight play an important part in their communication."[10] As Roberts realized, by utilizing a silent language, horses and humans can relate to each other more effectively, coming into a partnership based on *listening*. What this means is that the meeting of the minds between horse and human is actually a meeting of bodies—a blending of neurons, perception, and cellular intelligence.

Between 60 and 80 percent of our communications with each other and with other beings are nonverbal, spoken in the bodily languages of movement and touch—our conscious and unconscious gestures, postures, physical attitudes, and facial expressions. We are "talking" all the time but often unaware of the subtle dimensions of our exchanges. *This* is the *somatic self*—the bodily, intuitive dimension of our being that reveals itself through our "felt sense" of what is happening moment to moment. Eugene Gendlin, philosopher and originator of Experiential Psychotherapy, used this term to identify the pre-conscious, pre-verbal knowing that arises spontaneously from the continually shifting sensory/emotional landscape of the body. Thomas Hanna created the word "somatics" in 1976 to name approaches to mind/body integration, including movement studies and therapeutic practices that focus on internal physical perception and experience.

To have a more vibrant experience of our connectedness with ourselves and other beings, we must become more fluent in this awareness and expression that is our first and most essential language. Becoming "fully human" means discovering and remembering that *your* body is not separate from *my* body or *your horse's* body...or any other body. Our Common Body is the ground from which compassion and inspiration springs.

BODY-MIND CENTERING®

Body-Mind Centering® (BMC[SM]), developed by Bonnie Bainbridge Cohen, "is an ongoing, experiential journey into the alive and changing territory of the body. The explorer is the mind—our thoughts, feelings, energy, soul, and spirit. Through this journey we are led to an understanding of how the mind is expressed through the body in movement. The qualities of any movement are a manifestation of how the mind is expressing through the body at that moment."[11] BMC is the embodiment and application of anatomical, physiological, psychophysical, and developmental principles, utilizing movement, touch, voice and mind to investigate the body's systems: fluids, organs, endocrine glands, bones, muscles, skin, and connective tissue.

In a movement class with Bainbridge Cohen, she asks us to *move from our fluids*, entering the briney seas of our own bodies—cerebrospinal, lymphatic, cellular, interstitial, venous, and arterial blood—and to allow our feeling of the distinct quality of each fluid to inform our movement and our consciousness. Under her direction I could feel the quiet, resting lake of the cells, the smooth river of venous blood, the weighty pounding of the arterial pulse, the slow hypnotic flow of the cerebrospinal river. I was clearly aware of the unique sensory and consciousness "profile" of each. Bainbridge Cohen says, "The interplay between our conscious and unconscious mind is fluid and flows in both directions all the time. The conscious and unconscious are a continuum of one mind." For many, the unconscious mind erupts through the body as panoply of symptoms and hurts: bodily expressions of what lies unexpressed and unconscious. Bringing consciousness to the body through each of its systems is a way of experientially unraveling and differentiating the Common Body, discovering how our bodies reflect and echo our relationship to the world around us, and in the process, opening us to a universe of feeling, possibility, and understanding. It is a powerful method of *somatic inquiry*—a profound practice of asking a bodily question and listening for the answer.

Several years ago, BMC practitioner and horsewoman Sandra Jamrog came to the barn to help me with my horse Amadeo, who was suffering with a suspensory ligament injury. She showed me how to feel *into* his leg, differentiating with her touch between the ligaments, tendons, bone—even distinguishing between the marrow and periosteum. I watched her hands investigate his body as if she were feel-reading a topographic map: her touch discovering all the subtleties in his leg—little changes in density where the energy did not flow and where she could sense a block in one or more physical structure. I wondered at the time if and how the disruption in Amadeo's body mirrored a disruption in my *own* body or possibly some deeper fracture in the fabric of our relationship.

TRY THIS

FINDING CONNECTION, FEELING THE PATHWAYS

🕑 10 MINUTES

PURPOSE: Too often we feel our bodies as a collection of disconnected parts, or as an undifferentiated whole. That fragmentation or lack of feeling can communicate to our horses in the form of tension or a lack of fluidity and responsiveness. Our *fascia* is a continuous, elastic, connective tissue that connects every part of our bodies. "It both divides and integrates all other tissues and provides them with semi-viscous lubricating surfaces, so that they have independence of movement within established boundaries of the body as a whole."[12] Learning to feel the elastic connectivity in our own bodies helps us find a more harmonious, fluid connection with our horses.

1. Sit or stand comfortably relaxed, with the spine floating gently upward and the legs and feet rooting downward.

2. "Release" your eyes so they can wander where they want. Invite them to explore directions you may not usually look, and allow them to travel in a leisurely way and to linger. Notice how the movement of the eyes, head, and neck transmits in continuous pathways through the rest of the body. For example, if your eyes move diagonally upward and to the right, and then toward the back diagonal, can you feel how that diagonal travels through your body, all the way to your feet? Don't try to create the pathway; simply *notice*. If you feel any kind of obstruction or lack of feeling, just pause and breathe, allowing the breath to softly open a channel of connection.

CONTINUED ▶

3. Slowly raise your right arm, letting your eyes follow your hand as it reaches up. As you do this, feel how that movement travels in a continuous pathway down that side of your body all the way into your right foot. In that extended position, take a moment to gently move your fingers and toes to wake up the distal ends of the body. Become aware of how your lungs support and expand this movement.

4. Repeat on the opposite side, reaching the left arm up, following with your eyes, and feeling the transmission of that movement all the way through the body to your left foot, again noticing how the "contents" of the body support the "container."

5. Now try the same movement of the right arm, but focus on feeling the pathway as diagonal, traveling through the body to the *opposite* leg and foot.

6. Reverse sides, stretching the left arm, connecting contra-laterally to the right foot. Imagine the internal elastic connectivity of the fascia opening to allow this movement.

7. *Feel* all three dimensions of the body as you do these movements: front/back, side/side, up/down, and diagonal. Again, *visualize* the lengthening stretch traveling through the fascial network.

8. On your horse, at the walk, practice this expansive, meandering movement of the eyes, allowing them to move where they want, taking in the details of your horse's body. Be interested in what changes in your body, your awareness, and your horse's movement as your eyes move more freely and expansively.

9. Come to a halt and remove your feet from the stirrups. Holding the reins in your left hand, lengthen your right arm up, following softly with your eyes, and feel that movement traveling down the same side of your body into your right foot.

10. With your feet still out of the stirrups, using the right arm, repeat the lengthening, but feeling the movement diagonally to the foot on the opposite side. Then repeat both movements with the left arm. What changes do you feel in your horse's movement? In your body?

The Body and the Dance

I began dancing seriously in college, and although I didn't realize it fully at the time, dancing was a way of diving into the deep waters of my body, of trying to find myself. What I discovered in dance was a rich and hidden world of emotion, feeling, and expression. In a college production of *The Trojan Women* by Euripides, I played Cassandra, the wild seer. The director, David Mayer, wanted the role to be danced and pushed me to express Cassandra's terrifying visions through movement. Dancing her made her indelible. Years later I can still feel her ferocity and the way my movement pushed the character into the realm of magic and power. I began then to understand that the body was a portal to ways of knowing, feeling, and being that I had barely touched in my youth.

The body is also a muse—a gateway to inspiration. Several years ago I experienced a stunning, sudden absence of creative inspiration. After years of choreographing dances, I felt "dance-less," emptied out, silent, and motionless. I continued to ride and found that over time, the waves of my horse's movement and their simple presence softened my resistance, bringing fluidity, musicality, and inspiration back into my body. By attuning to them, I was able to feel myself more clearly. From my dreams, I began to remember gestures, ways of flying across space as a dancer, all of the images tethered to the rhythms of the horse, to that shared breath and movement—the reciprocal softening of two bodies to each other.

In a movement improvisation class I was taking, teacher Nancy Stark Smith asked us to move, first from our skin, then from our muscles, and finally from our bones. As I moved, I could clearly feel the "voice" of each layer. *Moving from my skin* felt like gliding across a glassy lake, a small eddy here, a complicated backwater flowing under the armpit, across the shoulder, and then a sluice down the back, and I found myself connecting with the whole pliant outer envelope of my body. *Muscle movement* brought a feeling of resistance and power—a tensile, elastic engagement. There was a clear change in my breathing and a heightened energy. *Bone dancing* was like being transported into a whimsical Dia de Los Muertos party, with loose, jangly, unhinged motion—a skeleton blown by wind and music, with a dense stillness at the marrowed center of each limb. With all three explorations I felt more clearly my connection to the earth and the other dancing bodies in the room. Embodying these discrete layers was a way of becoming more aware of and connected to everything around me.

TRY THIS: SKIN, MUSCLE, BONE

⊘ 10 MINUTES

PURPOSE: Skin, muscle and bone are three of the many systems in our bodies that include organs, fluids, nerves, glands, and connective tissues. Learning how to differentiate and move from each of these can help us discover a more sensitive, expressive, and playful quality in our movement, and a richer connection with our horses.

1. Sitting or standing, turn your head to the right, feeling the movement initiated by the skin of your right cheek. Turn to the left initiating from your left cheek.

   Now do the same movement from the skin *inside* the cheek. You may need to gently touch it with your tongue to awaken the sensation there.

2. Raise and lower your shoulders, intentionally engaging the powerful muscles of your shoulders and back. As you do this, clench your fists and feel the muscular engagement through your hands and arms. Release and soften.

   Now raise the shoulders from the skin and notice the difference in the quality of your movement.

3. Lift and lower, or shrug your shoulders from the bony skeletal structure. How does that change the quality of your movement and the quality of expression?

4. Repeat these movements, each time getting clearer about the layer of the body that is initiating. Can you feel the subtle differences? Is there an emotional quality present? Notice what feels the most familiar, the most like "you."

5. Shift your exploration to different parts of the body. For example stand or sit from the whole envelope of your skin, from your skeleton, or intentionally add the power of your muscles to the movement.

6. When you are riding or walking with your horse, play with moving your attention from your muscles to your bones to your skin. Feel the relationship of each of these layers to the corresponding one in your horse. Pay attention not just to the anatomical differences, but the emotional and sensual qualities of each. How do those changes in perception affect your movement and your connection with your horse?

7. As you ride, can you feel these layers of your body receiving sensory information from your horse? Can the sensation of the skin/muscle/bone of your legs on the horses's sides and your hands on the reins be felt in other parts of your body: your back, your throat, your face?

LEARNING TO LISTEN

Horse
With him
here, now
skin to skin
warmth spilling
one into the other.

breaths
a lattice of
drawing in,
drawing out.

the heart is a
cave that holds our
boisterous blood
our twinned pulses
bound in this moment

after all, the only and
most precious.

Paula Josa-Jones

Amadeo, my lovely, complicated Andalusian, is my riding partner and my teacher. When we first met, my hips were failing, worn ragged from years of dancing. Riding had become difficult, and I needed to find a horse partner that was easier on my body than my wide Friesian, Goliath. Just outside of Madrid, I was introduced to Amadeo, a gleaming dark bay. I was able to sit all his gaits—walk, trot, and canter. He was a beautiful, extravagant mover—soft and open in his strides. I felt like I was riding a cloud.

What life with Amadeo has often felt like: chaos and connection, love and connection, and never sure which it will be.

But by the time Amadeo arrived in the United States, sitting on any horse was agonizing for me. I had two successive hip replacement surgeries, and it was nearly eighteen months before I could safely ride again. When finally cleared to mount a horse, my body was a foreign territory. The delicate proprioceptors surrounding my hip joints had been terribly disrupted by the surgeries, my joints replaced with titanium and porcelain. My body did not know where it was in space or motion. Riding Amadeo I was tentative and fearful. He read me perfectly and knew that, "Go," really meant, "Don't," or "Slow." That became our agreement: I asked and he refused. To make matters worse, he was skittish and reactive, perfectly mirroring my newfound nervousness. I struggled with my failures as a rider and my frustrations with this beautiful, inaccessible horse. I had occasional good rides, but mostly it felt as if we were speaking two very different languages. Even as I became stronger and bolder, it seemed that our confused communications were hard-wired.

Amadeo and I moved to a new boarding facility nearer my home. Soon after we had settled in, I took him out of the barn for a graze and to walk around the stable area. On either side of the main barn doors were two large statues of horse heads. As we came back from our walk and were approaching them, I felt him suddenly go "on the muscle." He became 1,200 pounds of tension, fully alert, head up, tail flagged, blowing like a stallion—a timebomb at the end of a rope. My heart pounding, I spoke softly, trying to ease him back inside. Suddenly without warning, he spun and shot out his hind leg—fully extended—slamming his shod hoof into my leg. Everything went black and starry for a moment. All I could manage was to stumble into the barn and melt down the side of the wall as someone took him from me. I was in bed for three days after, unable to walk, and had a hoofprint with an egg-shaped lump of scar tissue in the middle of my thigh for almost two years. I felt betrayed, angry, scared.

Our Horses, Ourselves

After, I felt my anxiety growing on the way to the barn. Our rides felt more like a bitter, old argument than a friendly conversation. I sensed him watching me, waiting. My mind skittered: "I'm not breathing, my mind is rushing, I'm not with him." With each ride, my expectation grew for him to misbehave, stop, or buck, and of course, reading my mind and body perfectly, he did just that. He threw his haunches to the left, curled his neck, tightened his body, and began an exaggerated, stilted, Spanish walk, bucked, or drifted sideways or crowhopped. When my trainer Brandi rode him, he was fluid, moving with ease and elegance. I tried not to take it personally. One day Brandi offered to encourage him to find forward with me in the saddle by motioning with a longe whip from the ground. At first he seemed confused, then he bucked, and trotted briskly off. I gave him a looser rein and in rising trot, followed Brandi's instructions to urge him to *really move forward*. The result was astonishing: he surged into a big, extravagant trot, something that I had rarely experienced with him. I felt nearly out of control, a little scared, and at the same time *thrilled*.

As I came down the long side of the arena toward the mirrors though, I could see that my sternum was dropped and my shoulders slightly braced—a defensive posture that definitely did not say, "Go!" At that moment, I let my breath flow, relaxed my shoulders, and felt another pulse of energy under me. It occurred to me that all this time I had been riding Amadeo with my foot on the accelerator and the brake at the same time.

The problem wasn't that Amadeo was frustrat*ing*, but that I was frustrat*ed*. I remembered the words of my first trainer, Tom Davis, "Your frustration has absolutely no place in your riding." And yet there I was, a dozen years later, my riding stuck in the cul-de-sac of fear and reactivity. I was embarrassed by my own limitations and realized that it was not about making small changes in my riding habits, but about completely changing the nature and the ground of the conversation I was having with my horse. I decided to take a complete break from riding Amadeo. I had to catch my breath, unravel my frustration, and see if I could soften and open the gates to possibility again.

Eight months later I still was not riding Amadeo. Finally, I began to work with him on the ground, longeing him in a big circle on a loose line. My hope was that it might be a way to open a new understanding in our fraught relationship. I wanted to appreciate more about the link between my movement cues and his responses, and to build a more "feeling," body-focused conversation between us. Slowly I began to figure out certain cues, how to express them more clearly with my mind and movement, and to better understand what he was telling me with his responses.

I visited another farm where a trainer who was longeing a horse said to me, "I am waiting to feel his mind in my hands." I immediately understood that she was talking about a bridge between the consciousness and behavior of the horse

Working with Amadeo on the ground helped me "find" him—in my hands and my body.

With Amadeo—walking together, being soft together.

and the sensation and understanding of that in her own body. My next time working with Amadeo was different. I could feel and see when I had him "in my hands" and when I didn't. When I saw his eyes going toward the outside of the arena, looking out the big doors, I softly "sponged" (squeezing and releasing) the longe line with my hand, and thought, *with me*. His inside eye came back to me, and his ear turned in toward me. In that moment I felt that I was listening to him, and that he was also listening to me. I realized I didn't want just his *mind* in my hands; I wanted to feel his whole body, his breathing, his connection to the ground, his focus—and even his distraction and reactivity—so that *my* whole body was a receptive sensor for his.

Focusing this way, I felt no fear. One day a horse walked by the arena as we were working. Amadeo exploded, prancing and blowing like a stallion, all big muscle taut at the end of my line. Miraculously, I did not panic or react, but softly asked him to move forward, and focused on breathing and grounding my own body, repeating mentally, *with me, with me*. Within a few minutes, he was calm.

My friend, the sculptor and painter Peggy Kauffman, once said, "I never sold a horse, I just learned how to ride the horse I had." When she said that, I'd thought, "Yes, but..." because I could not imagine riding Amadeo after so many months of *not* being able to ride him. But as I thought about her words, I began to believe that it might be possible.

THE LETTING GO

*"When we don't know where our support is coming from,
the first thing we do is hold."*

Bonnie Bainbridge Cohen
Movement Artist, Researcher, Therapist

When composer and choreographer Meredith Monk was growing up and learning to ride horses, she thought that riding was about gripping to hold on. Later in life she learned that riding actually has nothing to do with holding on, but rather *letting go*. This "opening" to the animal, its movement, and all the sensations in the body is something that she has needed to learn not only with horses but in all areas of her life.

"It's like letting go of everything, like letting go of any crutch that you have to stay on this huge animal," she says. "It's something about trust and knowing that it has to do with balance. And actually the more relaxed you are the more balanced and aligned you are. The more I stay out of the way of the horse the better rider I am. What I learn from riding now I seem to need to learn from every aspect of my life."[13]

Dropping Your Focus

Eventually I was riding Amadeo again, but we were changed. In the time away from riding, I had let go of much of my anxiety, along with urgency. My focus had dropped into my body; his body. I was paying attention to what I was feeling physically and mentally: to the tension or softness in my hands, the balance or imbalance in my seat, the right and left evenness of pressure of my feet in my stirrups, the feel of the drape of each leg on his sides. My hands: were they quiet or jittery? Did I feel my spine "like a flowing column"? And my sternum: had it "fallen" onto the front of my spine like a clump of heavy wet leaves or was it floating softly, opening to the way my horse was lifting under me? Was I happy

RESTING, FINDING SUPPORT

🕐 10 MINUTES

PURPOSE: In our rushed, highly technological, media-infused world, we rarely take the time to rest and let go deeply and intentionally. These habits of hurrying, and the associated, chronic tension transmits into every part of our bodies, and therefore, our horse's bodies. Allowing for moments of deep rest, consciously releasing our bodies into the support of the floor, or any surface, can be profoundly restorative. Over time, this can help rewire your nervous system, creating a more settled body-mind, which in turn will support a more balanced relationship with your horse.

1. Lie down on your back on the floor in a quiet place, with a folded blanket or towel under your head.

2. Notice where there may be tension or where you feel like you are "holding" your body in a particular position, and allow those parts to yield into the support of the floor. Be aware of the pliant, elastic, skin container of your body, and its contents of bone, muscle, fascia, organ, and fluid. Imagine that your whole body could soften and widen across the floor like a balloon filled with water.

or worried, distracted or focused? When I was frustrated, could I find a way to be more playful and balanced?

At the same time I listened to what Amadeo said to me through his body. Was he tense, braced, sticky in his movement? My answer was always to try to feel any tension in my own body more clearly, to breathe more consciously without straining, and to invite softening from him with my own softness whenever I felt stiffness or resistance. I was looking for more ways to connect the *inside of me* to the *inside of him*. When he was balanced and quietly taking the bit from my hands, holding it steady in his mouth, and moving forward with a feeling of buoyancy and confidence, I felt we were in sync. I could see the arch of his neck and the small fan of lashes on his inside eye. Other times when he fussed and tossed his head, and the reins got "wavy," I could feel that we had fallen out of balance; that I was not *there* in the way that he needed me to be.

Amadeo's ears were like two separate animals: They never waggled, like some horses that are confident and relaxed. His were like wild antennae—one cocked back to me, the other poking out and around anxiously, or both pricking straight

3. Close your eyes, taking time to feel your eyes and eyelids soften, become heavy, and settle back into the supporting concave hollow of the eye sockets.

4. Feel your lips resting on the arch of your teeth. Release any expression from your mouth and face, letting them become spacious and peaceful. Let your tongue soften and widen inside the hollow of your mouth. Allow gravity to release and shift your bottom jaw down toward the floor, at the same time letting the top jaw unhinge and float upward, so that your mouth relaxes slightly open.

5. Release the skin and the inner chambers of your ears so that your hearing expands both inward and outward.

6. Breathe, without shaping the breath, just following the movement of the breath with a soft, open focus.

7. Notice anywhere in the body where you feel restriction or where the breath does not flow. Imagine sending your breath there, and visualize that "closed" place flowing open on the river of your breath.

up toward *something*, looking for trouble. I kept my attention on him, not the trouble, and breathed, thinking, "Don't worry, nothing there, I am here." Suddenly his ears fell apart like two halves of a peach and I felt that he had settled and his mind was back in the game. I listened for the snorts and growls that told me he was breathing and relaxing, his body opening to the movement. When that happened, I relaxed, and my eyes could soften and take in all that was around us: the green fields with their horses, the lines of black fence, ducks on the pond, a truck grumbling by on the road, wisps of clouds in the pale sky, and the thickets of hoofprints in the arena sand. I felt the cold snap of the air on my face, the currents of chill as we moved forward, him in his thick brown coat, me in my layers. I imagined our hearts beating separately...then together and together and together...

COMMON BODY MEDITATIONS

🕙 20 MINUTES

PURPOSE: Imagery, imagination, and simple movement meditations can be a way to connect more deeply with yourself and your horse. Using imagery softens the hard edges of our thinking and moves us toward a more creative and expansive way of experiencing. These three simple meditations remind you to settle yourself and begin where you are, taking the time to be fully present in your relationship with your horse. It is important to drop into "horse time," letting go of any need to hurry. If your time is limited, do just one and feel it fully.

1. Stand still, beside your horse. Be two islands in a sea of air. Imagine all your cells—yours and your horse's—floating in this sea. Feel the connection through both of your legs and feet, extending down into the ground. Feel your horse's hooves connect to the ground in the same way. Listen together to the sounds that you are hearing; the landscape you are seeing together.

Stand beside your horse—two islands in a sea of air.

2. Breathe quietly together. Notice the shared pattern of your breathing, the filling and emptying rhythm of inhalation and exhalation. Feel your breath sluicing into every part of your body and your horse's body. Imagine that breathing dissolves the separateness of your bodies—that you and your horse become a single "landscape."

While near your horse, breathe with him. Just breathe.

3. Walk beside your horse with a relaxed, rhythmic, and steady stride. Be aware of your footfalls and your horse's footfalls. Now, run beside him. Let his movement catch you like a wind. Feel the swirl and eddy of it. Join him; become a herd.

Run with your horse; become a herd.

The "Deep I"

Another way of experiencing the Common Body is through what spiritual teacher and author Eckhart Tolle speaks of as the "Deep I." By this he means a way of looking outward to the world without the references or habitual frames of thinking, personality, personal history, judgment, or analysis. When we look outward from the "Deep I" we are simply present, in a state of awake awareness. We are conscious of being conscious. Riding from the "Deep I" is a way of stepping out of the currents of busy-ness of body and mind and being able to observe the whole, without the limitations of commentary or identification with what we judge to be "good" or "bad." In my experience, this perspective has a "winnowing" effect on our riding—stripping away the habitual, unconscious, and unnecessary habits of body and mind that we carry with us. Resting in the "Deep I" is a portal to "becoming one" with the horse and the moment.

"Owning up to being an animal, a creature of earth. Tuning our animal senses to the sensible terrain: blending our skin with the rain-rippled surface of rivers, mingling our ears with the thunder and the thrumming of frogs, and our eyes with the molten gray sky. Feeling the polyrhythmic pulse of this place—this huge windswept body of water and stone. This vexed being in whose flesh we're entangled. Becoming earth. Becoming animal. Becoming, in this manner, fully human."

David Abram
Becoming Animal: An Earthly Cosmology (Pantheon Books, 2010)

THE EARTH AND THE COMMON BODY

During a choreographic residency in Monterrey, Mexico, I visited the harshly beautiful La Huasteca Canyon with composers Pauline Oliveros and Arturo Salinas. We drove deep into the canyon in Arturo's tiny car, following the ragged tracks of other vehicles along the shallow, broad belly of the now-dry Santa Catarina River. As we drove deeper into the canyon, we neared a razor-sharp, silvery mountain with flanks that resembled those of a spread-winged eagle. Then the track blurred, grew indistinct, and we were bumping and scraping in the water's narrowing old course, finally stopping where we could go no further. In the falling dusk, we walked in the dusty river's path, reaching a point where the canyon became a thin, enclosing gorge. There we saw the carved traces of the water's path down rocky undulations where it cascaded during heavy rains into the parched bed of the river. In the deepening, moonless dark, we made sounds—Pauline and Arturo with conch shells, me with my voice and my movement—a music and dance of the place, its creatures, and the night. The reverberations flew around us like bats, until they shivered off, dying into the surrounding mountains. That night I wrote impressions from my movement in my journal:

> *I am occupied: a skinny cow seeking shade and water; a gasping fish, its belly scraping the scorched riverbed; a frog, dried skin sticking to its bones. My voice is a clatter of stones spilling from my mouth, my belly. Limbs sprout the harshly beautiful joints of cacti that grow in the river's margin. The ragged talons of the mountains jut from my spine. My body is both the earth and what walks upon it.*

Later in an improvisational performance with Pauline, those images of the canyon are carved into my movement and her sound. We dance and sing our Common Body. Diving deep into the rich waters of the body dissolves our feelings of separateness and lets us, as horseman Monty Roberts says, "join up." It is that moment when we feel and breathe across the divides of skin, mind, species, age, gender, or any other imagined separation.

CHAPTER TWO

THE HEART OF THE MATTER: CONNECTING AND CENTERING

Let yourself be silently drawn
by the stronger pull
of what you truly love.

Rumi
Illuminated Rumi
(Crown Publishing, 1997),
translated by Coleman Barks,
used by permission of
Coleman Barks.

THE HEART AND THE HORSE

One day I was talking to horse trainer Jayne Marino of Mistover Farm in Pawling, New York, about teaching a movement workshop for riders at her stable. I told her the class was not for strengthening the core muscles or stretching, but about "waking up" and "opening the body" from the inside. This involves developing awareness of unconscious movement and mental habits, creating a clearer experience of the body—of connections between the parts and differentiation among them. In this way, we become more sensitive and responsive to our horses and more aware of our own bodies.

Without heart, riding can become a disembodied technique—the pursuit of a skill without the vital ingredient of spirit or soul; what Mary Oliver calls "that wild silky part of ourselves."[15]

"Yes!" Marino exclaimed. "Riders forget that the *actual* 'core' of riding is *coeur*!"

That elegant play on words (*coeur* means "heart" in French) is exactly right. In his book, *Free Play: Improvisation in Life and Art* (G.P. Putnam's Sons, 1991), Stephen Nachmanovitch tells the story of a friend who teaches riding by insisting that at first her students learn to control the horse by weight and thought, instead of the mechanical aids of reins and spurs. "This means becoming one with the horse—loving the horse," he writes.[14]

The Heart of Play

Prayer

Our problem—may I include you?—is that we
don't know how to start, how to just close
our eyes and let something dance between
our hearts and our lips, we don't know how
to skip across the room only for the joy of the leap.
We walk, we run, but what happened to the skip
and its partner, the gallop, the useless and imaginary
way we could move through space, the horses we
rode before we knew how to saddle up, before we
had opinions about everything and just loved
the wind in our faces and the horizon in our eyes.

Stuart Kestenbaum
"Prayer," *Prayers & Run-On Sentences*
(Deerbrook Editions, 2007), used with permission of the publisher.

Sometimes the reason we were first drawn to horses gets lost. We lose touch with the playful, joyous part of being with them. We become automatic and hurried—fragmented in our attention.

Musician and author Stephan Nachmanovitch says that the German word *funktionslust* means the pleasure of doing for its own sake, having nothing to do with the pleasure of fulfilling a goal or attaining a particular end. Play is the heart of the creative process. "As play, the act is its own destination. The focus is on process, not product. Play is intrinsically satisfying. It is not conditioned on anything else. Play, creativity, art, spontaneity, all these experiences are their own rewards and are blocked when we perform for reward or punishment, profit or loss."[16]

When riding, if *goals* overtake the relational and exploratory parts of the practice of riding, play can fall by the wayside. Riding becomes another job. "Improvisational riding" is playful, having to do with meandering, getting lost, taking

One of my dancers, Ingrid, and Pony at play.

unexpected turns, responding intuitively to what is arising in the moment. Play researcher Stuart Brown says, "Play is the swing off the rhythm in music, the bounce in the ball, the dance that delivers us from the lockstep march of life. It is the 'meaningless' moments that make the day memorable and worthwhile. I believe we live in a playful universe."[17]

How do we play with our horses? And how can we reconcile playfulness with the goals of riding? One key to bridging play and goals is the cultivation of enthusiasm. According to Eckhart Tolle, "Enthusiasm means that there is a deep enjoyment in what you do plus the added element of a goal or a vision that you work toward. When you add a goal to the enjoyment of what you do, the energy field or vibrational frequency changes. A certain degree of what we might call

Ingrid and Pony finding connection, listening to each other.

structural tension is now added to enjoyment, and so it turns into enthusiasm."[18] The effect of enthusiasm is to add direction and purpose to the more meandering, open-ended quality of play.

> *"Once there is a certain degree of Presence, of still and alert attention*
> *in human beings' perceptions, they can sense the divine life essence, the*
> *one indwelling consciousness or spirit in every creature, every life-form,*
> *recognize it as one with their own essence and so love it as themselves."*

Eckhart Tolle
A New Earth (Penguin, 2008)

The Heart of the Matter: Connecting and Centering

PLAYING WITH GOALS

🕐 10 MINUTES (OR ALL DAY!)

PURPOSE: Learning to be playful and improvisatory in our daily lives can help us become less rigidly focused and goal-driven with our horses. This more expansive approach is nourishing for the horse—and for us.

1. **Washing your face:** Take longer than usual to wash your face. Splash the water slowly, letting your hands linger over the surface of your face. Smile into the mirror. Use the towel, softly, gently. Apply lotion as if you were carefully painting your face with beautiful colors. As you touch your face, close your eyes and enjoy feeling the landscape of your features.

2. **Making the bed:** Make the bed as quickly as you can. Let it be wonderfully messy. Now make it slowly, being intentionally careful and enjoying every detail of what you are seeing and touching. Now lie down on the made bed and savor its softness and comfort before going on to the next thing.

3. **Grooming your horse:** Groom your horse with the intention of making a sensual connection with your companion. Imagine that your brushes are touching not just the hair and skin, but all of the layers of the body, turning on the lights in each cell. Can you groom without mentally or physically rushing? As Vipassana meditation teacher Narayan Liebenson says, "When eating, just eat. When walking, just walk." When grooming, just groom. Let your mind become quiet. Remember to breathe.

4. **Riding your horse:** While riding, notice your habits. How do you usually begin? What can you do differently today? One very skillful rider at our barn has a different map for each day. Some days she rides out first. Other days she may take a short walk outside the arena in the middle of the ride. She might ask the horse to do something out of the blue, like "Just go," and off they gallop, exuberant, spontaneous. There is no discernable formula—she is always in the moment, playing with all the possibilities. I see her responding to her horse; how he feels that day. In response, he is keenly attuned to her. I can see her goals developing, but they are arising from the waves of her enthusiasm and joy.

Learning and Listening with Heart

Horses can teach us a great deal about ourselves if we are willing to listen. On the ground or in the saddle, finding harmony with a horse is like sitting with a Zen master or practicing yoga. In yoga, where you place your feet and hands, the details of how you move into and out of a form, the support of your breath and intention, are all essential to that *asana*, or pose. Being with horses requires both yogic mindfulness and a receptive, friendly mind. There is nothing terribly abstract about being around a 1,200-pound flight animal. You have to be in the moment. When we listen, horses—with their clarity, honesty, and generosity— will teach us again and again what is really important: softness, balance, connection, and love.

As a beginner rider I could not decode what I was feeling in the saddle; it was all a jumble of sensation and motion. Tom Davis, my trainer at the time, described learning to ride as being like trying to listen to 500 radio stations at once. I couldn't begin to sort out all the different parts of what I was sensing and feeling: hands, reins, feet, stirrups, legs, the horse's flanks, his footfalls, his balance, my seat in and out of the saddle, the voice of the trainer, breath, ears, eyes! My trained dancer's body felt illiterate. It did not feel like my own—and in fact, it was not—because sitting on a horse, you become a part of another body, sharing breath, movement, skin, muscle, and bone.

As I spent more time riding and being with horses, I was drawn into a vortex of questions for which I had no answers: questions about the nature of communication, relationship, and body language. I hungered for more than the grooming and riding. I wanted to speak with them through my body with gesture, play, and touch, meeting the horse in the shared landscape of body and movement, to become more fully attuned in ways that were unknown, even unimaginable to me at the time. I wanted to know: *How can I be understood and how can I better understand? What is communication with a horse, actually?* I became troubled by other questions: *What is the role of force, domination, and control in this delicate relationship?*

I remember seeing horseman Monty Roberts giving a demonstration at a large equine event and feeling uneasy as the horse ran in circles in a round pen, eventually allowing Roberts to put a halter on his head and lead him. Roberts explained that in driving the horse away from him, he was establishing a herd hierarchy in which he was the leader and the horse learned to follow him.

In Carey Wolfe's *Zoontologies: The Question of the Animal* (University of Minnesota Press, 2003), philosopher Paul Patton asks, "Could there ever be a purely nonviolent method of training the horse, or is the very idea of training inseparable from a kind of violence to the horse's intrinsic untrained nature?" He notes that all the riding aids are "part of a larger somatic framework of inter-species communication...embedded within a larger sensory field of touch, pressure, body contact, and attitude, including eye contact." He quotes English cavalry trainer

Henry Wynmalen, who says that riding must "endeavor always to detect what is the lightest possible aid to which our horse will respond, and on the discovery of this lightest possible aid, to continue trying to obtain response to a lighter one still." However, Patton concludes, "Appealing as I found this idea, I could not help but think that it was also a lure or an illusion that served only to mask the reality of a relationship that was fundamentally coercive."[19]

When I read this I felt a plunging despair. If paddocks, stalls, tack, and riding were all part of the subjugation and coercion of these beings I so loved, how could I continue? I felt that I had interpreted the horse's cooperation and acquiescence as an agreement, a choice. The whole question of relationship and right action was blown wide open.

Should I stop riding? I could not imagine it. Riding a horse is a miraculous language of skin, bone, nerve, and fluid, shared rhythms—a vibrant poetry of the flesh. At its very best, it is improvisatory—an unfolding jazz played by two bodies sharing a vernacular spoken in touch and movement. I could not imagine giving up the exhilaration, delight, and sensuality that I experienced in riding. But does the horse love any part of that? I realized that I had to *feel*, not *think* my way into an answer that was right for me.

Horsewoman, poet, and philosopher Vicki Hearne says that when you ride, you must "learn not only to read what your skin tells you but also to be, as it were, kinesthetically legible to yourself."[20] This means that we must be able to read our own skins in order to be physically intelligible to the horse. Most of us do not speak the language of the body with any fluency. Hearne goes on to say, "Horses have continually to forgive us for what must seem to them to be extraordinarily blunt and clumsy communication most of the time."[21] To be with them *fully*, we must become bilinguists, consciously and continually threading between the specific vocabularies of our two distinct physicalities and perceptions.

Reading this, I began to understand that feeling my own body more clearly was a way to become less "blunt and clumsy," in my communications with my horses, both in and out of the saddle. What I did not know at the time was that becoming more conscious of my body—moment to moment—and seeking greater softness and subtlety in my riding would spill into other parts of my life in profound and unexpected ways. Perhaps the greatest surprise was that my riding practice could lead me to greater self-compassion.

Dressage trainer and author Erik Herbermann says, "It is up to us to initiate harmonious resolutions to any negative cycles which occur. The horses do not know how to do so, and tend to continue to resist (that which they perceive to be our resistance against them) until we help them out of their cul-de-sac by dissolving the resistance in ourselves first. In this way we give them nothing to be against in the first place."[22] Through their physical responses, horses show us *exactly* when we are helping and when we are obstructing through tension or harshness. Cowboy and Aikido master and author Mark Rashid said in a work-

OPENING WITH HEART

🕐 10 MINUTES

PURPOSE: Imagine bringing a quality of openness and vulnerability into your riding and your time with your horse. How would that feel in your body? In your mind? Practice this meditation:

1. As you breathe, feel your lungs surrounding and "holding" your heart. Visualize the heart expanding into this cradling support. Picture your horse's heart enfolded by his lungs.

2. Can you bring this quality of nurturance into your body and mind as you ride? As your legs drape on the sides of the horse, can you imagine them like another pair of lungs, surrounding and supporting the heart of the horse?

3. Instead of looking for what is wrong, what needs to be improved, or some difficulty with your horse, focus on what is pleasurable: your legs receiving the warmth of the horse's sides, the undulating sensation of your hips in the saddle, the softness of his eye.

4. While you are riding, try saying out loud, "How can I help?" and notice how that changes the conversation between you and your horse.

shop I took with him that we want to ask ourselves, "How can I *help* the horse do what I want him to do?" *not* "How can I *make* him do it?" Because of our big brains and the big egos that accompany them, we often default to *making*, not *helping*. We direct, we push, we demand. *Helping* requires us to listen and feel. *Helping* engages our more generous, receptive, and willing selves.

On the "good" days with Amadeo, when I was able to open my heart, mind, and body to him *and to myself*, I did not feel that he had surrendered to me, but that he was able to expand into an expression of his own exuberance. I was approaching what Vicki Hearne describes as the moment when "the horse thinks and the rider creates, or becomes a space and direction for the execution of the horse's thoughts."[23] To do this requires—in addition to the language of pressure, touch, and balance—a willingness to take full responsibility for your physical and emotional presence and participation in that relationship. To open to our shared vulnerability and imperfection in this relationship, on the ground, in the saddle— to open and open and open.

"The capacity for unmediated knowledge of us is not unique to horses, but because we ride them, because they carry us, it is particularly hard to avoid noticing not only that horses know us but that they know us without yielding their own volition, which continues to belong to the horse."

Vicki Hearne
Adam's Task: Calling Animals by Name
(The Akadine Press, 1982)

"Anything forced and misunderstood can never be beautiful. And to quote the words of Simon: If a dancer was forced to dance by whip and spikes he would be no more beautiful than a horse trained under similar conditions."

Xenophon
The Art of Horsemanship
(Dover Publications, 2006)

HELPING, NOT MAKING

Several years ago I went to a clinic being offered in our neighborhood by someone who was an "expert" in "natural horsemanship." My wife Pam and I went with our daughters, Chandrika and Bimala, and brought some folding canvas chairs to sit and watch. The instructor was working with a beautiful and very nervous young Arabian stallion. She kept shaking the lead rope at him, explaining that it was a way of getting his attention and making him move away from her. Each time she shook the rope, she increased the pressure, saying in a sarcastic tone, "Hello? Hello?" The rope was like a dancing snake; the little stallion was clearly upset, wide-eyed, head straight up in the air, and doing anything he could to get away from the lead and the person on the other end of it. I could feel my stomach tighten and my daughters' consternation as they watched. Suddenly the clinician walked up to the horse and struck him hard in the face, turning to explain that she needed his attention and his respect. In a single movement, all four of us stood up, closed our folding chairs, and walked out, the girls' eyes streaming with tears. She called after us, noting in front of the other auditors that we obviously didn't know anything about horses.

The little stallion *had* learned a lot that day. He learned about distrust; about violence and fear. He did not learn about softness, dependability, curiosity, or cooperation. A frightened animal (or human) cannot listen or learn—he or she just wants to get away from the threat. Instinctually, we often respond in kind to the tone of another person: For example, if someone is harsh with us, we are harsh; if someone is impatient, we are impatient. A hard-wired part of the more primitive section of our brain puts us in an endless loop of reactivity and rage. But that does not work well with horses. For one thing, they outweigh us by around ten times. For another, they can always pull harder and run faster. To step out of the fight cycle, to make a *real connection*, we have to move within, listen to the body, observe the mind, and settle our nervous system.

My dressage trainer told me how one day she was speaking to a group of her young students following a competition. She praised them for their focus, their seriousness of purpose, their willingness to learn, as well as the emotional and physical balance they showed with their horses. She remarked that she had not seen anyone lose her temper or punish her horse if the horse happened to miss a jump or make an error during the test.

Then the second trainer began to speak. "Riding is war," she said, and then proceeded to tell these aspiring riders that they had to constantly fight for control of their horses, that they had to treat competitions as if they were entering a battle. Above all, they must force their horses to obey, no matter what. "Hold the reins tight and kick them on."

There is a way to be with horses that honors their nature by listening and responding with sensitivity, and another way that violates it with force and domination. The same thing can be true of how we treat our own bodies. Real partnership demands that we find a way to be at one with our horses, and by extension, ourselves.

Renowned horse trainer and life coach Klaus Ferdinand Hempfling says that horses, because they are so much larger and stronger than us and so quick to react, can easily expose our imbalances and shortcomings as riders...and as humans. Feeling inadequate, we resort to using more and more force—a pattern that can spiral out of control into an adversarial and punishing relationship rather than one that is cooperative and friendly. The unfortunate results show up in our bodies and the bodies of our horses—as tension, anxiety, or injury, as unconscious habits or problems in our horsemanship and relationship with the horse that remain stubbornly unresolved. Caught up in the struggle, we miss the opportunity to experience the beautiful, shared landscape of sensing and feeling that is the Common Body.

According to Alexandra Kurland, author of *Clicker Training for Your Horse* (Sunshine Books, 2007), when a horse is made to do something via force or exhaustion—lying down is the example she uses, but she could easily be speaking of loading a horse into a trailer—his essential nature is violated and he simply gives up. When this happens, the movement or action you've trained may be "poisoned" forevermore because "at the heart of that behavior, in the formation

SETTLE DOWN

🕐 5-10 MINUTES

PURPOSE: Sometimes when our nervous system is overwhelmed, or we find ourselves in a vortex of reactivity, we need simple strategies to settle ourselves and find an emotional and physical balance. As you become more settled, that equilibrium will transmit from your body and mind to your horse.

1. **Breathe.** Whatever you are doing, make breathing a part of it. Pause and take a few easy, conscious breaths. Whatever you are doing, intentionally bring a quality of flowing breath to the activity.

2. **Pause.** Simply slow down and then stop what you are doing, and come into stillness. If you or your horse feels agitated, allow the "hot" energy of that activation to disperse and quiet in the stillness, taking as much time as you need.

3. **Smile.** As you breathe, invite a soft smile and let the sensation of that smile percolate through the rest of your body.

4. **Orient to pleasure.** Look around and notice something you find beautiful or pleasing. Pause and absorb the details of what delights you. Enjoy the richness of your sense perceptions. Can you let this pleasure permeate your body? What is the difference between *seeing* and *looking*, between *hearing* and *listening*?

5. **Change the activity.** If you have been riding a particular exercise, do something different—for example, take a walk with your horse or end your ride early. When you encounter a challenge in your work, change your perspective, or simply "let it go" for now, knowing that you can begin again when the time is right.

6. **Interrogate the feeling.** When you begin to feel tense, flustered, or anxious, take a moment to ask what is happening in your body, in your mind, or with your horse. Let the sensation in your body be a cue to "get quiet" and tune into what is triggering this feeling. Then breathe consciously for a few moments, and allow it to dissolve.

of it, the horse *gave up*.... You may applaud that the horse lay [*sic*] down, but if you can see what is at the heart of that training, it is hard to applaud."[24]

It is, of course, possible to go back and teach the behavior a different way, but if you use the old cues, you will see the deadened response again. Kurland reminds us that it is possible for a performance to be beautiful and exciting and at the same time truly honor the horse, working with the horse's willing participation.

"You can teach the horse to bow and have the horse love to bow," she writes. "You can teach the horse to lie down and have the horse love to lie down. Or, you can teach the horse to lie down by taking its leg away so that the horse thinks it is going to die, because when you take the horse's leg away, you are pulling the horse down in the way a predator would pull a horse down."

The important question is this: Do our relationships with our horses (spouses, children, friends) evoke cruelty or kindness? What are the intentions that define our relationships? Mark Rashid says that humans are not very good at making connections—that we spend a lot of our time *disconnecting*. This is a particular problem when we then want to join with our horses and each other. We haven't practiced listening, feeling, and acknowledging the other being. On the other hand, Rashid says that we *are* good at creating "openings." I believe that means that the big human brain is flexible, improvisational, and good at generating options and possibilities. To find those options and openings, we have to take the time to look inwardly and become willing to feel ourselves more deeply, both physically and emotionally. Sometimes this requires the intentional dismantling of old habits, and sometimes it can happen on an exhale.

SOFTENING, OPENING

During a four-day workshop with Mark Rashid, I found myself looking again and again at the mouth of his horse, Baxter. I loved the roundness of it, the soft way that he held his jaw, the easy line of his lips, and the fact that he never opened his mouth or struggled with the bit. The reason for that was that there was nothing to struggle against. Rashid's hands on the reins were flowing, generous, and yet effective. He was always consciously offering *softness*. Baxter, in turn, was a peaceful, quiet, balanced horse, which showed me that he was working with a feeling, connected, and kind rider.

In that same workshop, I was riding a lovely, young, blue roan Quarter Horse named Sam, who had, as Rashid said, "an industrial-strength brace" that showed up in the way he resisted the bit, throwing his head. Sam would hit the bit so hard that he would back himself up—like a wave striking a sea wall. He could not soften, and apparently, neither could I. With me still in the saddle, Rashid held my reins without pulling, using a neutral but firm contact that resulted in Sam backing himself all the way across the big paddock—not because Rashid was pulling (he wasn't) but because Sam was simply reacting to *his own* resistance.

HELPING, NOT MAKING

🕐 10-15 MINUTES

PURPOSE: In riding (and in our human relationships) sometimes control overshadows communication; harshness and impatience displace softness and connection. We are riding by making statements and declarations, forgetting to ask the questions. Learning to practice self-compassion and self-help can teach us to become more generous and patient in our relationships with our horses. Learning to listen to our own bodies helps us listen to our horses.

1. From a standing position, slowly lower your body to the floor, settling on either your right or left side. Let the body yield deeply into the floor, seeking ease and comfort. As you settle, breathe gently into this restful connection. When you feel the need, shift slowly to another comfortable position, using your hands and arms to help protect your joints from bumping the floor. Again, settle deeply and comfortably. Ask yourself how you could be more comfortable and make those adjustments.

2. Begin to rise slowly to a standing position. Instead of pushing yourself up quickly, go slowly, helping your body move in a smooth and supported way to standing. Pause along the way. Look for a leisurely unhurried feeling. You are not "making" yourself stand, you are "helping" your body find the most easeful and gentle way to rise.

3. Repeat this sinking and rising a couple times, letting your movement be slow and langorous, each time discovering more ways to help your body change level and position on the floor with greater ease and flow.

Rashid showed me what he does with the reins with an exercise on the ground: On one end of a pair of reins, I was the "horse," bracing my hands and arms. On the other end, he softened my resistance with something invisible that felt like warm water moving up the lines to me. He never changed the position of his hands or arms. He was sending intention, he explained, and "going underneath" my stiffness—something he learned through his practice of Aikido. The solution was not mechanical, he told me, but happened by finding the connection between the *inside of the rider* and the *inside of the horse*. And he said that if you aren't connected to yourself, there is no way you can connect to the horse.

The easy round softness of Baxter's mouth on the bit.

Through a simple exercise off the horse, Rashid showed me how to communicate softness through the reins.

Baxter easily moving back as Rashid asks with softness and intention.

BREATHING RHYTHMS

🕐 5 MINUTES

PURPOSE: We often forget to breathe, or we breathe shallowly, irregularly. We hold our breath, sometimes for a long time. Breathless, our bodies stiffen and "close." Mark Rashid's intentional breathing exercise is a way to remind us to breathe more fully and consciously. Over time, this practice can become a natural and instinctual part of our riding and our daily lives.

1. Standing with your feet beneath your sit bones and your knees slightly bent, place your hands on either side of your navel, so that you can feel both your lower ribs and your belly.

2. For the next several minutes, breathe in on three counts and out on four. Focus primarily on the horizontal dimension of the breath, feeling your ribs widen and narrow laterally as you breathe in and out. When thoughts arise, gently put your mind back on the breath. Remember that even as you count, you are looking for an easy, restful quality, letting the breath enter and leave the body without effort.

3. Try breathing with this in-on-three-out-on-four count when you are riding. You can change to in-on-four-out-on-five or any other rhythm that feels comfortable. Breathing with an intentional rhythm is a good way to find out if you are breathing continuously or only occasionally. Breathing consciously also communicates a quality of relaxation and consistency to your horse, helping him to relax, too.

4. Now let go of counting, while staying softly aware of the breath. Can you allow the breath to penetrate all of the spaces and tissues of the body? Can you feel the breath as a bridge connecting your body and your horse's body?

What I felt was not just a change in the sensation in my hands or a mechanical "fix" in the reins, but a quality of open-hearted kindness in the contact—making connection with heart.

When I got back on Sam and took up the reins again, Rashid told me that instead of meeting Sam's resistance with my own resistance, to just picture my hands moving toward the horse's mouth, without actually shifting their position in space. This dissolved the bracing in Sam...and in me—the beginning of a reliable softness between us. When I asked him to back up now, he moved backward in a smooth, easy motion. Rashid explained that Sam had felt my intention for him to move backward, and because there was no force or restriction, he simply began to flow like a river in the direction I had visualized.

During the clinic, Rashid also saw that I was not breathing—at least, not in a way that would allow me to soften or continue riding for very long. With a smile, he said, "An exhale would go a long way here," or "When the wheels come off, try exhaling." He instructed me to breathe in on a four-count and breathe out on a five-count in rhythm during the walk, then to maintain that rhythm in the trot. As I rode with this conscious breathing, I felt Sam begin to breathe differently, too, his stride opening and lengthening. And then Rashid pointed out, with a chuckle, that I was actually smiling!

What Mark Rashid taught me while I was riding actually applies to everything: "When things are falling apart, let that be your cue to breathe." Beyond that, I could feel in my own body and mind how the breath also created an opening to qualities of soft, open-hearted engagement with my horse.

LESSONS LEARNED

Testy Pony

I am given a pony for my birthday, but it is the wrong kind of pony. It is the kind of pony that won't listen. It is testy. When I ask it to go left, it goes right. When I ask it to run, it sleeps on its side in the tall grass. So when I ask it to jump us over the river into the field I have never before been, I have every reason to believe it will fail, that we will be swept down the river to our deaths. It is a fate for which I am prepared. The blame of our death will rest with the testy pony, and with that, I will be remembered with reverence, and the pony will be remembered with great anger. But with me on its back, the testy pony rears and approaches the river with unfettered bravery. Its leap is glorious. It clears the river with ease, not even getting its pony hooves wet. And then there we are on the other side of the river, the sun going down, the pony circling, looking for something to eat in the dirt. Real trust is to do so in the face of clear doubt, and to trust is to love. This is my failure, and for that I cannot be forgiven.

Zachary Schomburg

Sometimes what appears to be the "wrong pony" is actually the one that helps us make a leap of faith. Many of the horses in my life have seemed like wrong ponies, but they have taught me the right lessons. I wasn't always willing to listen or able to hear, but these ponies were patient and persistent. They taught me about feeling my body, noticing my emotions, and being more connected to the present moment and another being.

Empty the Mind, Open the Heart

In her book, *Dressage with Mind, Body & Soul* (Trafalgar Square Books, 2013), Linda Tellington-Jones[25] tells a story of a Hungarian stallion named Brado, who had been slated for the US Olympic Eventing Team. But Brado did not like to jump ditches, which ultimately kept him from competing. Tellington-Jones was at the Pebble Beach event course, one of the premier courses in the country with many natural water ditches, and since she had successfully competed in eventing for many years, she used the opportunity to see if she could change Brado's mind about such obstacles. The first thing she did was *empty her mind*, mentally picturing that he could choose to go forward on his own. According to Tellington-Jones, emptying the mind is "a great way to stop unwanted left-brain chatter or negative thought and leave room for positive outcome." She learned about emptying the mind when she read *Judge Dee and the Blind Samurai:* A legendary, unbeatable fourteenth-century samurai prepared for combat by emptying his head of thoughts "like a hollowed gourd." In doing that, he was prepared for whatever might arise rather than confused by a mind full of expectations and fears.

"I sat quietly, not allowing Brado to go left or right or back, but not urging him to go forward," writes Tellington-Jones in her book, "and simply held the intention that he would lose his fear and go forward when he felt safe and confident. In a few minutes he walked forward on his own, jumped the ditch easily, and I never had one stop at a ditch in the years I competed with this wonderful stallion."

Alexandra Kurland notes that with horses (or spouses, children, friends) we can become distracted by all the things we *don't* want; we feel we have to react to unwanted behaviors. "If the horse is nudging us we feel the need to elbow the horse away. The horse is pushing at our pockets, looking for a treat, so we feel that we should be doing something with the lead line to send the horse away." Her advice is that rather than focusing on all the things you *don't* want, look for what you *do* want and give *that* your attention.

"We must learn to be aware of everything but to be non-reactive to it," she says. "This creates an enormous shift in people. You can have bad things happening around you, but you do not have to be reactive to them. As you focus on the one or two elements that you *can* reinforce, and you find that those elements become magnified. Other pieces of good behavior then begin to emerge and to add onto that central core of behavior that you have been reinforcing."

Our Horses, Ourselves

What horses have taught me with great precision is that focusing on what I want instead of the problem is the key to finding both the solution and greater connection. Giving attention to what I *don't* want only adds energy and momentum to the negative thing. For example, if I am riding and focusing on the terrible quality of my shoulder-in, that situation is unlikely to improve. Instead, if I take a moment to picture a clear, flowing image of the shoulder-in that I want, that feeling will more often than not transmit to the horse. As classical horseman Erik Herbermann says, "There is a saying in carpentry, 'Let the hammer drive the nail.' So too in riding, we should let the aids inspire the horse to respond as we wish, rather than trying to move the horse's body with our own physical effort. Dance your horse forward; do not push him."[26]

In a workshop with Linda Tellington-Jones, I watched as another attendee brought her horse into the arena, dragging him behind her like a bag of heavy sand. She looked frustrated and angry, and more than a little embarrassed by her horse's "bad behavior." Tellington-Jones took the line from the student and showed her how to lead the horse with an enthusiastic "Let's do it!" attitude,

TRY THIS

TRY THIS: LET'S DO IT!

 5 MINUTES

PURPOSE: Bringing a quality of "Let's do it!" to your horse and to your other interactions with humans and animals in your life invites qualities of enthusiasm and playfulness to those relationships.

1. Begin walking, and as you walk, mentally repeat the words, "Do it!" over and over. Imagine a stern quality in your voice, like a scolding coach or an angry parent urging you on. Notice your body and your emotions. Does your body feel heavy or tight? Do you feel resistant or frustrated?

2. Now turn to face a different direction and breathe in and out in a soft, easy rhythm, three or four times.

3. Start walking, mentally saying the words, "Let's do it!" with a quick, eager quality, as if you were being invited to dance by a playful partner. What shifts do you sense in your emotions and body? Is there more lightness and ease in your step?

instead of a demanding, "Do it!" The change was immediate as Tellington-Jones playfully invited the horse to join her at the walk, and he relaxed, stepping forward with her easily.

As a choreographer, I am used to telling dancers where to move, what kind of movement I am looking for, and what needs more or less "juice." Over the years I have learned that when my direction is infused with the "Let's do it!" feeling, the results from my dancer-collaborators are confident and generous. When I am anxious or frustrated, the whole process of working with others becomes strained and "sticky." It is the same with the horse, whether in the saddle or on the ground: If I respond to my horse with anxiety, fear, or anger—if I think, "Do it!"—*that* is what will be reflected back to me, rather than playfulness, openness, ease, and flow.

OPENING ALL THE WAY

Consider this passage from Margery Williams' *The Velveteen Rabbit* (Harper Festival, 2006):

> *"It doesn't happen all at once," said the Skin Horse. "You become. It takes a long time. That's why it doesn't often happen to people who break easily, or have sharp edges, or who have to be carefully kept. Generally, by the time you are Real, most of your hair has been loved off, and your eyes drop out, and you get loose in the joints and very shabby. But these things don't matter at all, because once you are Real, you can't be ugly, except to people who don't understand."*

The Skin Horse is talking about the time it takes for body and mind to soften, for self-consciousness and self-importance to be worn away, for demands to become less insistent, for the ability to listen to deepen, and for our hearts to open. As that happens, we become more connected to our horse and human friends—and ourselves.

In the film *Pina* (2011), the great choreographer Pina Bausch tells a dancer who is struggling with the motivation for her movement, "Just dance for love." In the same way, we should ride for love, nothing less. There is nothing like stopping to take in the sun, the trees, the hills while standing next to a horse that is choosing to be there, to be near you in that full-hearted, breathing moment.

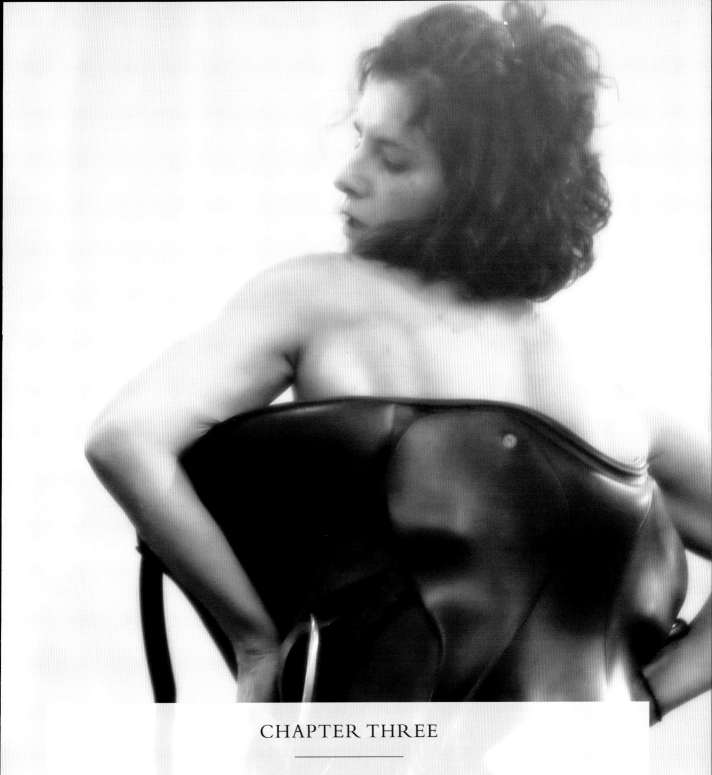

CHAPTER THREE

THE LIMITS:
OPENING THE GATES

It is not dark that scares me, but the limit
Which places the house in its field, the horse in its stall.

Ann Lauterbach
"Carousel," *Before Recollection*
(Princeton University Press, 1987)

UNDERSTANDING THE LIMITS

What constitutes a limit? Is it the body, the mind, the stall, the bridle and reins? Is it our belief that we are separate entities; living lives essentially independent of each other, unable to feel ourselves part of a larger whole? How can we listen more deeply and hear what is being communicated by the natural world—an oak tree, a horse, a singing wren, a friend? How do we negotiate these limits of body, mind, heart, and spirit? Except for wild herds in places like the American West or Chincoteague, the Camargue in France or Mongolia, horses live within the confines of stalls, paddocks, and work. They inhabit the spaces we permit, their freedom cut to fit our needs and demands, completely dependent upon our care and feeding.

Like our horses, our bodies express our limits: habitual postures, aches and pains, and a lack of feeling, expression, and imagination are all part of the boundaries that we expect and endure. Habits of mind become engraved in our tissue, cells lose elasticity and fluidity, and our bodies become little stalls instead of open pastures. These physical, mental, and emotional contractions can be reflected in our work, relationships, and health, impeding our ability to live joyfully. The good news is that our bodies can also help us feel and release these limiting beliefs, tensions, and anxieties, and horses can play a crucial role in this process of moving toward greater freedom of body and mind.

According to anthropologist David M. Guss, in tribal societies, "A system of reciprocity existed in which all living things took part."[27] In other words, what many think of as more "primitive" cultures were not limited by *dualism*—the "them and us" worldview that is deeply rooted in many aspects of contemporary thinking, particularly in relation to other species. Guss observes that in tribal societies, connections with other humans, the natural world, and all nonhuman forms of life, were continually reaffirmed by song, dance, dress, and other cultural forms. "This ceremonial life of the tribal person was a constant dialogue, with interspecies communication both ordering and transforming it. This was the magical ingredient

50

that seasoned every action, dissolving the individual into the greater reality while at the same time defining his relationship and responsibility to it."[28]

Perhaps this is the most devastating limit we experience: the loss of an embodied, numinous relationship with nature in all its forms, what spiritual teacher Eckhart Tolle calls "a web of interconnected multidimensional processes."[29] Sculptor and horsewoman Gillian Jagger (who I speak further about in chapter 7) says, "If we continue to care only about our own species, we will set ourselves adrift from the larger and necessary connective force of the whole...what Henry More (1614–1687) called the spirit of nature, the soul of the world, the *anima mundi*."[30]

Dissolving Our Limits

Is there a reliable, readily available way to dissolve our limits, to deepen connection to the larger whole? In an article in *The New York Times*, David DeSteno, a professor of psychology at Northeastern University, states, "Meditation fosters a view that all beings are interconnected." In his work with psychologist Piercarlo Valdesolo he has found that "any marker of affiliation between two people, even something as subtle as tapping their hands together in synchrony, causes them to feel more compassion for each other when distressed. The increased compassion in meditators, then, might stem directly from meditation's ability to dissolve the artificial social distinctions—ethnicity, religion, ideology, and the like—that divide us."[31]

For a time, we lived across from a farm. People would drop off cats, and several of them made their way into our yard, which is how we expanded our population of cat companions. One day a young mother cat appeared in our garden with three kittens. While we kept the kittens, the mother was very feral, so we spayed her and then released her. I named her Mamacita. We built a little shelter outside our door with a heated pad where we would feed her daily. It seemed that she wanted to stay, but we could not touch her, and she would flee if she saw us.

I spent many hours, and soon many years, sitting quietly, waiting, allowing Mamacita to sniff my fingers, then eventually she let me touch her head. One winter she decided that living inside was preferable to the cold, and she hid in our living room, declining to leave when we offered her the outdoors. Again, I would enter, lie down nearby or sit quietly and wait. After perhaps six years, I was able to hold her. It is now ten years since Mamacita first appeared. She lives in a small room off my studio with a cat door. When I come in to feed her, she calls plaintively to me, and does not eat until we have had a luxurious long snuggle. She still has her spooky, fearful, hiding moments, but for the most part she has overcome the limits of her wildness.

I tell this story to demonstrate that meditation is not only sitting on a cushion. It includes moments that invite awareness and a quiet, receptive mind. Touching and being touched, dancing, singing, and writing can all be forms of meditation when we bring intention and conscious focus into the heart of each moment.

Sitting quietly with no expectations and a quiet determination to connect with a fearful cat can be a form of meditation. Riding or working with a horse from the ground can also be profoundly meditative. I learned from a Mustang stallion how to create connection through a meditative approach. It meant letting go of expectations and the limits of my own desires and goals, to help him, over time, begin to break free of the limits of his fear and past experiences.

Nelson and the Limits of the Wild

He had read of rhythm in the Book
Of the Free-Thundering Hooves. He dodged
My hands, my ropes, my notions
Exactly as though no human
Ever fed him.

Vicki Hearne
"Ibn, Who Wouldn't be Caught," *Nervous Horses*
(University of Texas Press, 1980)

Nelson was beautiful. A dark bay with a thick stallion's neck and a white star, a long tangled mane, and a stocky, muscular body. He had "swagger" and everyone who saw him had a "Wow!" moment—he was that striking. Nelson was a Mustang, rounded up with his herd by the Bureau of Land Management using helicopters, and it was reported he was one of the craziest horses ever seen upon capture. He tried to climb the 10-foot fence of the pen, and because of his age and his irascibility, his prospects for survival or adoption were bleak. Equine Advocates,[32] a rescue and sanctuary for horses, mules, and donkeys in upstate New York, heard about him and brought him and a buddy to live in a beautiful three-acre field on their property. When Nelson's companion passed away, Nelson remained in the field on his own as Equine Advocates sought an appropriate pasture mate for him. They would eventually find another Mustang that needed a home, which provided Nelson the companionship of a fellow traveler from a common background, and both horses a comfortable and safe home for as long as they needed.

A few people could approach and pet Nelson, but it was always on his terms. He ruled the field with its copse of trees at one end where he could hide and the expanse of rolling pasture. Visitors gazed at him—the powerful stallion in the open field—bearer of the fraught history of the wild horses in the American West. Nelson was a dreamcatcher—an emblem of wildness and wilderness. But he was no longer free or wild and could not quite figure out how to adjust to his new world.

Our Horses, Ourselves

Nelson on the alert in his field.

At first Nelson would not pick up his foot, but even a slight shift of his weight got a "Yes" click, reinforced by a treat. Allowing me to stroke my hands down his leg was a big "Yes!"

I spent many hours with Nelson and came to see that he was, in fact, *limited by his own wild nature.* I wondered if it was possible to "open the gates" for Nelson to a *different* kind of freedom. I had the honor of working with him, using a combination of Clicker Training and Tellington Method touch and groundwork.

Clicker Training, developed by behavioral scientist and animal trainer Karen Pryor, uses the positive reinforcement of a food reward—something that the horse will actively work for—to make clear the connection between a requested behavior (standing still, being led, lifting a leg) and the "Yes" sound of a click. The Tellington Method helps horses become more emotionally balanced and less reactive, and therefore more able to listen to and work with their human partners. One component of the method is the Tellington TTouch—a collection of circles, lifts, and slides done with the hands and fingertips over various parts of the horse's body. TTouches have been scientifically shown to balance brain wave activity and give the animal (or human) a sense of calm and safety by "turning on the lights of the body at the cellular level," according to Tellington-Jones.

In my experience, both Clicker Training and the Tellington Method profoundly change the instinctual predator/prey dynamic between horse and human. Both methods are based on asking a question with touch or movement, and listening for a response. This is significantly different from many methods of conventional horse training, which often involve telling, rather than asking. With Nelson, I used one kind of touch as a way of asking, "Does this feel okay?" If he moved away, I knew that the answer for the moment was "No." I would make a subtle variation in the quality or placement of my touch and ask again until I found the "Maybe" or the "Yes."

At the beginning of my work with Nelson he was extremely wary, fearful, and reactive. He had no idea who I was or what I might do. To be successful in communicating with him, I could see that any new information had to be introduced in a way that was gradual, clear, and digestible. That meant that Nelson had to be able to understand and accept each part of what was being asked or offered before moving on to the next step. My ground rules were that I couldn't skip steps, push an agenda, or rush goals. At the same time, it had been two years since Nelson had his hooves tended to—there was a sense of urgency to safely and humanely manage routine hoof care without resorting to tranquilization or trauma.

Many horses enjoy a good scratch, but at first Nelson did not want me to touch him. His skin literally shivered when I got close enough to place my hands on his back or neck. He was guarded, vigilant. It was frustrating not to be able to touch Nelson—I wanted to stroke and calm him. Nelson had other ideas, though, most of them involving the other side of his field or wherever I was not. So I introduced each touch or movement—raising my hand, moving toward him—very slowly. I used "air" touches, slightly off the body, with the more neutral back of my hand and experimented with different qualities and durations of touch on different parts of his body—the "safer" places at first being the right side of his neck and shoulder.

A week later, after repeating some of the things we had done before, I began adding new touches and then asked him to pick up each of his legs on a movement cue. He was patient and trying hard, not spooking or evading. After 20 or 30 minutes, I removed his rope halter, and instead of just moving away, Nelson placed his chin on my left shoulder, his nose touching my cheek. We stood like that for at least a minute; he was breathing me in and I was breathing him in. I felt that we were dissolving his loneliness—that I was helping him to understand that he could make different choices, not just the automatic default of leaving. In a way, Nelson was stuck in his wildness; addicted to running. For his whole life, flight had been his first line of defense. What Nelson and I were doing was "opening the gates" to other options—creating a familiar, shared vocabulary of movement and touch so that he could find his way out of the cycles of fear and reaction.

Nelson greeting me, and the beginning of our dance that day.

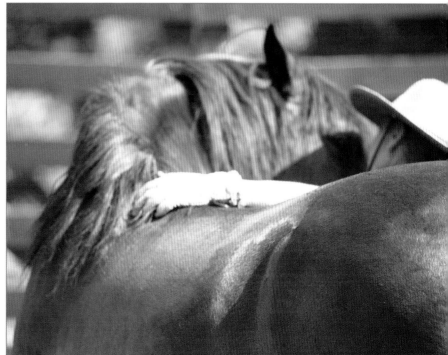

Taking in the sun together.

Here are some of the things I learned from Nelson:

- To be okay with what I don't know.

- The value of steadiness, of commitment and humility.

- How to begin again, and how to keep going and trust my intuition in the presence of a big, fast and sometimes fearful animal.

- How unsettled I could become when he was nervous and how to quiet my mind and body more easily and quickly.

- The meaning of love and devotion.

- How to re-orient to the present moment when I become distracted or overwhelmed.

Nelson was a patient teacher. He showed me how to trust stillness, quiet my mind and body, and take small, progressive steps. When I felt him breathe, felt the tension drain from his body, saw his eye soften, I knew that we were finding a different kind of freedom for us both—entering the fullness and the flow of what was happening right there, in that moment. Working this way, we were removing limits for both of us, bit by bit.

THE LIMITS OF DESIRE

We know the horses are there in the dark
meadow because we can smell them,
can hear them breathing.
Our spirit persists like a man struggling
through the frozen valley
who suddenly smells flowers
and realizes the snow is melting
out of sight on top of the mountain,
knows that spring has begun.

Jack Gilbert

HUMMING OPEN THE GATES, FINDING FLOW

🕐 10 MINUTES

PURPOSE: Using a humming sound sends a vibration throughout the body. In my experience, we can feel this sensation most clearly by visualizing it reverberating in our bones or our cells. Using sound this way helps awaken a feeling of aliveness and connection in the body. Try humming as you groom your horse or begin your ride. Notice how that sound brings you more fully into the present and brings more focus into the body. Can you feel your sound traveling through the reins to your horse's mouth? Can you feel the hum into your seat and hips, transmitting to your horse's back?

1. Lie on your back and take a few moments to become aware of all the sensations you are feeling: the rhythm of your breathing, your heartbeat, the vibration of your nervous system, and the heaviness or lightness, warmth or coolness, tension, or relaxation of the parts of your body as they rest on the floor.

2. Take a few conscious breaths, feeling the movement of breath not just in the chest and belly, but throughout your body, including the parts that are touching the floor.

3. On the next exhale hum softly, keeping the tongue, throat, and jaw relaxed and open.

4. Now focus on feeling the vibration of the hum in your bones, beginning from the sensation at the core of the body, around the sternum and ribcage, and then spreading outward to the periphery. Imagine the skeletal system transmitting vibration and vitality throughout the body, all the way from the top of the skull to the small delicate phalanges of the fingers and toes. Continue this "bone humming" for several minutes.

5. Once you have a clear sensation of the hum, shift your attention to your cells. Picture the watery body of each cell receiving and transmitting a fluid "hum-vibration." Then picture the hum moving on into the communicating interstitial fluid that surrounds each cell.

6. Continue humming on each exhale, sending the hum throughout the body. Feel the hum as an internal massage, letting the warmth and vibration of the sound reach deep into the spaces inside, nourishing the whole body.

When my daughter was seven and first saw the ocean at Lucy Vincent Beach on Martha's Vineyard, she raced into it. Recently adopted from Nepal, she did not speak English and did not understand, "Wait! Stop!" We stood frozen for a moment, and then ran into the cold waves with her. We called our Nepali friend Abish and said, "Please tell her not to run into the ocean! Please tell her it is dangerous!" He did—but the next time she ran straight into the ocean again anyway. A "water child" called by her nature, by her desire. Somehow she knew that she would be rescued, no matter what.

What does it mean to approach each day as a leap of faith, running into the waves of the unknown? A leap of faith cannot be planned. It can only be danced like a surprise tango in the moment of its arrival. Too much anticipating may mean not leaping at all, but instead walking cautiously around. Leaping is a way of bursting through our limitations, of diving into the deep.

There are passions that devour us, pushing us to leap, tossing us over the hurdles of our fears. In his book *Callings* (Harmony, 1998), Greg Levoy tells a story about a boy who so loved a drawing of a Wild Thing sent to him by Maurice Sendak that he ate it. Levoy believes: "Passion is a state of love, and hunger. It is also a state of enthusiasm. Which means to be possessed by a god or a goddess, by a Wild Thing. We move toward a kind of divine presence because through our passions, we are utterly present."[33] Callings are born of our passions. They are portals, opening to what beckons us irresistibly. Answering a calling means letting go of control and limitation—diving in and being carried into the deeper unknown, swept out beyond the enclosures of the familiar and the safe.

Horses call us. They are a heady mix of mythic and earthly, vulnerability and power. Often we come to them through the magical, yearning doorways of our childhood. Our bodies also call. Often they call for food, warmth, shelter, comfort, and rest. They can call loudly, persistently with pain and disease, pleasure and desire. Our clues about what the body wants may come from dreams, sudden insights or serendipitous events. The body can be sly, dissolving our resistance, pushing us toward what the heart desires. When we do not answer, we tempt the demons of hunger, illness, or may enter a state of suspended animation that Levoy says can be both "soul withering and bone dissolving."[34]

Artist Marion Laval-Jeantet and her creative partner, Benoît Mangin, share a particular calling. Since 1991 they have been exploring the physical and emotional connections between humans and animals under the name *Art Orienté Objet*. Their art is political, bridging science and art to disrupt our usual expectations of what "art" and "science" are supposed to look like. In the controversial work, "May the Horse Live in Me" (*Que le cheval vive en moi),* Laval-Jeantet wanted to experience what physiological and psychological, emotional, and spiritual changes she would experience by introducing foreign animal antibodies into her body. Horse people often say that horses are "in the blood," meaning that there is a carnal, elemental kinship between themselves and the horse. Laval-Jeantet arranged with a laboratory to be injected with horse blood plasma. She called her work "a symbolic gesture from a visual artist and performer, whose aim was also to challenge ethical barriers that man fixes between himself and the animal." During the performance itself, Laval-Jeantet donned stilts with hooves and walked with a horse in what she called a "communication ritual." The audience grimly watched her be injected with the equine plasma, and again watched as the "hybrid" or "centaur" blood was drawn from her and freeze-dried.

The mythological character of the centaur, the half human, half-horse creature caught between the two natures, fascinated Laval-Jeantet. She says, "I felt horses are mysterious and contradictory, in terms of conceptualization. They are shy and strong, docile and rebellious at the same time." She says that she had almost no experience with horses prior to the project, except to "cuddle them when we would meet in the countryside."

The first stage of the project was to engage Sabine Rouas, an ethologist, to introduce Laval-Jeantet to a real horse to give her a physical experience that would add an experiential and emotional dimension to the work.

Laval-Jeantet says, "The challenge for Sabine was twofold: to teach me to understand the reactions of the horse and to teach the horse what we wanted from him, which was totally new. To walk with me, accept that I am wearing stilts and would be as tall as him, to have him come to me when I call, allow me to touch his head (as he hated it especially), to react peacefully to my every move, even though he did not know me.

Marion Laval-Jeantet with her prosthetic hooves.

In an earlier work, Laval-Jeantet used prostheses and movement to explore the relationship between herself and a cat.

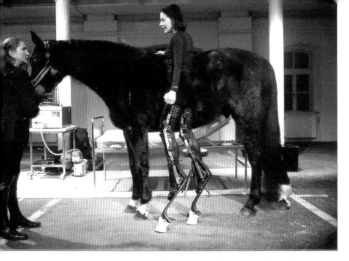

Laval-Jeantet with the ethologist Sabine Rouas and the horse.

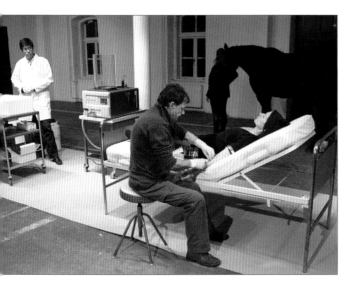

Drawing Marion's blood during the performance.

"Initially, the horse and I were a little scared. But [Rouas] calmed my fears by teaching me to move around the horse and groom him. It took almost ten days to be with each other and cease seeing each other as foreigners." Laval-Jeantet says that this particular horse had been considered hopeless, difficult to educate, and no longer able to be ridden. That was one of the reasons the owner allowed him to be part of the project. However, they saw a transformation in the horse as they began working with him. "Within days, a horse that was sullen, distant, rebellious, became an accomplice, capable of handling a completely new situation."

The injections of horse plasma took place over a period of several months in slowly increasing the amounts. Laval-Jeantet refers to the process as "mithridatisation," after the Persian King of Pontus, Mithridates VI, who supposedly built up an immunity to poison by regularly consuming small doses over a period of time. Injecting foreign animal antibodies and immunoglobulins could have resulted in a life-threatening allergic reaction. But the hope was was that the horse's immunoglobulins would bypass the defensive mechanisms of her immune system and enter her bloodstream to bond with the proteins of her body.

Laval-Jeantet explains that immunoglobulins are biochemical messengers that control the glands and organs of the endocrine system, which is also closely tied to the nervous system. During the performance, and in the weeks after, she experienced not only alterations in her physiological rhythms but also of her consciousness, which were characterized by heightened sensibility and nervousness. She describes it this way:

"The first response, within one hour after the injection, was fever, which was going up and down. When my blood was taken for a sample to preserve it as 'centaur's blood' it became completely clotted after only ten minutes, which is a symptom of strong inflammation. This direct response made the strongest impression

Our Horses, Ourselves

FOLLOWING A CALL, FOLLOWING THE BODY

🕐 10 MINUTES

PURPOSE: Most of us have either forgotten how to listen to the body or become experts at ignoring or overriding its voice. With our horses, we often move automatically through a set sequence of activities each time we are with them. Here is a simple way to learn to listen to and respond to the body with movement. This exercise is about staying with one thing until the body wants to do something else. At the beginning of this exercise, limit your movement choices to three simple actions: standing, sitting, or walking.

1. Begin standing. Stand until you feel an impulse from your body to walk or sit down. Notice what that impulse or sensation is like: Is there a quality of impatience or uncertainty? Is that feeling coming from your mind or from your body? Don't move until you feel a clear impulse *from the body*, not from your mind.

2. Sit or walk until you feel like changing to one of the other two movement choices. Again, wait for the impulse to come from your body, not your mind.

3. If you were to add one more choice what would it be? Lying down? Running? Turning? Stretching your arms overhead? Add one more movement option and see what happens as you let the body decide what to do next and for how long.

4. As you improvise, notice any mental or emotional responses. Maybe at first you feel nervous about getting it wrong or remembering the "rules." Become curious about what will happen next. Don't try to figure it out; just move when moved.

5. Now, as you go through your day, notice those moments when you feel an impulse for a particular movement from your body. Most of us have so completely extinguished this ability to listen to the body that it may take some practice before you are even aware of these small impulses. Maybe you want to stretch, to stand, to shake your hands or even your whole body, to yawn or make a sound. Following the body is the opposite of thinking of or planning a movement. As movements arise spontaneously from the body, follow them with a compassionate inner witness. Notice how this practice of allowing movement to percolate from the body nourishes creativity, imagination,

CONTINUED ▶

CONTINUED FROM PAGE 61

and "aliveness" in other parts of your life, offering new ways of moving and connecting with your body.

6. With your horse, before you pick up your brushes to begin grooming, let your hands move in a spontaneous and exploratory way over your horse's body. Let them linger wherever they want, slowing and speeding up as the impulse arises. Imagine that your hands are on a journey with no destination, no timetable—a leisurely tour with unexpected interruptions. Imagine that your hands can listen to the horse's body and allow it to tell you where to travel next.

7. As you ride, let each transition in gait or direction come from an impulse that you feel arising from the shared body of you and your horse. Try *feeling* the shift rather than planning it with your mind. Instead of riding a "test" or a set sequence of movements, try improvising from this listening practice. Notice what changes.

on me. During the next two days other atypical reactions occurred; then came a paroxysm, which lasted for over a week. During this period, which still seems to me drastically anarchic, I could sleep no longer than one hour at a time, then I woke up for another hour and then fell asleep for another short period of time. My nights were totally fragmented, I had an absurdly strong appetite, and when someone knocked my arm I used to panic. In spite of that I felt incredibly strong...I was talking to immunology doctors about it, and particularly with one immunologist who specializes in horses. To him it was obvious that all my reactions that have not been entirely of psychological nature were very much typical for a horse."[35]

Laval-Jeantet says of her experience, "I was not in my usual body. I felt hyper-powerful, hypersensitive, hyper-nervous and very different. Perhaps this was the emotionalism of an herbivore? I could not sleep. I probably felt a bit like a horse."[36]

The experiment of sharing blood or biological "cross-dressing" with another species is both disturbing and intriguing, connected to a lineage of body art pioneers like Carol Schneeman[37] and Marina Abramovic.[38] Laval-Jeantet took the idea of "horses in the blood" beyond what most of us would imagine or attempt. Her calling, her desire to join with the horse and the questions that drive it are provocative and poignant: What is it to consume what consumes you? To change yourself chemically and biologically to come closer to what you love and want to understand?

62

With all respect for Laval-Jeantet's curiosity and ferocity as an artist, and her generosity in sharing her story, there are other, simpler ways to bridge the limits of our understanding of another species that involve movement, touch, and listening. That can begin with a practice of "following the call"—feeling *how* and *when* the body wants to move, and allowing that inner voice to guide us into action.

THE LIMITS OF THE BODY

John Killacky and his beloved childhood pony Raindrop.

John Killacky was a dancer first. After a successful performing career, he experimented with creating his own choreography, but found that making dances was not nurturing, not his true calling. He traveled to India for ten weeks, visiting a Tibetan monastery in the Himalayas, seeking his next direction. When he returned, he began to run marathons, and over the course of the next decade, he ran six of them.

During that time, he was working as the company manager for Laura Dean and then Trisha Brown, both major figures in American modern dance. Over the years, he established himself as a major curatorial and programming voice in the dance world, curating first the performing arts program at the Walker Art Center in Minneapolis and then the Yerba Buena Center for the Arts in San Francisco. At the time of this writing, he is CEO and Executive Director of the Flynn Center for Performing Arts in Burlington, Vermont. Before dance, though, Killacky's earliest love was horses, and one Shetland Pony in particular.

"When I was a young boy my father sold cattle at the Chicago Stockyards," he says. "Gay boys and their daddies often have complicated relationships, and we were no exception. However, on weekends, I often tagged along with him on country trips to meet with farmers. Farm visits were safe ground, wonderful bonding time between the two of us—quite different from our tumultuous relationship at home. One rainy day in 1962 on a farm in Milledgeville, Illinois, a Shetland Pony mare gave birth to Raindrop, a beautiful roan filly. I had never seen anything so miraculous. I was smitten. Whenever my dad was in the area for business, he would drop me off at the farm and I would spend the day playing with the pony. She was the best friend I ever had, as well as my escape from unpleasant realities at home."

In high school, Killacky's life was filled with activities other than horses, and the connection dimmed further as he entered college "although I kept photos of Raindrop as a reminder of unmitigated joy," he says. It was later that things took a catastrophic turn: He was living in Minneapolis, directing the performing arts programs at the Walker Arts Center, when following a spinal surgery he became paralyzed, losing much of the function in his legs. He had no sensation on his right side; no awareness of location on his left. "It's complicated to walk," Killacky says. "My legs are heavy with neuropathic pain. I navigate the world slowly, assisted by a cane."

He must continually work at strengthening his lower limbs. In the warmer months, he walks in the evenings with his husband and Border collie, "And me with two walking sticks—intently micro-calibrating and adjusting my bifurcated stride." At the gym he sets the treadmill to its lowest setting, practicing pushing through on his left foot. "'Heel to toe, heel to toe' becomes my kinetic mantra. In the pool, cold water quiets spastic muscles, diminishes the pain. I bend knees, flex feet, swing legs, and then swim to strengthen my core. Time is suspended between three strokes and a breath as I do laps." Killacky's yoga practice helps him to stretch, re-center, and find balance. When he cannot do a pose, he visualizes the movement. "The soles of both feet have almost no connection to the ground, so I stand on mystery with faith that somehow the world will hold me up. All this not to get better, just to persist."

Killacky was living and working in San Francisco when he began to feel a strong desire to reconnect with horses. An online search led him to a Shetland Pony farm in Moss Landing; he went to the Santa Cruz County Fair to watch their ponies compete.

"The instant the Pleasure Driving classes began, I turned to my husband and said, 'I think I can do that,'" he remembers. "Soon I began learning to harness and drive a pony in a cart with a very patient trainer. In my first competition, driving the big-boned pinto mare, Candy, beginner's luck and clever Candy won us six blue ribbons. I was hooked. Once again Shetlands became instruments of salvation, this time allowing me to move freely and once more dance in the world—exhilarating for this middle-age balding guy who ambulates with a cane."

Our Horses, Ourselves

John Killacky competing in California with Fog Ranch's Candy.

With his brothers, Killacky traveled to their hometown of Chicago and took a day trip to find the pony barn in Milledgeville where his childhood buddy, Raindrop, had lived. He went to the Village Hall and asked about the farm, there learning that Raindrop had lived a long life and eventually died of colic, and getting easy directions to the old property.

"When I stepped on the porch to knock on the door, I was bursting with joy," he says. "I remembered those wooden steps where I would take off my shoes before going into a warm kitchen for lunch and homemade pie. No one was home, which allowed my brothers and me to explore. The fields where I used to run with the ponies and shady grove of trees were as I remembered them; however, the cattle pens were overgrown, the corncrib burned down. The pony barn was quite derelict, a completely ramshackle structure. My brothers saw abandoned detritus, but I saw majesty, remembering the trophy and tack rooms. Here I was, next to the very stalls where I would spend hours brushing and being with my beloved Raindrop."

Today John has a new Raindrop that he is teaching to drive. Pacific Raindrop is young and green, with soft, inquisitive eyes, and a tuft of downy mane between her ears. When I visit him it is cold and muddy—a typical Vermont spring day—and I wonder how her little body is adjusting to the change from balmy California. Killacky lets me take her out into the ring on a lead line where I try out a bit of Clicker Training to get a feel for her. She is a savvy pony, a little uncertain but curious, working out the meanings of her new home and human partner.

"In working with my pony," Killacky says, "I must first understand the world through her eyes, her smells, her experiences, her fears, and her relationships. Only then can we begin to communicate and make progress. Nothing can be imposed from a human perspective; I must first meet her on her terms. And what we learn together on one side often has to start all over again when we change directions."

In learning to drive, Killacky was able to connect with the balanced, able-bodied part of himself. Sitting in the cart behind the pony allowed him to feel the joy of fluid movement and the rhythm of his body in a different way.

Killacky driving "Raindrop Number Two"—the new equine companion named after his childhood pony pal.

"I find a different kind of mobility with my Shetland. I harness her up to a two-wheel open cart and off we go with me seated behind her. Gravity cannot compromise our dancing together, since legs are not engaged in driving. I communicate through my arms, voice, and whip. Long reins are offered with firm, but giving hands as we work on gait changes. For these fleeting moments, I am *not* disabled."

Killacky feels that being a "novice" horse person at midlife is gratifying, that it is sublime to learn through the advice of those at his new barn, from teenagers to an amazing woman in her eighties. His work with the "new" Raindrop gives him a self to explore that is completely different from his art world identity.

"The ex-dancer in me loves diving into what Buddhists call 'a state of unknowing,'" he says. "The beginner's mind is amazingly open. Acquiring new skills is unexpectedly rejuvenating. Laughter at failure and learning from mistakes propel improvement. Thrilled to do my best, whether first or fifth, is so freeing; it used to be all or nothing."

Killacky also speaks of the importance of opening to what is on the periphery of our vision and our awareness. He observes that human eyes, like other predators, are oriented to see what is straight ahead. We hone in, whereas horses have peripheral vision, allowing them to see what is coming in all directions. Learning to use his peripheral vision has helped with his walking.

"Before, I focused intently, looking down and placing one tentative foot in front of the other," he says. "Now I embrace the larger world around me as I ambulate more assertively at home, in my office, on the street, and with my pony at the barn."

Killacky says that as he drives in his cart, he must embrace the entire arena: "Imagine the world opening up in startling ways. Space and light are transformed. No place is more important than another; the image behind is equal to that in front." There may be five or six other riders in the arena at the same time, and the animals—human and horse—are all keenly aware of each other. "The herd mentality is always present. One misstep can set off all the other horses,

BEGINNER'S MIND, BEGINNER'S BODY

🕐 10 MINUTES

PURPOSE: Zen master Shunryu Suzuki says that "beginner's mind" is an empty mind and a ready mind, a mind that is ready for anything and open to everything. "In the beginner's mind there are many possibilities; in the expert's mind there are few."

Letting go of any real or imagined "expertise" opens the door to new discoveries. Beginner's mind allows us to relinquish control of *knowing* and instead attune to the wisdom of what is arising in the moment. That listening and feeling awareness also allows our horses to show us the more subtle signals that we may otherwise have missed. Begin with this simple walking meditation. You may want to try this before you spend time with your horse, noticing how it changes the feeling in your body and the quality of your interaction.

1. Stand outside or inside, in an open area free of obstacles. Notice what is in front of and behind you—and then above and below and to each side.

2. Begin walking slowly, paying attention to the details of your walking—each part of how the foot leaves and then reconnects to the ground. Notice all the little balancing adjustments your body makes to accommodate moving this slowly. Walk without a feeling of going anywhere specific. Simply walk with the intention of being fully present in each part of every step.

3. Stand still once again, opening your awareness three-dimensionally to what is around you.

4. Begin walking again. Let your breath deepen and connect to the steady slow rhythm of the walk. Walk slowly in a curvilinear path, pausing occasionally and visualizing the line of your movement unspooling behind you, feeling both where you are going and where you have been. Continue this walking meditation until you feel your mind untether from any sense of urgency or impatience.

5. Now just stand, letting your body settle into stillness. Breathe into all three dimensions: forward/back, up/down, side/side. Expand your awareness and your sensing in all directions.

Killacky and Raindrop.

OPENING TO THE PERIPHERY, DISSOLVING THE EDGES

🕐 10 MINUTES

PURPOSE: Often our visual sense becomes so predominant that it limits our experience of other sensory information, including our capacity for inner knowing and intuitive wisdom. We often have a hierarchical view of the parts of our bodies, assigning more importance to some parts than others. For example, "My hands are more important than my elbows," quite forgetting that without elbows we would not be able to bring objects toward ourselves, or pull ourselves to standing! This creates a bodily fragmentation that may mirror how we see and feel our horses. This exercise helps the eyes become part of the "democracy" of the body's sensual experiencing. As our eyes relax and soften, there is a cascading, releasing effect on the rest of the body. That softening in us is then transmitted to our horses.

1. Sitting or lying down in a comfortable position, allow your eyes to simply receive what they see with a soft, open gaze. Let go of any need to understand, penetrate, or hold onto what you are seeing. Imagine seeing from the back of the skull, as if you are standing at the back of a large room, looking out into the distance.

crow-hopping sideways off stride. Staying calm and centered is essential for a productive working session."

Killacky brings that same peripheral awareness to his more meditative, non-working moments with Raindrop. One day, she started refusing to go back into her stall after a workout. This went on for weeks, until a friend at the barn suggested spending more time with her after a training session and before putting her away. Now Killacky slows his hands as he takes off tack and brushes her down.

"She stands quietly, contentedly watching the other horses being groomed as cool summer breezes wash over us," he says. "Ten minutes of extra hands-on time and she goes back in her stall with no hesitation. In the pasture, I stand next to her as she grazes and try to experience the world as she does—180 degrees and beyond. As I give myself over to the horizons, the interconnectedness of us all becomes obvious...as if my pony and I become porous and dissolve into the expanse."

2. Become aware of your peripheral vision without changing the position of your head or eyes. As your vision expands to the periphery in all directions, do you feel more relaxed or expansive?

3. Close your eyes and observe the play of light and dark on your closed lids. Then open your eyes and allow them to refocus and simply receive what you are seeing, all the way out to the periphery.

4. Alternate opening and closing your eyes. Change your body's position slightly each time you close your eyes so your perspective is different each time you open them.

5. Can you imagine seeing and sensing in all directions with all the cells of the body? Experiment with becoming more peripheral with *all* your senses: consciously tasting and smelling the subtle undercurrents of flavor in your dinner, listening to the vast and complex aural web of sound, experiencing touch with the whole map of your skin and the multi-dimensional geometry of your movement in space. Let your awareness and your senses meander and savor, taking in what is familiar and what you have never experienced before.

THE LIMITS OF OUR NATURE

At one time I lived in a small cottage in the woods set on a small rock outcropping above a swamp. The basement was cave-like, dank with dark ledges of rock at the back. One day I came down to check a fuse and saw a small head peering out from a crack under a stone step. I did not know what it was. I watched it. It watched me. When I approached, it withdrew. I started to visit it daily, sometimes more than once. It was a salamander, with blue-black oily skin and rows of yellow orange spots that went from the top of the head down the body.

Over the next several weeks, I began to feed her lettuce and bits of vegetation and leave a small plate of water, then sit and wait to see if she would come out to eat. She did, sliding out, spot by spot, pulling the food back into her cave. One day she was all the way out and I managed to gently catch and carry her to the nearby swamp. Loosed into the black, leaf-littered water, she wriggled under cover.

Our limits, imagined or real, often cause us to hide like this salamander, staying motionless, undetected, and hopefully safe. The little salamander is like the part of us that is hiding, that is not fully out, that does not want to be seen—the part that is not quite at home.

For Susan Richards, horsewoman, social worker, and writer, horses have helped her come out of hiding and feel more at ease in the world of humans. Horses are deeply woven in her family background, coming down through generations via her grandmother and great-grandmother. I first discovered her work when I read her book *Chosen by a Horse: How a Broken Horse Fixed a Broken Heart* (Mariner Books, 2007).

It was a hot, late August afternoon, and we were sitting on the shady porch of a restaurant in Rhinebeck, New York. We ordered iced tea and cold, fresh pea soup as I set up my computer to record. When I asked her about how her life with horses began, she said that as a child horses were as if someone threw her a lifeline and she just grabbed it.

"I was aware that something huge and important was involved. You know, it happened after I lost my whole family, and the very next thing I remember is this ecstasy about horses and having horses become the centerpiece of my life."

Richards was a tentative child unsure of her place in the world; someone who did not have a lot of confidence, physically or mentally. Horses and horse paraphernalia were all around her—a universe of smells, sounds, and sights. In her grandmother's attic was a trunk of riding clothes: "brown leather field boots that laced up the front, handmade in England; wool tweed riding jackets with leather buttons and small tailored waists; linen breeches with leather leg patches; and wide hipped jodhpurs with fitted calves."[39]

Unlike many people who are drawn to horses later in life, Richards was tossed into the horse world... her grandmother gave her a horse of her own when she was five. In *Chosen by a Horse* she tells this story:

*"Her name is Bunty," my grandmother proclaimed, handing me the lead line
as she herself marched out of the pasture, leaving me alone with my new
pony. Standing at the other end of the lead, I squinted up at the fat white
body slung between two sets of shaggy legs with a tail that swept the ground
at one end and dark narrowed eyes under thick lashes at the other. It was
like leaving me alone with a chain saw. I knew I was in mortal danger, but
I was holding a horse. My horse. The best thing that had ever happened to
me. I wish I could say I was a natural from the start. That I hoisted myself
onto her back, and, with a willow twig for a crop, went for a wild gallop
around the field. But the truth is, I had no idea what to do. I stood trembling
in my pink sundress, staring at the pretty pony until she lunged forward and
removed some of the baby fat packed around my upper arm.*[40]

Even as a very young child, Richards was aware that the physicality of horses
is huge—they are beautiful and completely who they are. She didn't always see
that authenticity in people, but she always saw it with horses, and that was very
attractive to her. She felt that if she could stay near that energy, make her life
centered around that energy, she would be okay.

"I know this sounds corny, but I am a Sagittarian and my sign is half horse,
half human, and I feel like that is what I am. I always felt that when I was on a
horse, I was magnificent, I was beautiful, I was athletic, I was confident, I was
happy. I was an extension of this animal."

For Richards, limits were in the human world, whereas horses gave her a
sense of feeling and expression. They helped her understand and navigate the
complicated and confusing world of people. She found that observing horses
was like reading good writing.

"I love that horses are so understated," she says. "If a horse is communicating
with you, it's likely very subtle so you have to really listen. I love understatements.
I love writers who write that way. And I love having to pay attention to an animal
just to figure out what's going on. I am a good listener, and I listen to animals
and to horses that way. I have four dogs now. I know them. I know who they are. I
listen. I like walking them along so I can listen to what's going on with them. And
horses give you that opportunity to really listen."

During a recent trip to Wales Richards was hiking with a friend in a place
where there were wild ponies everywhere. They stopped to watch, and one pony
was nibbling another pony and her friend asked her, "What are they doing?" As
Richards explained, she realized that not everyone sees it, not everyone understands all of the communication going on between horses. For her, reading their
movement is like being a part of the herd.

"I had two couples in my pasture, and I just loved watching them and how
they communicated and how one couple would communicate with the other couple. It was like watching fire—endlessly interesting."

READING THE HUMAN HERD

🕐 10 MINUTES

PURPOSE: Becoming a more skillful and astute observer of the human world helps us to better notice what is happening with our horses—what they are seeing, how they are reacting, and what may be causing their responses. As you observe, notice what is in the foreground and background, including your central and peripheral vision. Use all your senses and notice how your body is responding as you watch and listen. Remember, observation includes the observer!

1. While sitting in a café, train station, airport, or just walking down the street begin to observe the patterns and interactions around you in your human herd.

2. Look at the choreography of the movement: the ways people move around or with each other, their proximity or distance. Do they feel isolated or part of a larger whole? Notice moments when two or more people appear to be synchronized in the spatial or expressive aspects of their movement, and other moments when there is no observable affinity.

3. Notice differences in movement qualities: slow or quick, forceful or delicate, tense or relaxed. How does physical tension or relaxation express through others' bodies? Are they vigilant, awake to their surroundings, or oblivious? How is this reflected in the way they move or their body attitude? How do these observations affect you as you watch? Are you breathing?

She found herself observing human interactions as if she were watching a herd of backyard ponies. She could work out the hierarchies, the signals, the personalities of the horses and then the humans. She found that horses were both a sanctuary from the human world and a bridge into the more threatening, incomprehensible existence of people. "I avoided humans. I couldn't wait to get home and be with my horses," she admits. But from all those years working with horses, she felt that she came to understand people through them and to become more forgiving. "People are animals; we're very flawed, and that's not our fault. Through the horses I was able to see the beauty of my own species."

Horses also gave Richards a way to become more comfortable with physical contact. She was never a physical person...now she can hug a friend, but it took her years to be able do that. "I'm not the person that reaches over and touches

Our Horses, Ourselves

4. What assumptions do you make about people because of their movement behaviors?

5. How are they using their eyes? Are they making eye contact? Can you tell if they are narrowing their focus, restricting themselves to looking only forward, or orienting themselves more expansively?

6. Do others' movements use a lot of space (large sphere around the body, also called the *kinesphere*) or are they closer to the body (small kinesphere)? How does this reflect the ways that you use space?

7. Be aware of what is happening in your own body as you observe other people in your environment. What gives you a sense of recognition and excitement? Which qualities or movement dynamics feel like "you" and which are less familiar, even uncomfortable or threatening? Do you sense yourself as a part of this human herd as you are observing? Be curious about the moments when you feel connected to or separated from your herd.

8. Finally, notice how this more detailed and specific way of observing movement qualities—relative tension or relaxation in the body, the subtle movements of tail, head, eyes, and ears—can help you become more conscious of your horse's body language. Again, include yourself in your observations. What is the relationship between your movement and your horse's?

your arm. But I'm very physical around an animal. The smell, the touch—it's that tactile experience that I love with them."

Listening to Richards, I realized that what fascinates me is this feeling of being *an animal among animals*—horse and human (and human and human) feeling each other in a bodily, neuroceptive way (how we assess safety or danger), rather than through language and the performative parts of our personality. It also means learning how others in our herd smell, sound, and move. Not thinking about it too much, but *feeling* it, and reciprocally allowing oneself to *be* seen and felt. This takes practice and also a kind of unstylish courage.

One afternoon I watched my friend Carlos do some repairs on the heating system in my house. Carlos is a big man with a wonderful, dense, stocky physicality. If he were in my herd (and he is), I would feel good grazing near him, keeping him in my peripheral vision, because he is so nicely connected to the earth—a big, warm, safe presence.

How can you read and join your own human herd? Become quiet. Stop talking. Stop thinking *about* and start feeling *into*. Begin with breathing. Don't just look *at*, but let it—the tree, the bird, the dog, the man, the woman—move *into* you. Blend, even for a moment.

LISTENING BEYOND LIMITS

Sheila Ryan and Mijoy.

Sometimes the limits are in our insistence on thinking or analyzing, when the answer may be one that requires a more intuitive, embodied approach.

Ethologists argue endlessly about the emotional lives of animals. They debate about our attribution of emotion to animals, and what constitutes animal intelligence. Dr. Marc Bekoff, in his book *The Emotional Lives of Animals*, notes that, "When it comes to anthropomorphic language, I've noticed a curious phenomenon over the years. If a scientist says that an animal is happy, no one questions it, but if a scientist says that an animal is unhappy, then charges of anthropomorphism are immediately leveled."[41] Animal communicators, or those who claim to have a psychic connection to animal bodies and minds, are often dismissed as charlatans or fabricators of stories about the animals they "talk" to.

I first met intuitive healer Sheila Ryan when she was helping my veterinarian figure out what was going on with my beautiful young Friesian, Tsjalling. Ryan was a typical horse-crazy girl. She started riding at around eight but wasn't interested in the competitive jumping and eventing that so many other girls found thrilling. At the age of sixteen, faced with having to choose between riding lessons and a car, she chose the car, and didn't ride again until midlife. During a particularly difficult time, she began to study alternative healing therapies, animal communication, and Native American traditions. She studied with Grandmother Twylah Nitsch, an elder with the Seneca tribe, learning about animal totems and how we can communicate with the earth. She studied native traditions such as the vision quest, sun dance, medicine wheel, and the shields of the directions, to name a few—teachings that had not been shared with non-native people in the past and were now being taught in an effort to bring people together in understanding.

Ryan describes her first psychic communication in this way: "I was married to a very challenging partner, and in an effort to retain my sanity I would spend a lot of time out in the yard gardening. At one point I was building a stone wall, and I was very frustrated because I didn't know what I was doing. All of a sudden I heard a voice say, 'I'm next,' and when I turned around and saw this rock, and I put it on the wall and it fit like a puzzle piece into the rock I was working on. I started to hear the rocks talk to me, and they told me how to build this 80-foot long stone wall in a matter of a few days."

Ryan's Arabian, Mijoy, was everything that you are not supposed to buy for a first horse: She was sick and very green, often even dangerous. To better understand Mijoy, Ryan began to experiment with psychic communication.

"One day, I put the saddle on her and went to get her bridle, and she took one look at the bridle and started to flip out," Ryan says. "One of my friends said, 'Well, why don't you ask her?' I asked her and she told me that her teeth were killing her. I thought, 'Well, that is strange because I just had her teeth done.'"

Ryan hired another vet who tranquilized the horse and did her teeth, focusing on the back ones, which the first veterinarian had failed to do properly. After the appointment, Mijoy settled completely, and when other boarders at the barn saw the results of Ryan's communications with her Arab, they began to ask if she could "talk" to their horses. Ryan's techniques produced similar success time and time again: Over the years veterinarians have confirmed that areas horses "complained about to her" were, in fact, in need of medical attention.

One woman requested a consult for her older, upper-level dressage horse that had stopped eating. The horse was dropping weight rapidly, it was wintertime, and she didn't know what to do. When Ryan put her hands on the horse, he told her, "I would rather die than stop working."

"I heard that very clearly in my mind," says Ryan. "When I said it out loud to the horse's owner, she burst into tears. She said she was only trying to be good to him. She had been standing outside his stall a number of weeks earlier and thought to herself: 'He is an old man; I have all these acres of land at home, maybe it is time to retire him. He has worked hard for his living, maybe it is time for him to relax.' Well, he must have heard her, because that was when he stopped eating."

The owner put the old horse back in a lesson program the next day and he started eating.

"That was probably four years ago and he is still working," Ryan says. "He loves his kids; loves to go around in circles....This case happened at the beginning of my work with horses, and I said to myself, 'Oh my god, this stuff works.'"

Ryan tells another story about a horse she was asked to see because he had stopped drinking water when in his stall. When she walked in to see him, the horse looked at her and then looked at the water bucket. She walked over to the water bucket, put her hand in it, and got a big electric shock. It was a heated bucket and had shorted out. The horse was refusing to drink because every time he did he got zapped.

The Journey with Tsjalling

"Hearts are there to be broken, and I say that because that seems to be just part of what happens with hearts. I mean, mine has been broken so many times that I have lost count. But it just seems to be broken open more and more and more, and it just gets bigger. In fact, I was saying to my therapist not long ago, 'You know, my heart by now feels like it has just sort of dropped open, you know, like how a big suitcase falls open. It feels like that.' And that's the way I'm used to my heart feeling. The feeling of the heart being so open that the wind blows through it."

Alice Walker

Shambala Sun, January 1997

My trainer Ellie Coletti and I noticed early on that when my three-year-old Friesian Tsjalling was walking, his legs meandered before finding the ground and he seemed to have difficulty with his balance. His stifle (equivalent to the human knee joint) locked frequently, immobilizing his hind leg. Initially we attributed all of this to his size, his rapid growth, and his youth, and were not terribly worried. Our vet confirmed that the symptoms are not unusual for a young horse that was growing rapidly. But unsure, I asked Dr. Sharon Doolittle, a veterinarian, chiropractor, and medical intuitive to look at him. Finding various imbalances in his spine, she worked to correct them over a period of several months. The corrections did not seem to hold, and she began to look for an underlying cause. As a medical intuitive, she often "feels in her own body" what the horse is experiencing, and she said she felt a dull pain in her head when working on Tsjalling.

One day I got an urgent call from my trainer: While she was riding Tsjalling, he stumbled and went down to his knees. She was fine, he was fine, but now we were really worried.

Dr. Doolittle suggested a consult with Sheila Ryan. At the end of the session, Ryan placed her hands on Tsjalling and asked if there was anything that he would like to tell us. He said he appreciated our efforts to help him; that he was doing his best. But according to Ryan, there was a static quality to his communication, as if he were trying to speak through a barrage of radio signals, and like Dr. Doolittle, she also felt pain in her own head when she approached him. She described the pain as "blinding."

After two trips to Cornell Equine Hospital in Ithaca, New York, and many possible diagnoses and treatments, it was clear that Tsjalling was getting worse. Cornell could not give us a conclusive diagnosis because it was too dangerous to fully sedate a Friesian—the breed is very sensitive to anesthesia medication. Back at home, most of the time Tsjalling appeared to be comfortable, the same sweet boy we all loved, but at times his behavior was erratic and explosive. He became violent, kicking out, pulling away, or recalcitrant, refusing to move. There was concern for the safety of the staff at the barn.

Then one day while being led from his paddock into the stable, Tsjalling lashed out with his front legs, bucked, and reared violently, ripping away from his handler. He galloped wildly around the property, before he suddenly stopped, looking dazed, as if he had no memory of the incident.

I called my good friend, animal communicator Kate Reilly. She "reads" horses' bodies at a distance, often in great anatomical detail, and prefers that owners tell her only the name, size, age, and appearance of the horse, without any information about symptoms or previous diagnosis. She confirmed that Tsjalling was in extreme pain. She said I must consider euthanasia, reminding me that animals do not regard dying with the same emotional attachments and fears that we do. They accept and understand death in a way that we humans do not.

I find it hard, even now, to think of the journey I took with an exquisitely beautiful, and—on the outside—seemingly healthy horse to the large animal hospital for the purposes of euthanasia. It was a crisp, sunny, fall day and Tsjalling was as radiant as I had ever seen him, his coat shining like ebony. His beautiful neck arched like a swan to take the carrot from my hand. I walked him into a stall to wait as the attending veterinarian called the insurance company. Everyone admired him; wanted to touch him. I stood with him, feeling desperately sad. The hideousness of the situation was that I did not know for sure that I was doing the right thing. I was taking a leap of faith with him—standing at the abyss and praying that the decision was the right one.

I led him outside to a small grassy enclosure where Tsjalling cropped grass unconcerned, as if to say, "Look at this day! Can you feel the sun on your back? Can you taste this beauty?" I wondered if he knew that he was about to die. Did he sense my distress? Was he at peace with what was about to happen?

The vet suggested that I not be present when he went down. My wife Pam and I walked to where we could not see him and waited for the injections to take effect. We both whispered the Buddhist chant, "*Om tara tutare ture soha*," the Tibetan words spoken at death to help the soul find its next auspicious incarnation. We heard him fall to the ground, and I struggled to turn and walk back to him. Between his lips were pieces of the bright green grass he had been eating when he died. I stretched myself out next to his body and wept. The journey was over. My beautiful friend was gone.

I waited anxiously for the results of the autopsy, required by the insurance company, which would also confirm the "rightness" or "wrongness" of the decision. Three days later, the veterinarian called. The first thing she said was that she was certain that 80 percent of Tsjalling's symptoms and behaviors had been caused by severe pain: compression on the spinal cord and permanent neurological abnormalities that could not be treated. It was unusual to see such gross changes, she said, and the autopsy confirmed that my beautiful boy suffered from a type of Wobbler's disease. I heard words like "multiple lesions," "vertebral instability," "secondary changes in the cartilage," "remarkable changes in the articulating facets," "genetic predisposition." I was breathing hard as I listened, relief flooding me. I had done the right thing. I called everyone who had helped with Tsjalling—to grieve, yes, but also to share the relief that he had been released from his suffering.

Ryan thinks everybody receives messages from horses...they just don't know how to interpret them. She says working with horses and humans requires intuitive alignment, and she has to get "empty" and quiet enough within to hear what is being transmitted.

Sheila Ryan and her client Alex.

"I think we are all vibrating molecules of power," she explains, "and if you get yourself in the right state of mind, which means being able to shut down the chatter, and get clear enough, you can translate those energy feelings or fields...if you ask the right questions, then you can get the answers. It is possible to ask vague or incorrect questions and get answers that are misleading, so you need to make the questions very clear. It is not so much the technique, but rather the clarity of the questions."

When asked how she begins to connect with a horse, she says, "I take a nice deep breath, exhale, and shut my brain off. I stop *trying* because there is nothing to do. I become an empty room and let horses walk into the room and present to me what they want to present."

Ryan has found a way to open the gates between herself and the horse by releasing any limiting expectations or preconceptions and simply listening. What she has found is that the horse is always there, waiting to be heard.

UNRAVELING THE LIMITS

On an unusually balmy December day I went to see Nelson with some holiday carrots. He was very soft and friendly from the beginning, seeming to echo the quiet peace of the day. I could feel him looking at me, waiting. So I began our dance by asking him to move around me in a small circle, to stay calm while responding to the "Go" and the "Whoa" signals from my gestures and movements. He was relaxed when circling to the right, but still uncertain moving to the left. I asked him to keep trying on that harder side, and suddenly the exercise opened into something surprising. I began to improvise more freely with changes of direction and with different kinds of movement cues than ever before. I used my hands, my body, the lead rope, and the wand. For the first time ever, nothing seemed to rattle Nelson. He seemed to want to stay in this dance with me. Even after I opened the gate of his catch pen so he could move out into the large field, he stayed with me—no halter, no lead rope—just moving together; being still together.

Everything about my work with Nelson had been an improvisation. At the beginning, our movement vocabulary was very small, very careful. But in that moment, our language was suddenly expanding—new options, more choices, and greater flexibility—all springing from a reservoir of trust. There was a more reliable continuity from one day to the next, and the fragments of our interactions were weaving into a whole cloth. The new openness between us was deepening and penetrating, reminding me of the comparison of meditation to dipping a cloth into dye. The first 100 times, it is said, the color will rinse away, but slowly and steadily, the color begins to take and deepen.

CHAPTER FOUR

THE SPACE BETWEEN TWO MINDS: TOUCHING THE BODY

You've heard it said there's a window
that opens from one mind to another,

but if there's no wall, there's no need
for fitting the window, or the latch.

Rumi
Illuminated Rumi
(Crown Publishing, 1997),
translated by Coleman Barks,
used by permission of
Coleman Barks.

THE LANGUAGE OF TOUCH

Capprichio is a gorgeous black Andalusian stallion with long braids reaching down his legs, a massive neck, and glossy black coat. He is trained in all of the elegant, showy movements of Grand Prix dressage: pirouettes, flying changes, flowing lateral movements. To feel Capprichio lift himself up into a *passage*—a lofty, slow, elevated trot—is ecstatic, breathtaking. Sadly, in our eleven years together, this wondrous horse has struggled through one injury after another. He has a degenerative disease of the suspensory ligaments, the architecture of connective tissue that provides support for the lower legs. He has had stem cell injections, platelet-rich plasma injections, hyaluronic acid and cortisone injections, acupuncture, nutritional supplements, chiropractic—but the progression of the disease is inexorable. There have been months of rehabilitation, followed by months of wonderful rides, and then once again, a sudden, often inexplicable re-injury.

During Capprichio's last recovery, I came to the barn to "tack walk" him—a twenty-minute walk under saddle to help him maintain his fitness as we were waiting for the ligaments

Capprichio and Ingrid Schatz in the dance "Pas de Trois" with rider Brandi Rivera.

Our Horses, Ourselves

to heal. I groomed him, wrapped his legs, and began to collect the saddle and bridle, when I felt him watching me and stopped. I realized that I was preoccupied with worry, moving through my preparations in an automatic, distracted way. I stood with him quietly, and then put my hands on his back. For the next hour, my hands explored, caressed, and massaged his body. I leaned into him, felt him take the weight of my body and press back. There was no feeling of separation between us, no sense of me as a "doer" or "fixer," but rather a soft bodily conversation free of saddle, bridle, bits, and agenda.

> *"The primary sense organs of touch and movement are located throughout the body—in every cell. Touch is emphasized in the skin. Movement is emphasized in the proprioceptive and kinesthetic receptors in the joints, ligaments, muscles, and tendons, the interoceptors of the organs, and the vestibular mechanism of the inner ear. Movement and touch develop simultaneously. Touch is the other side of movement. Movement is the other side of touch. They are the shadow of each other."*

> Bonnie Bainbridge Cohen

Touch is a sensory language that we speak with not only our hands, but our entire body. Touch is how we connect, explore, and soothe. Touch brings us into a visceral and immediate sensual relationship with the world around us. When coupled with our other senses, touching is one of the ways that we draw close, decode, and savor. Touching dissolves our separateness, and is the most intimate and feeling way that we bridge the sacred space between two beings. *How* we touch—the quality of intention, receptivity, and listening that we bring to that act—defines our attention to and caring for each other. It has all the potency and potential of prayer. Touching is always a shared act, whether we acknowledge it or not. David Abram, author of *The Spell of the Sensuous* (Vintage, 1997) and *Becoming Animal* (Vintage, 2011), calls the phenomenon of being touched by what we are touching "reciprocity." He suggests that we are a part of all that we touch and behold, not a separate entity that is only the *toucher* but always, inextricably, the *touched*.

"As breathing involves a continual oscillation between exhaling and inhaling," he writes, "offering ourselves to the world at one moment and drawing the world into ourselves at the next, so sensory perception entails a like reciprocity, exploring the moss with our fingers while feeling the moss touching us back, at one moment gazing at the mountains and at the next feeling ourselves seen, or sensed, from that distance..."[42]

Touching a Horse

How does this happen?
When did you find yourself so engrossed
by your hands' touch,
such trembling in your heart
that your mind gives up?
When did you make this leap?
How can you not repeat this over and over?
How can you not change everything
for just and only this moment?

Pam White

For Pam White—painter, horsewoman, and my wife—there is sensuousness in handling her materials that reminds her of how she feels touching horses. "I love how the paints or pastels feel as they are applied, or the way a particular paper or canvas feels under my brushes and hands." She spent the first several years with her Friesian gelding Sanne learning his body, "speaking" to him with her touches, exploring every part of him, and introducing herself as she mapped his body with her hands, conscious of how he was touching and changing her at the same time.

Conscious, intentional touch creates more gentle, generous, and embodied relationships. It is not always important to figure out the content of what is being communicated between you and your horse, as thinking can interfere with the feeling quality of what is actually happening in the moment. It can also take us into a task-like mode, making touching a job—something to do and finish— rather than savoring the experience and allowing the act of touching to transmit from the horse to our bodies and minds, and from us to the horse.

Rumi's vision of a window opening from one mind to another from the beginning of this chapter echoes what physicist David Bohm calls "undivided wholeness in flowing movement." According to Bohm, "We have reversed the usual classical notion that the independent 'elementary parts' of the world are the fundamental reality, and that the various systems are merely particular contingent forms and arrangements of these parts. Rather, we say that inseparable quantum interconnectedness of the whole universe is the fundamental reality, and that relatively independent behaving parts are merely particular and contingent forms within this whole."[43]

Touch is a way of opening Rumi's windows, dissolving separateness, and experiencing this feeling of "undivided wholeness in flowing movement" between us. In learning to deeply feel and calibrate our touching, we may also become more conscious of the importance of measuring and balancing our verbal

Our Horses, Ourselves

PRESENCE, GIVING, AND RECEIVING

🕐 10 MINUTES

PURPOSE: Learning to be more intentional and conscious about the way we touch our horses is an essential part of creating a more embodied and friendly relationship, one that includes the horse as partner and collaborator.

1. Place your hands on the horse's neck, back, or ribcage. Let your hands, shoulders, and arms relax and soften with this contact. Make your intention to simply make a connection with that part of the horse's body without any kind of "doing." Notice the horse's reaction to being touched in this deliberate, unhurried way.

2. Breathe, and feel the rhythm of the horse's breath, and the warmth and the texture of his coat.

3. Notice the sensation of *giving* and *receiving* through your hands, of both touching and being touched.

4. Slowly shift your hands to another part of the horse's body, noticing his response as you move and resettle them. If he is nervous or moves away from the contact, stand quietly with your arms relaxed at your sides and just visualize placing your hands on your horse.

5. Exhale and slowly place your hands again. Can you soften your touch so that there isn't a reaction, as if you were, as Phoebe Caldwell suggests, "slipping into the water without causing a ripple"? Feel how your hands are supported by and connected to your whole body.

6. If you feel any urgency or effort in your hands, body, or mind, take a breath and release it, just resting in a companionable stillness with your hands in contact with the horse. Can you let go of any feeling of being a separate being—even for just a moment?

7. When you are riding, try to bring this same sensitivity and clarity to the way that you tack up, and to the moment that you pick up the reins and make a connection with the horse's mouth. There shouldn't be a reaction or bracing, or any interruption in the smooth flow of energy or the quality of shared communication between you.

communications, and taking responsibility for the impact of our words and how they land in the holy space between us.

Refining Touch

Shannon is at the barn tacking up her horse, Rafi, who stands in the stable aisle on the crossties. She reaches for the brushes and hoof pick in an absentminded, off-hand way, and curries his coat with strong, circular strokes, bringing up the loose hair and dirt. Then she brushes him with a stiff brush, flicking off the debris. Her strokes are quick, forceful, and business-like. Rafi moves away from her brushing, paws with his front leg, and she yells at him, "Stop it! Stand still!" He freezes momentarily, and then resumes his nervous pawing, as she tosses on the saddle pad, then the saddle, tightening the girth and snapping the stirrups down.

Many of us would not like to be touched in the way that we touch our horses. Our touch can be perfunctory, more about "handling"—the execution of a series of tasks—and performed with little relational intention or awareness. But there is another way of touching that is conscious, intentional, and sensuous. The horse's skin is extraordinarily sensitive, able to feel and move the precise spot where a fly has landed with a twitching shiver. Our own naked skin is also an elaborate map, able to perceive everything from the delicate movement of air through the hairs of the arm to piercing pain. Our skin is the pliant, protective boundary between what lies outside of us and what is held within, containing specialized receptors for pressure, temperature, vibration, and pain.

Horses and humans share the fact that when we experience pleasurable stimulation, it transmits a message to the brain releasing oxytocin, a neurotransmitter sometimes referred to as the "cuddle hormone." That hormonal response is an integral part of our mammalian ability to relax into a state of well-being and social recognition. Harsh or careless touch triggers the horse's (and our own) fight-or-flight response, shutting off our ability to connect socially or learn because our nervous system is overwhelmed by a barrage of frightening or unpleasant stimuli.

The Touch That Teaches

According to Linda Tellington-Jones, the intent of her Tellingon TTouch bodywork (a collection of circles, lifts, and slides done with the hands and fingertips) is to activate the function of the cells and awaken cellular intelligence, by "turning on the electric lights of the body." It has been shown to help the horse think rather than simply react, and it enhances the horse's ability to feel his own body and motion. It is a practice that helps us to become more skillful and conscious in the ways that we touch our horses.

Tellington-Jones touches horses with the skill and subtlety of an artist. Her work is as ephemeral as that of a dancer, but its traces remain in the horses she touches. Her "art" is etched into the cells and the memories of thousands of

SHARING GROOMING

🕐 10–20 MINUTES

PURPOSE: Grooming is not just about cleaning your horse. It is a way of waking up the skin and underlying tissues and making a bodily connection with him. Including your own body in the process can be a part of your warm-up and another way of creating a "felt sense" of the relationship you share.

1. Groom your own body as you groom your horse. (This practice will encourage you to keep your brushes clean!) Use the curry down your legs, hips, arms, and on your shoulders. Use the same kind of strokes and pressure that you use on your horse's body. Notice how it feels: Rushed? Harsh? Or pleasant? Stimulating? Do the same thing with the brushes, noticing your body's responses to the different textures, stiffness, and the quality of stroke that you use for each.

2. Now let your hands wander slowly over your horse's body with your eyes open. Imagine your hands are "feel-reading" the landscape of your horse's body.

3. Repeat Step 2, this time with your eyes closed. What more do you notice when your eyes are closed?

4. Now groom your horse, remembering what felt good to your body. Take your time, and continue to explore the horse's body with your brushes and hands. Be less efficient and more curious. What if that is all that you do together today?

horses over the past six decades. Tellington-Jones asks participants in her trainings to open their hearts to horses, whom she sees as teachers and guides. Her intention is to create a mindful, generous reciprocity between horse and human.

At a workshop in Western Massachusetts, Tellington-Jones, her eyes narrowing, watched Rowan, a huge, six-year-old draft horse that belonged to the Providence, Rhode Island, police force. At the time she had just celebrated her seventieth birthday, but I had seen her climb without hesitation onto a horse that women fifty years younger would hesitate to mount. I had—more than once— seen her take a horse through a series of gentle training steps, ending with her cantering around the arena, smiling broadly, with the horse wearing nothing but

The Space Between Two Minds: Touching the Body

a saddle and guided by a loose rope ring around his neck. But on this day, she was not riding—at least not yet.

Rowan was used for crowd control but was having trouble because he was easily spooked (not a good quality for a police horse). Tellington-Jones observed him for several minutes as Manuel, his rider, walked him back and forth in front of the class. She said quietly, "He doesn't feel his body; he has no idea where his feet are." She felt that because he was so big and had probably grown very quickly, he could not feel where his body began and ended. We could see that he was tentative with his feet, as if he was wearing someone else's too-large shoes. When he turned, he looked anxiously over his shoulder, as if his hindquarters were a surprise to him.

Over the next six days, Tellington-Jones instructed us in how to use various TTouches and ground exercises to help Rowan feel his body, and in particular, his legs and feet. We used small, circular TTouches all around the top of his hooves. We taught Rowan how to stand as we lifted one leg at a time, rotating the hoof and foreleg in small circles. This helped him find and adjust his balance while showing us where he was tight in his hips or shoulders. He learned to walk slowly and calmly through a maze structure created with ground poles to help him find his balance and learn to bend right or left as he negotiated turns. As he moved, pausing after each turn, we stroked his body all over with a long "wand" (similar to a dressage whip) to give him proprioceptive feedback and help him feel where his body was in space. By the end of the week, Rowan was a different horse. He moved his feet easily and confidently, and his rider, Manuel, was astonished by his transformation.

Tellington TTouch is not about telling the horse what to do or fixing a problem by manipulating the horse's muscles, but asking a question with your hands or movement and listening to the horse's response. Called "the touch that teaches," practitioners focus on supporting the horse's body in finding its own balance, and helping the horse think and feel rather than simply react. Tellington-Jones teaches her students that with touch, "less is more." This idea comes from her study of the work of Moshe Feldenkrais, who developed The Feldenkrais Method, "a process of organic learning, movement, and sensing to free you from habitual patterns and allow for new patterns of thinking, moving, and feeling to emerge" (www. feldenkraisinstitute.com). (In a Feldenkrais class, an individual performs specific movements—often based on developmental movement patterns or ordinary daily activities—that engage thinking, sensing, and imagination.) Tellington-Jones observes that by reducing force and pressure, becoming more subtle with the way she touches the horse, she can feel in greater detail, and so can the horse. Real-time biofeedback studies by Anna Wise, author of *The High Performance Mind,* found that during TTouch, the brain waves of both practitioner and recipient come into balance. She called this brainwave pattern the "Awakened Mind."[44]

Steadying Octango

Octango was a thirteen-year-old Dutch Warmblood, owned and ridden by his trainer Barbi Breen at Grand Prix—the highest competitive level in the sport of dressage. I had the opportunity to work with him during a Tellington Method workshop at Sky Horse Ranch in California. Octango had a history of being very spooky at shows, or any time he was separated from his favorite barnmate. He was afraid of sudden movements, and especially anxious and reactive when approached by a woman in a skirt bringing him his blue ribbon! Breen wanted to help Octango become steadier, calmer, and less easily rattled.

On the first day we observed that Octango was anxious and easily flustered, especially by the sheep grazing just outside the arena. Tellington-Jones got on, walking him slowly, with his head low and relaxed while softly stroking his neck, back, and hips. After a few moments, she circled close to the scary sheep, but now Octango seemed unconcerned, even relaxed when she stopped near them. When asked what she had done to create this change, Tellington-Jones replied that she was visualizing "smiling into the horse's cells," with her touches and bodily connection with Octango. By sending a friendly intention to the horse, visualizing his cells smiling, she was creating harmony and a calm connection between horse and rider. She also says that she speaks to the horse "from the heart—consciously feeling the emotion of joy and gratitude I will feel as the horse understands. The horse (or any other animal) gets the picture when the message comes from the heart."

Greg Braden, the author of *Secrets of the Lost Mode of Prayer* (Hay House, 2006), calls this kind of visualizing as "praying rain." It is a sensuous, embodied way of invoking what we desire, for example the blessing of a drenching down-pour. He sees this as different from "praying *for* rain," which invokes the feeling of lack, dryness, and parched thirsting of the land. The idea is that by visualizing the sensory details of what we seek to create—the darkening of the sky, the scent of rain on the wind, the rumble of thunder, or with our horses, a quality of ease and engagement in a transition, for example—actually attracts the outcome we desire.

The Touch That Invites

I use the "praying rain" way of visualizing when I am working with fearful, trau-matized, or injured horses. With Nelson, for example, I visualized a slow, friendly, playful conversation in touch and movement, bringing my nervous system into alignment with the state I wanted to evoke and support in him. Many horses have a more predominant hyper-arousal of the sympathetic nervous system. They are ready to flee at a moment's notice. When working with them, I have to settle myself into a calm, inwardly attuned state, tracking the relaxation of my body with focused breathing and active grounding.

I often worked with Nelson without any kind of restraint, so it was important that he not become excited because once he was moving at speed, it was hard to

Making a connection with Nelson.

bring him back into a settled, receptive state. Many times, I began my sessions with the Clicker Training he'd come to know, asking him to target by touching the back of my hand with his nose. When he did, I reinforced the movement with a clicking sound and a small piece of carrot. As we repeated the cue over and over, his touches became fuller and more intentional, as if he wanted to be sure I knew he understood the game, and that he was *choosing* to connect with me.

As Nelson allowed me to be closer for longer periods of time, I began to scan his body with my hands, calibrating the duration and firmness of my touch by his response. Scanning helped me feel for any subtle changes in temperature or texture on the surface of his body, which could indicate areas of tension or discomfort. My other intention with scanning was to help him feel his body as a whole—connecting head to tailbone, belly to spine, side to side, hip and shoulder to hoof—all of which helped him have a clearer sense of his physical self and a greater feeling of safety and confidence.

Scanning the Surfaces

Many years ago I had an experience of whole body scanning in a Delicious Movement Workshop taught by the dancers Eiko and Koma. These Japanese dancers are known for their extraordinarily slow and richly detailed way of moving. Lying on the floor with my eyes closed, I could feel where the sun had warmed the floor and how it, in turn, was warming my skin. We were learning a technique called "surveying," using the floor to explore and map the surfaces of our bodies. Moving with extreme slowness, we focused on parsing the detailed landscape of our skin, using the floor as if it were another body or a pair of hands. As I began to move, almost immediately I felt a flood of sensation. Eiko showed us how to survey not just the broad plains of the body, but the caverns, valleys, and hidden rifts: the spaces behind the ears, the backs of the knees, the armpits. As she moved, her body floated over the floor, morphing from one extraordinary shape to another, her long, black hair trailing like another limb.

It was an unbelievable challenge to stay on the surface of the body, rather than settling my weight comfortably onto the floor and into the underlayers of

Our Horses, Ourselves

SCANNING HANDS

🕐 10 MINUTES

PURPOSE: Use scanning to become more sensitive to the outer form and shape of an object, a person, or your horse. Use it to make your initial connection. How does this change your sense of what you are touching and its relationship to you?

1. While sitting or standing, place your left hand on your right shoulder.

2. With one slow, continuous stroke, slide your hand over the curve of the shoulder and down the length of the arm, over the hand, then continue the stroke up the palm, the underside of the arm up to the armpit.

3. Now stroke down the side of the body along the ribs to the hips, down your leg all the way to the foot. Slide your hand up the inside of the thigh, to the belly, and bring it to rest over the heart. Take a slow breath in and out.

4. Repeat this stroke on the same side, even more slowly and more lightly. Notice how, as you slow and lighten the touch, you are able to "read" more about the surface of your shoulder, arm, and side, and how the scanning hand is also being "read" by the surface it is touching. Note any subtle changes in heat, in texture, in contour, and sensation, and whether your body relaxes as you scan.

5. Take a breath in and out and then repeat the entire sequence with the right hand stroking down the left side of the body. Notice any differences from side to side. Is one hand more sensitive than the other? Does one side of the body feel more awake, softer, or fuller?

6. Try scanning a surface (another body, a chair, the floor) with parts of your body other than your hands—your face, hips, back, legs, or feet. How refined can your feeling become as you scan with these less familiar parts of your body?

7. As you are sitting reading this, take a moment to slowly let your hands scan the surface of whatever is near you, first with your eyes open and then with them closed. Use not just the tips of the fingers, but the palms and heels and backs of the hands, the wrists, and the lower arms. Notice

CONTINUED ▶

CONTINUED FROM PAGE 91

contour, shape, texture, smoothness, roughness, warmth, or coolness as you play with this.

8. Use a slow scanning touch to make a first contact with your horse's body, and to help you become even more familiar with the landscape of his body; able to discern any subtle changes that may indicate areas that need attention or support. Can you find something new in this landscape as you scan—something you have never noticed before?

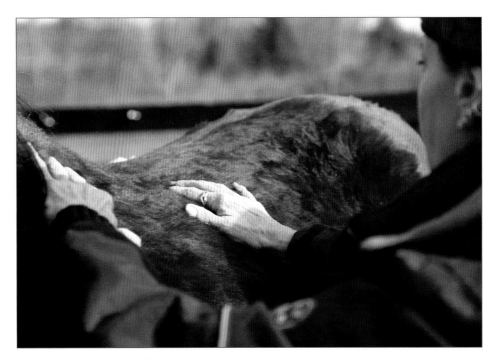

Touching a horse with soft, scanning hands.

muscle and bone. Surveying felt like hovering at the body's edges, as if I could be released from gravity, drifting across the outer terrain of my body. My tactile sense became electric, microscopic, giving me close-up and detailed information about my skin's surface and what it was touching.

Similarly, scanning—using one part of the body to move slowly and lightly over another part—gives you detailed information about the surface you are touching and its relationship to the underlying tissues. Tellington-Jones uses a

Our Horses, Ourselves

scanning touch as I had on Nelson—to look for subtle differences in temperature, and roughness or smoothness of the coat, which may reveal changes in the skin, underlying muscle and connective tissue. She starts on one side of the horse with her hand just behind his ear and slides down the body close to the spine. On a person, she begins at the forehead and traces behind the ear and down each side of the spine all the way to the heel.

TOUCH AND ATTUNEMENT

In Don Hanlon Johnson's book *Groundworks* (North Atlantic Books, 1997), Bonnie Bainbridge Cohen writes: "As we move in utero, our skin is stimulated by the amniotic fluid, the uterine wall and by one part of our body touching another. Thus we discover touch and movement in synchrony. Movement occurs at two levels, movement of our cells within the boundaries of the skin and movement of the body through space. Touch also occurs at two levels, cellularly and contact of our skin from the outside.

"The experiences of movement and touch in utero are primary factors in establishing our ability to comprehend and organize touch and movement after birth—to receive from outside and to express ourselves from within. These experiences also allow us to actively differentiate between what is occurring within the boundaries of our skin and what is occurring on the outside of our skin—to know who we are and who we are not."[45]

For over fifty years Bonnie Bainbridge Cohen has been an innovator and leader whose work has influenced the fields of bodywork, movement, dance, yoga, body psychotherapy, childhood education, and many other body-mind disciplines. Whether working with a baby with developmental challenges or teaching a group of professional dancers, Bainbridge Cohen's movement has the quality of an Aikido master, flowing seamlessly from high to low, wide to narrow, graceful and grounded at once. With her halo of white hair and startlingly clear gaze, she gives the impression of a being both flesh and air.

Bainbridge Cohen describes her work with touch and movement as an *attunement*...listening for a resonance between herself and the person with whom she is working: "I would say that I'm in a state of awareness. If I'm working with any area of someone else's body, I will go into that area of my body to see. In the process I become more open also. It becomes like two bells ringing on the same pitch. We can resonate each other."[46]

My own experience with her touch followed the replacement of my right hip. By chance, Bainbridge Cohen was visiting Martha's Vineyard (where I lived at the time), when I was recovering from the surgery. Besides being in pain, I could not feel my body as a whole; I felt as if there had been a complete severing between my upper and lower body (there had). Over a period of five days, she used the subtlest of touches to reweave my body's connections: muscle, nerve, organ, tendon, bone, fluids, and the subtle energy that flows in every living being. In her book, she describes a similar process with a young boy whose leg had stopped growing due to a traumatic accident. Following her work with him, the boy's leg, to the astonishment of his doctors, began to grow normally:

"Attuning to this delicate process is the key to bone re-patterning," she writes. "This process takes place within the cells of our bodies and is not easily obvious to others observing from the outside, because there is minimally perceptible change between us in either the practitioner's hands or in the client's body. These internal micro-movements also underlie our proprioceptive sense or knowledge of where all of our body parts are in relation to each other and in relationship to gravity and space, and our kinesthetic sense of perception of how we engage in movement. Cells change due to interaction with their environment. Therefore, deep trans-formation of tissue takes place when there is an ongoing dialogue between the practitioner and the client at the subtle level of the cellular matrix."[47]

Although I could not tell precisely what she was doing with her hands, I had the completely clear sensation of her listening to my body and answering with her own. These responses were not dramatic, but incredibly delicate, and at the same time fully legible to my body. Her touch had nothing to do with mechan-ical massage and everything to do with a conversation at the cellular level that enabled my body to rediscover itself and its connections with my new "cyborg" parts. I felt her touch speaking to each layer of injured tissue—in its own lan-guage—reweaving it into the whole cloth of my body.

Touch Using The Developmental Stages of Movement

According to Bainbridge Cohen, our movement can be understood developmen-tally as consisting of five basic actions: yield, push, reach, grasp, and pull. Often our conversations and physical interactions with our animal companions, chil-dren, partners, and ourselves, are defined by the "reach, grasp, pull" phases, and lack the grounding of the simple, essential *yield*.

To experience yielding, imagine that you are holding a sleeping baby on your shoulder, the feeling of that baby's body softening and molding itself to your chest and shoulder, and the reciprocity of your own body softening to meet the infant. Can you recall the experience of an embrace where you and the other person softened fully into each other, losing any sense of separateness, becom-ing for a moment, one body? Can you imagine yielding your hands onto the reins, and then finding a yielding quality of the reins with the horse's mouth, without changing the position of your hands, loosening or losing contact, but simply having the intention of *softening*?

Riding Is Contact Improvisation

Contact Improvisation is a flying, falling dance form based on the physical ex-change of weight between two dancers, creating constantly changing relationships through the contact of skin, muscle, bone, and their underlying structures. In Contact Improvisation dancers give their body's weight to another body, finding a point of balance between the two bodies that is fully committed and at the same time requires shared responsibility for weight and physical support. Like riders, their attention is focused on gravity, space, and connection with another. Dancer and educator Ann Cooper Albright says that "the experience of internal sensations and the flow of the movement between two bodies is more important than specific shapes or formal positions. Dancers learn to move with a consciousness of the physical communication implicit within the dancing."[48]

Pony yielding his chin into dancer Ingrid's shoulder.

Riders must learn to move with consciousness of the physical communication in the riding. Riding is a contact sport, a kind of Contact Improvisation, even, and a very different kind of touching, involving two bodies (one of another species) in a moving dialogue. Riding engages our breathing, bone-to-bone, muscle-to-muscle, blood-to-blood relationship with the horse. Usually when we think of riding, we speak of being carried by the horse, or of sitting deep into the horse, and of blending our rhythms with his. Each gait, each change of direction, tempo, and rhythm has a different somatic resonance in the body of the rider, requiring continual, sensitive micro-adjustments.

Dancer Karen Diego describes her experience of Contact Improvisation in words that remind me of riding: "We learn to take nurturing touch. We learn to allow our bodies to be supported, perhaps for the first time since childhood. We learn to give the center of our weight to another human. We decide to open ourselves through curiosity, sensuality, emotionality, and physicality. Body tissues soften and relax. Defenses come down. We open up."[49]

Whole Body Yielding

I watched as my dancers DeAnna Pellecchia and Ingrid Schatz rehearsed a piece with Escorial, nicknamed "Pony." Pony was trained to move and respond to cues without any tack or means of restraint and was an astute reader of human and equine body language. His trainer, Sarah Hollis, asked him to lie down, and after he settled on the ground, DeAnna moved slowly toward him and began leaning into him, shifting her weight over his back, hips, and shoulders. Pony looked

YIELDING

 10 MINUTES

PURPOSE: Yielding is the first way that we experience support as infants. It is the foundation of our sense of connection with the earth and our caregivers. Learning to use the yielding touch gives horse and human the shared feeling of deep connection and support. You can use the yielding touch with your horse, dog, cat, or a friend. You can also practice the yielding touch on your own body.

1. Gently place your hands on your horse's body. Allow your hand to find a place to rest. Notice any response to your touch and what you feel in all parts of your body as you make this contact.

2. Without pressing, gradually allow your hands to soften into the horse's body as if they are sinking into soft, warm mud. With each exhale, deepen the sensation. Feel how yielding into the surface enables you to begin to sense the deeper layers of the horse's body.

3. Now feel yourself yielding with the innermost parts of your hands—the small muscles around the bones. Without increasing the pressure of your touch, let the "sinking into mud" quality penetrate your arms, shoulders, chest, hips, legs, and feet.

curious, then a bit alarmed, and then over the next several minutes, he relaxed, allowing her movement to flow over and into his body. Ingrid moved in and joined DeAnna. Both women softened into Pony, their bodies arching, rolling, and folding over his, careful to calibrate the amount of weight that they gave him, and maintaining an even, slow pace so as not to startle him. They practiced yielding, interspersed with moments of reaching an arm or leg, lengthening their bodies into a new relationship with Pony's. There was a quality of pouring, surrendering—a breathing connection through the shared layers of skin, muscle, and bone. As Pony shifted his body, they adjusted their movement: pausing, slowing, and subtly changing their points of balance.

Most of us will not roll and balance on a horse like Ingrid and DeAnna. However, learning to yield our bodies into the support of the horse is a crucial part of riding—in particular developing a deep, balanced, and responsive seat. When we

4. Slowly release your hands from the contact as if you were lifting them out of warm mud, and yield into another place on the horse's body. As you move your hands, can you sense what part of the horse's body is "asking" to be touched? Pay attention to each phase: touch, yield, and lift.

5. Repeat this several times, staying with each yield for at least one minute so that you can fully settle and let go of any impatience or wanting to move on to the next thing. See if slowing each phase of the movement helps you feel more connected and centered. If your hands were speaking, what would they be saying?

6. Allow your touch to become more three-dimensional, creating a sense of volume in your hands. Without increasing the pressure, visualize the shapes of the underlying structures (muscles, organs), allowing your hands to both receive and transmit a sense this quality of three-dimensional fullness in the yield. Practice this by placing your hands on your own body first, just below the ribcage. Yield, closing your eyes and visualizing the shape and weight of the organs (liver, stomach, lower lobes of the lungs) with your hands. As your hands yield, feel your body yielding toward them in response.

allow that connection to be as fully weighted and connected as it actually is, we are acknowledging and committing to the profound, whole-body reciprocity of the relationship we have with our horses.

Pushing

Robert Wrigley describes a pushing, pressing touch in his poem "Kissing a Horse." Pressing his lips into his horse's underlip gives a familiar fullness and depth of contact that we experience with a hug, when we are held in an embrace or pressing another body to us. Sometimes pushing has the feeling of sending away, but here it is about connecting, drawing in. Can you think of a moment when you used a push with your horse to make a deeper connection?

Ingrid and DeAnna yielding and Pony supporting.

Yield your hands into an object as you hold it.

Three-dimensional, yielding hands on Amadeo's nose and chin.

Our Horses, Ourselves

WHOLE–BODY YIELDING

🕐 10 MINUTES

PURPOSE: Allowing the whole body to yield gives us a profound sense of receiving and accepting support. With our horses, practicing yielding and allowing them to truly support us nurtures qualities of trust and reciprocity.

1. Using a comfortable surface such as a bed, sofa, or physioball, experiment with yielding using different parts of the body: your head, ribcage, belly, back, or hips. Because this involves larger masses of the body, be clear about the difference in feeling between yielding and pushing (see more on this on p. 97). Instead, see if you can feel simply *yield* your body, the way an infant softens into the body of the mother.

2. As you yield, be aware of the difference between softening into the surface that holds you and *collapsing*. Yielding has a slower, more conscious quality of "giving" your weight and at the same time maintaining responsibility for your balance. Can you feel the underlying structure that supports you? Can you feel what is beneath that?

3. As you slowly shift from one part of the body to another, notice the gradual "un-yield" or separation phase, and the subsequent yielding with a different body part.

4. Try sitting down by yielding your hips into a chair. Be aware of how slowly you must move in order to yield, and notice how this action changes the quality of the movement. How is this different from the way you usually sit? Can you let yourself "be held" without collapsing?

5. Notice how yielding changes the way you handle everyday objects like dishes, books, or laundry. Pick up an object by yielding into it before grasping. How does this change the feeling of the movement?

6. Explore how yielding can become a part of touching and grooming your horse, handling his tack, sitting in the saddle, or picking up the reins. For example: try yielding, rather than pushing, your leg to support a turn, or yielding your hands onto the reins as opposed to gripping. Yield your feet into the stirrups. As you yield your hips into the saddle, feel the deep support of the horse, while remaining balanced.

Kissing a Horse

Of the two spoiled, barn-sour geldings
we owned that year, it was Red—
skittish and prone to explode
even at fourteen years—who'd let me
hold my face to his own: the massive labyrinthine
caverns of the nostrils, the broad plain
up to the head to the eyes. He'd let me stroke
his coarse chin whiskers and take
his soft meaty underlip
in my hands, press my man's carnivorous
kiss to his grass-nipping under half of one, just
so that I could smell
the long way his breath had come from the rain
and the sun, the lungs and the heart,
from a world that meant no harm.

Robert Wrigley

"BJ loved to have his ass scratched," Wrigley says. "One stayed to the side (he was always potentially cranky), but if one used both hands and scratched from the tail downward, he nickered happily—almost a kind of purr. Red loved to be petted around the chin and jaws and yes, to be kissed. If I stood at the fence and offered him a carrot, he'd nudge me gently on the shoulder, until I stroked his chin and gave him a kiss. Then he'd walk away, glad to be loved. Or so it seemed. As much as anything, he seemed to love to be touched, without any requirements upon him."

He says that horses taught him patience and gentleness. He learned that horses are "relentlessly graceful and embarrassed by clumsiness—their own and their riders'. I was, and remain, endlessly fascinated by their enormous musculature and their great sweetness."

We often default to pushing (or pulling) our horses for various reasons: hurry, impatience, frustration, or insensitivity. *Embodied listening* means assessing the situation—the horse stopping when you want him to move or pulling away from you for some reason—and then gradating the pressure and force of your response. This can help you communicate your intentions with greater kindness and skill, and engage the horse's cooperative spirit.

Reaching, Grasping, Pulling

Mark Rashid says that he is always paying attention to what he calls "feel," whether he is leading a horse, picking up a cup, touching his cat, or sitting down in a

YIELD TO PUSH

⏱ 15 MINUTES

PURPOSE: Learning to gradate our contact with the reins, our legs, or our hands on the horse's body helps us to be more refined in our horsemanship.

1. Explore how a yielding touch becomes a push by adding weight and pressure. Begin with a yielding touch and then gradually give more weight to the contact, gently pushing into your horse. See how sensitive to the difference in weight and pressure you can become, noticing when the yield becomes a push, and then, as you lighten the pressure, when the push becomes a melting yield. Is there a difference between *pushing away* and *pushing into*?

2. Explore the push by increasing or decreasing pressure. Have a yield-to-push-to-yield conversation with your horse, feeling his responses to you: are they muscular and reflexive (trying to "win") or gradated and sensitive? What are you giving to the horse and what is he returning to you? Can you find a balance as you meet each other's push?

3. Look for the feeling of a differentiation between skin, muscle, and bone in the contact. Make the push *active* versus passive. This is the difference between just leaning into and "turning on the engine" of your push. The push is not about being stronger, but about deepening the contact. Do you feel any change in the horse's response? Is he meeting your push or moving away? Notice what happens to your breathing, the tone of your muscles, and any emotional changes that occur as you push. Does pushing begin to activate the "fight" response of the sympathetic nervous system?

chair. That means knowing how much effort or force is needed to accomplish a goal. It also means setting an intention to be conscious, and whenever possible, offering softness. *Reaching, grasping,* and *pulling* are fundamental ways that we connect to the world around us; how we draw objects, people, and animals into our *kinesphere* (the area around the body whose periphery can be reached by easily extended limbs without stepping away from that place that is the point of support when standing on one foot). The quality of those actions, whether gentle and inviting or brusque and careless, sets the tone for what follows. Often, quick, tense, sudden, strong responses arise either from involuntary or self-protective patterns that we may not even consciously be aware of. When those unfeeling, undifferentiated reflexes govern how we touch and respond to our horses or other people in our lives, we can become caught in a repeating cycle of reactive habit—our own and our horses.' If my horse spooks as I am walking from the stable to the riding arena, and I become angry or frightened, bracing my body, shouting and yanking on the lead rope, I am amplifying and reinforcing that behavior *at both ends of the lead*. The same is true of how we react to our children, spouses, and co-workers. By cultivating awareness of how much force or quickness is needed to accomplish a task or respond to a situation, we can step out of our habits and fears, and gain greater flexibility, expanding the range of our possible responses.

Observe your patterns (habits) with reach, grasp, and pull. How quickly do you move as you reach? Are you paying attention to the quality of that movement and your horse's response? When you grasp, is it actually a grab? Are you using unnecessary force? What about the way you hold the reins—is there excessive tightening in your hands, arms, and shoulders? Can you soften? Notice when, how, and why you are pulling. What is your intention and what is the emotional background—that is, is it driven by impatience, distraction, anger? Is pulling masquerading as "suppling"? Titrate pulling action with the reins so that you ask for bend in small, soft increments. Imagine the result that you desire. Put the feeling of that ease and flow in your body before you begin. Use breathing to soften into the action. If things "fall apart," pause, take a breath, create a clear and feeling visualization, and begin again.

TOUCH STRATEGIES

Here are some basic strategies for refining touch, whether with a horse, another human, or an object. They are based on *Laban Movement Analysis*[50]—a system for describing, interpreting, and documenting movement developed by dancer and choreographer Rudolf Laban:

- **Slowing:** Play with the speed of your movement. How slowly can you move and still keep the intention and direction of the movement? How quickly can you reach without losing the feel of softness through your body or startling the horse?

- **Directness or indirectness:** Is your hand moving from your side to your horse's body in a direct way, or does your gesture take a more meandering, indirect path? Sometimes direct gestures, especially when coupled with quickness and strength, can be alarming to your horse. Play with letting some of your movements take a more indirect path, and notice if that quality of movement changes the feeling in your body and your horse's response.

REACH, GRASP, PULL

🕐 15 MINUTES

PURPOSE: The next developmental movement stages are the reach, grasp, and pull. These are how we take our *attention* and *intention* out into space, and how we bring the world to us or bring ourselves out into the world. We see this when a baby first reaches for a toy or toward a table to pull herself up to standing.

Becoming more mindful about how, exactly, we are using the elements of reaching, grasping and pulling with our horses helps shift our intention from *making* to *helping*, and allows both you and your horse to find a softer connection.

1. Before approaching your horse, stand quietly and take a few conscious breaths, checking in with your body. Is there tension anywhere? What is the sensation in the center of your body, from your throat to your belly? Is it hard, soft, open, closed?

2. Now, how would you like to be touched if you were your horse? Imagine that in as much detail as possible. Begin to reach toward him with that feeling in your body.

3. Clip the lead rope to the halter, then grasp the lead rope with a smooth, quiet gesture, closing your hand softly to make a connection. Pause and breathe.

4. Now step forward, drawing the horse with you by *inviting* him to join you. "Pulling" with force is not the feeling that we are after. Look for a joining, blending quality in your movement, as you create a soft pressure on the lead to gently invite the horse to move toward you.

5. If the horse does not respond, try again, this time with a clearer picture and intention of what you would like the horse to do. Look at your horse. Use your voice. Think of inviting him to the dance as you put a gentle directional tension on the lead. Imagine going underneath any superficial resistance to find a shared flow into forward movement.

6. Sometimes moving directly forward will seem to automatically engage the horse's resistance. This is often a signal that "I pull, you pull" has become a hardwired, shared habit—what Mark Rashid calls "inadvertent teaching."

CONTINUED ▶

These are the lessons we are teaching our horses (and ourselves) unconsciously. Each time it happens and you pull, you reinforce that pattern mentally and physically—for both of you. Instead of increasing pressure, see if a more flowing, indirect movement to one side or the other can "unhook" the resistance. Using your hand and arm in space in this more curvilinear way can open new possibilities for movement. *Look for the opening, not the resistance.*

7. Let that curving movement flow through your whole hand, arm, shoulder, and spine, all the way down to your feet, like a wave. Rashid says that horses are like water: they are looking for the path of least resistance. Can you find that in your own body? Let the horse tell you when you have it right. Remember to breathe.

8. Explore this sequence with both hands—dominant and non-dominant. Too often we become one-sided and frontal, forgetting that we are, in fact, three-dimensional beings!

- **Force:** Notice how much force or strength is needed to accomplish a task. Lifting a cup of tea requires less strength than a bag of groceries. Opening a heavy door is different from turning the page of a book. Because our horses are big and can react suddenly, we often approach them like that heavy door or bag of groceries. Instead, put the softness and fluidity in your body before you connect and see if that greater lightness and ease transmits to the horse, creating a response that is equally soft. Make the initial contact enough just to lift the weight of the lead rope and then see what is required. Remember that you are inviting your horse to join you, not dragging him along.

- **Tension or flow:** Like force, we can calibrate the amount of tension that we need for each action. *Flow* refers to the "goingness" or amount of control that we bring to a movement. *Bound flow* means that we are controlling a movement—like setting down a delicate teacup. *Free flow* has more abandon and an outpouring quality—like splashing water on our faces. Because horses are prey animals and can be easily startled by quick, unexpected movements, we tend to *bind the flow* of our movements to some degree when we are with them. However, too much tension transmits to the horse, so it is important to find the balance between free and bound flow, and track the horse's responses to our movement.

- **Shape in space:** Experiment with movements that are *spoke-like* (radiating directly out from the body), *arc-like* (raising your arm from your side), or *carving* (following a curvilinear path between your body and your periphery). As you tack up, explore how each of these shapes feels in your body and how your horse reacts.

As you expand your awareness of touch you become sensually awake to everything around you, making a connection not just of skin, muscle, and bone, but also spirit and heart. Whatever you are doing right now, close your eyes and allow your hands to feel whatever is near you. As you touch, become aware of a feeling of blending, becoming a part of what you are touching. Let that connection become *delicious*, full of breath and light. Learning to touch our horses, each other, and even the objects that we handle daily with mindfulness and compassion transforms not just the surfaces, but also the depths of our being.

You have to wait for touch
It doesn't just come to you
And it won't leave soon either
It's like a morsel of something
You've been waiting for a long time

Pam White

Pony choosing to connect with DeAnna.

CHAPTER FIVE

THE GLASSBLOWER'S BREATH:
FALLING TOWARD THE SOURCE

*Here's the
new rule: break
the wineglass
and fall toward
the glassblower's breath.*

Rumi

Illuminated Rumi
(Crown Publishing, 1997),
translated by Coleman Barks,
used by permission of
Coleman Barks.

THE BODY AS SOURCE

For Rumi, the "glassblower's breath" is the source of inspiration and connection. In breaking the wineglass, we come into the stillness and potency of the present moment. For poet Jane Hirshfield, the mule in the "tree's thin shade" is that quiet, breathing source, asking nothing, simply present, "calm and complete."

Hirshfield says that if she could choose what to do were she not a poet, it would be a Zen priest or a horse trainer. For her, the practice of Zen meditation is woven into her riding and all her time with horses.

"One reason I ride is because I wanted to *be* a horse, when I was a child," she explains. "Another is that it's a way of traveling through the world that's outside my usual immersion in words. Equally deeply, though, I ride because riding is a practice of mindfulness, of posture, of breath, of an awareness both broad and focused. Horse Zen is, like kitchen Zen, a practice that asks our whole attention. And then, you get the company of a horse. Which means it is also a practice of heart.

"I have always loved Hakuin Zenji, the great eighteenth-century artist, poet, and Zen teacher, not least for his saying, 'The saddle and the zafu are the same.' (A zafu is a Zen meditation cushion.) Perhaps Hakuin meant this metaphorically—perhaps he meant the journey and the practice are not different. But I like to think he may have been a rider, and meant it literally."

Horses are always in the moment, aware of smells, sounds, and sights, what is near or far, loud or soft, familiar or strange. They don't have the luxury of "tuning out" what doesn't fit their experiential picture. As prey animals, their attention to detail is the key to their survival. They have to practice what composer Pauline Oliveros calls the *unique strategy*—each moment, each breath is unlike any other. In their quickness to respond to threat, horses are not dissimilar from us. When things "hit the fan" we have a tendency to fly into full alert like a prey animal: run-run-run. Neuroscientist Stephen Porges, who developed the Polyvagal Theory,[51] calls this subconscious system for detecting threat *neuroception*: when the assessment of threat

Mule Heart

On the days when the rest
have failed you,
let this much be yours—
flies, dust, an unnameable odor,
the two waiting baskets:
one for the lemons and passion,
the other for all you have lost.
Both empty,
it will come to your shoulder,
breathe slowly against your bare arm.
If you offer it hay, it will eat.
Offered nothing,
it will stand as long as you ask.
The little bells of the bridle will hang
beside you quietly,
in the heat and the tree's thin shade.
Do not let its sparse mane deceive you,
or the way the left ear swivels into dream.
This too is a gift of the gods,
calm and complete.

Jane Hirshfield
"Mule Heart," *Lives of the Heart*
(Harper Perennial, 1997), reprinted with permission.

and safety is happening in the amygdala—a part of the limbic system—and not at a conscious level. At times these responses can be maladaptive, inaccurately assessing the relative danger or safety of what is happening. When our horses become excited or spooky, or when something else triggers our fight/flight/freeze response, the nervous system floods, and we go into a state of overwhelm. When this happens, the limbic system is activated, cortical activity is over-ridden and we enter a more primitive, reflexive state. As Somatic Experiencing® teacher Steve Hoskinson puts it, "The smoke detector is going off in the absence of smoke." At these times, we are acting out of the more primitive reptilian and limbic parts of the brain—all reaction and little, if any, logical processing. "On a neurophysiological level," Dr. Porges says, "our body has already started a sequence of neural processes that would facilitate adaptive defense behaviors such as fight, flight or freeze."[52] When activated, whether we are fleeing danger or preparing to fight, our sympathetic nervous system kicks in and we feel an amplified, defensive, adrenalized energy. Under conditions of extreme stress, where the sympathetic nervous system options of fight or flight are not available to us, the body may freeze. Immobilization or dissociation is triggered by a different, more primitive part of our nervous system, which Dr. Porges identifies as the unmyelinated, dorsal branch of the vagus nerve.[53]

The problem occurs for us as humans, and for our horses, when our neural alarm circuits become self-activated, conditioned to maintaining a state of hyper-vigilance, as the more we attend to fear, the more fearful we become, resulting in patterns of chronic arousal or shutdown. This happens often with trauma. The nervous system is on constant alert without access to its more settling cycles. We feel disconnected, continually apprehensive, even disoriented. We may feel anxious, angry, or frozen as a generalized state. As these conditions become habitual, they deepen their attraction and we lose our ability to effectively assess how safe or dangerous our situation really is, compulsively re-enacting cycles of over-reaction because *everything* feels threatening. We lose both awareness and our ability to observe and to maintain relative neutrality in relationship to our experience. Once that cycle is established in the body and mind, it is difficult, even impossible to be "in the moment" because our nervous system is tethered to past traumas or worries about the future.

The same can be true of physical pain. Chronic or severe pain can overwhelm the nervous system, making us jumpy and guarded, or overwhelmed by anxiety and depression. Even when the pain is localized, we feel that the whole body is fragile and unbalanced. The pain feels predatory, stalking us throughout the day, constantly threatening. Will it ever go away? Where is it coming from? What have I done to cause it? Physical therapies may be ineffective because the body and mind are so habitually attuned to the pain that they cannot shift the patterns of thought or movement.

Dr. Peter Levine, the originator of Somatic Experiencing®, a therapeutic method for treating trauma,[54] uses this analogy to explain this phenomenon: "According to the Buddha, 'When touched with a feeling of pain, the ordinary person laments, becomes distraught...*contracts*, and so...feels two pains...just as if they were to shoot a man with an arrow and, right afterward, were to shoot him with another so that he would feel the pain of [both]...' The first arrow in this teaching represents the actual pain. The second one represents the accompanying suffering and trauma. It is our *fear about pain* that causes this second arrow, a fear that creates a fertile landscape for chronic pain, distress, and anguish. As pain sufferers, we become so frightened of pain that we recoil from feeling *any* bodily sensations. It is as though we believe that by feeling our bodies we will be destroyed, or, at the very least, our conditions will worsen. Hence we remain stuck and so shoot ourselves with the second arrow."[55]

Horses, on the other hand, do not speculate about their physical pain, make up stories about it, or try to figure it out with language-based ideas. Even though pain profoundly affects their nervous systems, causing them varying degrees of stress, their experience of the pain or distress is in the present because they do not possess that part of the brain that allows us, as humans, to project our thinking into the future. They do not shoot that second arrow. For them time is simply *now*. Their fearful behaviors may have a component of memory, but they are not projecting that experience forward in time. When the scary triggering object or person reappears, they react. Temple Grandin calls this *associative thinking*.

"A horse trainer once said to me, 'Animals don't think, they just make associations,'" Grandin says in an interview in a 1997 issue of *Western Horseman*. "I responded to that by saying, 'If making associations is not thinking, then I would have to conclude that I do not think.' People with autism and animals both think by making visual associations. These associations are like snapshots of events and tend to be very specific. For example, a horse might fear bearded men when it sees one in the barn, but bearded men might be tolerated in the riding arena. In this situation the horse may only fear bearded men in the barn because he may have had a bad past experience in the barn with a bearded man."[56]

Titration, Chunking Down

One of the foundational principles of Somatic Experiencing is that of *titration*, meaning the introduction of small (sometimes *very* small) amounts of activation to help build resilience and capacity in the nervous system. Using the concept and practice of titration—learning to tolerate stresses by introducing them in manageable, digestible doses—is a useful tool for both our horses and ourselves.

It works like this: You know that your horse is frightened of a particular door or corner of the arena. To build his ability to tolerate that stimulus, you find a way to break that "obstacle" into smaller and smaller parts until you find the level at which the horse is able to be successful, with only a small reaction followed by a more settled state. Or perhaps you know that watching too much news interrupts your sleep and diminishes your general sense of well-being. So you titrate your exposure to the news, perhaps beginning with just the thought of the news or visualizing yourself glancing at the newspaper. You look for the smallest amount of stimulus that triggers a small reaction, or none at all. That demands that we learn to track the body, including any changes in breathing, muscular tension, and heart rate. Regulation requires awareness.

A second essential concept of Somatic Experiencing is that of *pendulation*. This is the practice of alternating between activation and returning to a settled body-mind state. Pendulation does not mean swinging wildly from high activation to a deep rest state but seeking a balanced oscillation between moderate activation and settling. Pendulation is a gradual re-calibration of the nervous system— one that takes place over time with continual repetition and practice—much like the changes that occur with the Tellington TTouch (see p. 53). It is not distraction or behavioral modification. Rather, by learning to consciously track the body's signals, the individual is able to sense when the subtlest signs of activation appear, and use that awareness to orient more fully to the present moment.

These principles of titration and pendulation can work with our horses. We have to become keen observers of our horses and ourselves, always looking for openings and opportunities to build and share greater softness and coherence. Somatic Experiencing teaches, "*Coherence is a measure of wholeness. When connected to the deep self, we feel 'whole.' Organization within body systems and cooperative, organized function between various physiological systems contributes to our sense of well-being, or wholeness. As coherence within any one body system increases, that system is more stable. As coherence between body systems increases, the overall organism as a whole becomes more stable.*"

For humans, one of the possible results of chronic emotional or physical overwhelm is that it creates an incongruity between our inner psycho-emotional landscape and our outward behaviors. We may try to act calm and unperturbed, while inside we're a tumult of anxiety, rage, or depression. My horses always show me when I have fallen out of balance, reflecting my emotional state like a funhouse mirror. Because *they* are "in the moment," their responses to us can call us back to ourselves in an immediate, bodily way.

Hirshfield says, "Riding an alert Arabian, you find that you must be in this very moment and no other—because the horse is and will respond to this moment differently in a heartbeat, if the moment changes. You find that your breathing and his breathing make a mutual awareness, that your feet are his feet, your eyes, his eyes."

One with the Herd

Hirshfield's observations are the key to *present-centered awareness*. Horse behaviors shift in response to what they see and feel emanating from us (more about this in chapter 8, "The Mirror"). Being with horses in a conscious way is a somatic process, because it involves awareness, bodily engagement, and inner "knowing." Focusing our attention in the body moment-by-moment is a way of moving out of the scramble of past or future thinking that obscures living wide-awake in the present. *Social somatics* (engaging our innate "herd-ness") can bring us into alignment with the bodies of our fellow beings of *all* species, leading to greater physical and emotional awareness, regulation, and empathy.

When Dr. Peter Levine says, "We are all born to participate in each other's nervous systems," he is not speaking in a species-exclusive way about humans only. This is also profoundly true with horses, dogs, cats, or animals we encounter in the wild. Understanding that this is a *socio-somatic* phenomenon, and that we are continually engaging with other beings at the level of the nervous system—and in fact *all* of the body's systems (see Body-Mind Centering, p. 9)—is the key to greater skill, sensitivity, and resilience in communication and social engagement.

My daughter Chandrika connecting with the herd.

As a teacher in movement classes I often invite students to respond to a stimulus—a sound, someone else's movement—as an animal might, instantaneously reacting to the source of that sound or movement from the body rather than the mind. Instead of *thinking about* what they just saw or heard, or trying to *figure it out*, students use the quick, neurobiological attunement that connects them to their instinctive, animal selves. The quickness overrides the tendency to try to sort things through. This kind of practice hones our abilities to speak and decode in the language of movement and the body. The greater our social and emotional intelligence, our inner balance, the more we are able to intuitively bridge the gap between others and ourselves.

When we practice *embodied* awareness we become more horse-like: sensitive, alert, and able to discern and differentiate our surroundings with more precision and subtlety. As Hirshfield says, "Zen pretty much comes down to three things— everything changes; everything is connected; pay attention."

Sometimes it is better just to stand like Jane Hirshfield's mule in the field, root our hooves down and feel the earth beneath us. Horse time is breathing time, hearts opening to the fullness of what is here *right now*.

"The longtime model used by psychologists is that of a 'spotlight' that picks out particular items of interest to examine, bringing some things into focus and awareness while leaving other things in the dim, dusty sidelines. The metaphor makes me feel like a headlight-wearing spelunker who can only see what is right in front of her in the darkness of the cave. Such a comparison can be misleading, because in fact one can still report on what was within one's peripheral vision at rates better than chance. And despite that spotlight, we seem to miss huge elements of the thing we are ostensibly attending to."

Alexandra Horowitz
On Looking: A Walker's Guide to the Art of Observation
(Scribner, 2013)

SOFT SEEING, BARE ATTENTION

🕐 10 MINUTES

PURPOSE: As we open our attention to the details of what surrounds us, orienting to our surroundings in a multi-sensory and unhurried way, we become more horse-like in our way of perceiving and connecting to the environment.

1. Stand outside with bare feet, feeling the warmth and texture of the earth and the movement of air on your skin.

2. Notice the flow of movement and sound around you: the swoop of a bird, the gentle movement of the leaves, and the scribble of an insect's flight in the air by your ear. Notice what is close to you and what is in the distance.

3. Close your eyes and listen to the play of sounds around you. Can you hear what is very near as well as what is farther away, including the sound of your own breath and heartbeat?

4. Slowly open your eyes to take in what is in front of you and what is in your peripheral vision, near and far. Let your eyes absorb what you see in a receptive (rather than active) searching way.

5. Now let your eyes wander wherever they want to go, taking in your surroundings: front and back, side to side, high and low, near and far. Can you feel how this soft, meandering movement orients you in the present, expands awareness of your surroundings, and settles you in a more relaxed way into your body? Use this practice of orienting with your eyes throughout your day as little recuperations, opening your attention outward, noticing the details of what you see, and how the movement of your eyes is felt throughout your body.

6. With your horse—on the ground or in the saddle—use this exercise to soften your focus, and through that, your whole body. As you do this, notice any changes in your horse. Is there greater relaxation between you?

SEEING THE MOMENT

Being with horses means knowing when is the right moment to move, to be still, to touch, or to give space, when to act and when to wait. Jeffrey Anderson is a master photographer who captures that right moment, what the master of candid photography Henri Cartier-Bresson calls, "the decisive moment." At the age of twelve, Anderson enrolled in a summer photography program at his junior high school. Within weeks, the clothing in his closet at home had been moved out and replaced with darkroom equipment.

Anderson's fascination with horses is life-long. "I cannot remember ever *not* being fascinated with these huge, dangerous, beautiful, gentle animals that channel every ounce of cowboy in my soul, while simultaneously serving as muse for my inner visual poet," he says. I had admired Anderson's photographs of Sarah Hollis's beautiful Andalusian stallions, Uther Pendragon and Regaliz, long before I met him. The play of light and dark, the quality of movement and stillness in his images was haunting and breathtaking. His photographs illuminated and revealed horses' bodies in ways that I had not experienced before.

"They are just beautiful from every angle at any time and in any light," he says. "And I am a photographer because I am literal and straightforward and can't draw or paint my way out of a paper bag. I cannot imagine a beauty beyond *equus caballus*, so I document what is in front of me. An art instructor could teach an entire semester of composition theory using nothing other than the horse and its parts. S-curves. C-curves. Rule of thirds. Vanishing point. Flow. Focal points: primary and secondary. In addition, the form of the animal is universally recognizable. Show a photo of the shoulder of a horse, or the mane, or the tail, to a passerby in Manhattan and they will tell you, 'That's a horse, right?'"

Watching Anderson photograph horses is like seeing a dancer in the

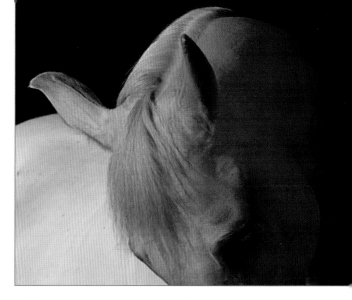

Jeffrey Anderson's photograph of the Andalusian stallion Uther Pendragon: "Light and Shadow."

Another Anderson photograph of Uther Pendragon, entitled "The Decisive Moment"—haunting and breathtaking.

Another "decisive moment" with Pony.

Ingrid dancing with Pony.

wings, hovering at the edges of attention and consciousness—an intimate, witnessing presence. Dancer Ingrid Schatz says, "He's on the ground or on a knee, moving right along with us. I'm sure he's not thinking about where he is or what he's doing; he's just being where the shot is." Anderson describes this process as a "drawing in" of the image. Knowing when to press the shutter to capture what he is witnessing is for him the *decisive moment*—what he says is *a willingness to be one with the image*, while at the same moment retaining an artist's ability to frame and shape it. For him, the process is visceral, emotional, and kinetic.

"While the decisive parts can be partially manipulated into proximity of each other, beyond that it is a matter of serendipity, of passion, of chemistry," he says. "Emotion sends a wave to my fingertip and the shutter fires. *Think* and the moment is gone. *Feel* and you will never miss it. The magic of equine photography lies in the unending flow of this energy. The horse is an emotional open book, like a child. The horse, any horse, every horse, is ready to give something real, honest, and palpable. I may not know what's coming, but something honest, something decisive, something perfect is always about to happen. I just have to turn off my thoughts and open myself to the moment. It's not always as easy as that may sound. Thankfully the horse is a constant stream of decisive moments. At any given time the most poorly bred, homeliest, unrefined equine will show some part of its body in pure, perfect artistic form. Somewhere on its body a decisive moment is happening."

Authentic Movement

One of Anderson's favorite collaborators is Sarah Hollis, the owner of Tintagel Enterprises and Tintagel Talent, a breeding and training facility and program for Andalusians and Drum Horses. Hollis is an equine performance artist, training horses for shoots for magazines like *Vogue* and *Harper's Bazaar*, as well as large-scale performances. Her training methods are humane, unique, and thoughtful. As she says on her website, "The Tintagel performance horses are taught to listen and understand human intentions very clearly. They are also taught to use options and think independently. This free thinking allows the horse performers to invent new and unexpected positions, poses or moves which may make the photograph or film more dramatic and unique."[57]

Ingrid and Pony.

Dancers Ingrid Schatz and DeAnna Pellecchia and I had been rehearsing for several months with Hollis's horse Pony, a performing liberty horse trained to move in response to her movement signals. She invited Anderson to come and shoot a rehearsal. He wrote afterward:

"Ingrid is tall and slender, with a timeless, classic dancer's build. DeAnna (Dee) is shorter, more compact, curvier, with biceps that demand attention. It would be natural to think of 'Ing' as the tall graceful one and Dee as the shorter, powerful one.

DeAnna and Pony.

That is exactly the problem with thinking. Very quickly into the rehearsal, Dee (the shorter, powerful one) arches nearly over backward under the horse... Shortly afterward she floats into an arcing leap that defies gravity. Within moments Ingrid (the tall graceful one) lifts Dee high into the air and holds her until the two mold together and slide gracefully into Pony's space, all three becoming one. Don't think, *feel*—authentic movement."

Authentic Movement[58] is an expressive, intuitive improvisational movement practice involving a mover and a witness. It was developed by dancer and psychotherapist Mary Starks Whitehouse, following her study with Carl Jung, and

Dancing with Pony.

her curiosity about translating his "active imagination" practice into movement. She wanted to know what would happen if her students and clients were to move without a specific intention. In the presence of a compassionate and non-judging witness, with eyes closed, maintaining a focus on bodily sensation and the flow of consciousness, the mover allows herself to respond to impulses arising from the body. The aim of Authentic Movement

TRY THIS

OPENING, SEEING

🕑 10 MINUTES

PURPOSE: Playing with space and vision can help us expand the body's sensing of and relationship to its surroundings. That in turn helps us become more spatially and kinesthetically aware as riders. Remember that horses are using their eyes multi-dimensionally or globally all the time, where our eyes are often fixed in a narrow focal way, excluding the periphery.

1. Sitting in a comfortable well-balanced position, close your eyes, letting them rest.

2. Slowly open your eyes, inviting them to stay soft and relaxed.

3. Repeat, alternating between slowly closing and opening the eyes, noticing both light and dark with equal awareness. As soon as your eyes are open, begin to close them and vice versa, so that you are blurring the distinction between open and closed, light and dark.

4. Now, with your eyes open, slowly turn your head and eyes to the right, initiating that movement from the eyes, and keeping the feeling of the eyes resting as they move. Now scan your eyes and head to the left. Repeat this two or three times, noticing how this gentle head turning travels down through the whole body. Can you differentiate between the motor act of moving the head and the process of assimilating what the eyes are seeing?

is not to make judgements about the authenticity or inauthenticity of one's own or another's movements. The aim is rather to "learn to be oneself in the presence of others," according to movement practitioner Eila Goldhahn. Can we "be ourselves" in the presence of the horse? Or are we always "performing" the role of owner, rider, expert, or novice? What does it mean to "be yourself"? And in this interspecies equation, who is the witness?

My dancers and I have found that practicing an eyes-open form of Authentic Movement with horses brings an honest and unadorned quality to our movement exchanges. This way of being with horses also draws on a responsive listening practice—one which follows the Authentic Movement instruction to "wait to be moved." This takes the ensuing movement conversation out of a planning,

5. Next, slowly turn your head to the right while moving your eyes to the left. Do the same thing to the other side. How smoothly can you move your head and your eyes in opposite directions? This may initially feel awkward and counter-intuitive, but as you do this non-habitual movement, you are creating new neural pathways—a more flexible and intelligent body-mind.

6. Imagine that you are standing in the middle of a cube. Scan your head and eyes (together) up and down along the four diagonal pathways, feeling how your whole body participates in this movement.

- Front/right/high to back/left/low
- Front/left/high to back/right/low
- Front/right/low to back/left/high
- Front/left/low to back/right/high

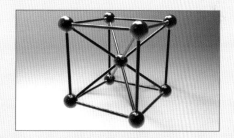

Move your eyes along the four diagonal pathways of an imagined cube.[59]

7. Now move only your eyes along these diagonals, keeping your head focused directly forward. Does this more contained way of using your eyes feel more familiar? Once again let the head and eyes slide along the diagonals, and see if this creates a sense of expansion and freedom of body and mind. You may feel a little disoriented as your brain sorts out all the directions—particularly in the backspace. Do this exercise without straining your neck or eyes; just playfully exploring the distant corners of your kinesphere. Remember to breathe!

choreographic form, and into a relationship based on attentive openness to whatever arises in the moment. Additionally, I have found that holding the intention to "be moved" encourages an instinctual and spontaneous quality in even my routine interactions with my horses, including riding.

"A horse will not bother with anything but authentic movement," says Anderson, "and a performance involving a horse and people can only succeed with the same honesty [and spontaneity] from all who are present."

DEEP LISTENING

In a church in Philadelphia a choir of singers is performing *Horse Sings from Cloud,* an improvisational music composition by Pauline Oliveros. I hear soft whinnies, clicks, kisses, hoof beats, shuddering outbreaths, and fragments of song. If I close my eyes, I can imagine being in the midst of a herd of horses somewhere in a vast openness of sage and rock in the West, or standing in a dark stable at night, surrounded by the percolating sounds of horses breathing, moving, and eating. The quiet in the church is palpable, and the sounds from the chorus weave in and out of that stillness—rising, building, diminishing, and then slowly resolving back into silence.

The score for this composition is an arrangement of words and suggestions for sounds that Pauline has given the musicians, containing images and compositional strategies, informing them when to make sound and the relationships of their sounds to the other musicians. There are no pages of notes, no time signatures, nothing to lock the voices into a single tempo or repeatable sequence of notes or sounds. The performers' choices are governed by listening to themselves, each other, and the space that holds them, and then following their own impulses and Pauline's compositional strategies about when and how to make sounds.

I first met Pauline Oliveros in 1990 during a residency at the Yellow Springs Institute in Pennsylvania where we were collaborating on *Skin,* a new performance work for which she was the composer and musician. Since then, we have collaborated on several major projects.

Oliveros is known worldwide as a distinguished composer, musician,

Composer Pauline Oliveros.

Our Horses, Ourselves

LISTEN TO WHAT YOU ARE HEARING

🕙 5 MINUTES

PURPOSE: Because Deep Listening is also a way of cultivating empathy and compassion, it is a powerful tool for inter-species connection. Deep Listening with horses begins with fine-tuning your perception of the shared world of sounds.

1. Simply stand with your horse and listen to any and all sounds around you, near and far. Be aware of the movement of your horse's ears: are they moving in response to something that you hear or something that has escaped your notice?

2. Listen for sounds that you have never heard before. What is the difference between *hearing* and *listening*?

and teacher. With a career spanning over sixty years, she is a leading figure in contemporary American electronic and experimental music through her pioneering work in electronic techniques, attentional strategies, teaching methods, inter-artistic collaboration, and improvisation. Deep Listening[60] is a practice that grew from her childhood fascination with sound. Oliveros describes Deep Listening as a way of listening in every possible way to everything all the time, and to notice when you are not listening and begin again. Such intense listening reaches beyond musical sounds to those that are a part of daily life, of nature, and of one's own thoughts.

"The key to multi-level existence is Deep Listening," she writes. "Deep Listening is not only to language and its syntax but also to the nature of sound and its atmosphere and environmental context. This is essential to the process of unlocking layer after layer of imagination, meaning, and memory down to the cellular level of human experience."[61]

Oliveros grew up in rural Texas, surrounded by the sounds of wildlife and the environment. Listening to the radio, Oliveros remembers that she "loved the static and tuning whistles to be found in-between the stations." For her, the moment of breaking through came in 1958 when she placed a microphone on her window ledge so that she could record sounds inside and outside the room. Even though she had listened carefully while recording, when she played the tape back, she discovered that the microphone had picked up sounds that had escaped her notice, perhaps because of an unconscious filtering of the sonic environment.

Her listening had been careful...but not *deep*. Oliveros feels that Deep Listening brings forth "acceptance before assertion, quietness before attachment, stability before change."

Ear Piece

Are you listening now?

Are you listening to what you are now hearing?

Are you hearing while you listen?

Are you listening while you are hearing?

Do you remember the last sound you heard before this question?

What will you hear in the near future?

Can you hear now and also listen to your memory of an old sound?

What causes you to listen?

Do you hear yourself in your daily life?

Do you have healthy ears?

If you could hear any sound you want, what would it be?

Are you listening to sounds now or just hearing them?

What sound is most meaningful to you?

Pauline Oliveros
Deep Listening: A Composer's Sound Practice,
(iUniverse, 2005)

Awareness and Attention, Global vs. Focal

For Oliveros, the distinctions between *global* and *focal* attention are not limited to sound. "While one's attention is focused to a point on something specific, it is possible to remain aware of one's surroundings, one's body movement of all kinds, and one's mental activity (in other words remain aware of inner and outer reality simultaneously)," she says. "Attention is narrow, pointed, and selective. Awareness is broad, diffuse, and inclusive. Both have a tunable range: attention can be honed to a finer and finer point. Awareness can be expanded until it seems all-inclusive. Attention can intensify awareness. Awareness can support attention."[62]

I have observed some interesting relationships between Oliveros's sonic attentional observations, and the way that we use our eyes. Once when I was with my autistic godson Jacob, I noticed that if I looked toward (not at) him in a soft and general way—focusing equally on foreground and background, and including the periphery—rather than using a more narrow and pointed focus, he seemed to be calmer. Global vision is (as best we understand) how Jacob sees the world. When I join him in that way of seeing, he often opens to other ways of connecting.

Our Horses, Ourselves

GLOBAL AND FOCAL SEEING

🕐 10 MINUTES

PURPOSE: As we become more cognizant of how we are using our eyes—including what kind of intention they carry—we gain more insight into our own emotional state. Both predator and prey animals observe our eyes to determine threat or friendliness. When we gain greater clarity about what how we are using our eyes and what they are expressing, we become more conscious and friendly partners for our horses and human friends.

1. Try softening and broadening your focus when you are in conversation with another person. Can you see both the person and what surrounds him or her? Can you see what is at the edges of your vision as much as what is at the center of your gaze? How does this shift in focus change your perception? Does it change the quality of your interaction with the other person in any way? Notice your breathing and the relative quality of tension or relaxation throughout your body.

2. Now try a gentle oscillation between a *focal* and *global* view: Look directly at an object, and then broaden and soften your focus so that the object becomes no more important than what surrounds it. Go back to looking at the object more directly, and then expand out again. Notice how this gentle fluctuation between focal and global is felt throughout your whole body.

3. When grooming, tacking up, riding or simply spending time with your horse, experiment with using a broader, more diffuse, and inclusive focus, and see how that changes what you sense physically in your body and in your horse. When using a global focus, do you feel more relaxed? Does your horse?

4. When riding in an arena, try not using a direct focus to pick out cones, dressage letters, or other markers. Instead, look in the direction of where you are going while maintaining a soft, global focus. This is *not* the same as "spacing out" (when you realize that you have been ruminating and were not conscious of how you got from one place to another). It is an intentional and more relaxed way of using your eyes.

5. In the saddle, practice expansively scanning your focus from side to side, up and down, or on a diagonal, including your backspace. Can you do this

CONTINUED ▶

The Glassblower's Breath: Falling Toward the Source

CONTINUED FROM PAGE 123

without your eyes needing to pick out specific objects or points of interest along the way? If you find this to be disorienting, pause and allow your eyes to rest on a single place, then continue to experiment with your focus.

6. Try moving your eyes along the same pathways but this time pick out specific points of focus along the way. Notice how you feel in your body and breath. Is it different from when you rode with a global focus?

During one of my weeklong visits to Jacob and his family, I noticed that when we were outside with Jacob, his mother Jo-Ann was using her eyes continuously in a strong, piercing, direct way. She was used to having to watch her son this way—always alert, ready for the unexpected, always at least moderately activated. There wasn't a recuperative break in that focus, and the tension in her eyes seemed to permeate her whole body. I invited Jo-Ann to let her vision soften, to try watching Jacob in a more peripheral, casual, global way. I suggested that she also intersperse moments of letting her eyes meander softly, aimlessly, instead of being always focused, laser-like, on Jacob. Within several moments, I could see a shift in her breathing pattern, as well as a releasing of her body into gravity and a significant expansion and relaxation in her chest and shoulders.

Most of us use our vision in a direct, focused way. We are often honing in, excluding the periphery, or trying to minimize distractions. The way we use our eyes mirrors our psychophysical state—"on" and "ready to go." When we turn that sharply focused gaze on another being, it can trigger the nervous system to respond defensively or at least become mildly activated. I have found that this also happens with horses. Unconsciously using our focus in a direct or penetrating way may trigger their flight response or cause them to be more reactive when we approach.

Deep Sounding

During an early rehearsal for *Skin*, Oliveros led us in a sonic meditation called *Teach Yourself to Fly*.[63] These are notes from my journal:

> *We begin lying in a circle, heads together, in stillness and in silence. First, she asks us to expand our attention to sound outward and inward, opening our awareness of sound as far as possible. Sounds filter in: the whoosh of a blower in the room, birds high and low, the shock of a car's passing, the distant whispers of wind in the trees. As the minutes pass, the sounds become*

clearer—more elegant and discrete. At one point, I hear the rush of my own blood. The sensation of all this listening was as if my ears had dropped open like mouths. I was aware that my left ear and my right ear were hearing differently, seeming to hold themselves open to the sound each in its own way: my right ear like a broad tunnel, my left slightly cupped, protective. From this place of expanded listening, we begin alternately making sounds and listening. Exploring different sounds, different durations of silence, listening to each other as our sounds blend and collide. Emerging from this practice I felt huge, my awareness clear, inclusive, and delicate.

I imagine that this is the way animals hear: a vast sonic tapestry infinitely richer and more nuanced than our own. I think about the flicking, rotating ears of horses, the giant canopies of the elephant's ears, the long pendulous flaps of the bloodhound that gather and direct scent and sound, and the delicate, flicking ear-cups of cats. What is sound like for each of them?

TRY THIS

SOUNDING IN, SOUNDING OUT

 15 MINUTES

PURPOSE: Like their vision, horses' hearing is inclusive and highly differentiated. Learning to listen with more clarity and subtlety helps us better feel and understand their sensory world, which in turn helps us become more attuned. As you play with this sounding practice, pay attention to the way sound travels out into the space around you, how sound moves toward you, and how both resonate in the body.

1. Lie on your back, arms and legs resting comfortably. Sense the weight of your body on the floor; be aware of what you are giving to the floor and what the floor is giving to you. Can you let the body softly yield into the floor?

2. Imagine your ears "falling open like mouths" to receive the sounds all around you—near and far, and inside your body, including your breathing, heartbeat, the gurgle of your tummy. What sounds are in the room? Let your listening bloom out in concentric rings: to the street outside, to a thousand feet away, a mile away. Can you imagine expanding your hearing to even farther than that?

CONTINUED ▶

3. Bring your attention to the breath and the exchange of *inside* and *outside* which occurs with each breath. Let your breath become audible as you exhale, first as just a sigh, and then audibly, as a hum or an "ahhhhhh."

4. Experiment with making each of the long vowel sounds as you exhale. Where do you feel each vowel resonating in your body? Imagine the sound as an internal massage, reaching into the bones, the cells, the nerves, sending small ripples through the fluids of the body.

5. Now send your sound out into the space around you. Alternate making sound with silence. There is no preference for any particular sound and no sense that your sounds must be beautiful or correct. But be as interested in your silences as you are your sounds. If you feel like moving as you make sound, notice which parts of the body want to move and how. Be curious about both movement and stillness, sound and silence. Gradually come back to silence, letting your sounds subside into breathing. Notice any differences you feel in the way your body is resting on the floor, as you continue to listen to all the sounds (and the silences) around you, near and far.

6. As you ride, listen, including any sounds in your awareness. Warm up by playing with vowel sounds at the walk. Where do you feel each vowel resonating in your body? In your horse's body? Does he seem to like one vowel sound more than another? Perhaps that is related to where in your body (and his) that particular sound is resonating.

INTENTIONAL TRANSITIONS

Traveling on the train from Connecticut to New York City, I was reading Phoebe Caldwell's book on her practice of Intensive Interaction and autism, *Delicious Conversations* (Pavilion Publishing, 2012), hoping to learn how better to communicate with my godson. I was struck not only by her descriptions of autistic hypersensitivities, but by her observation that the autistic brain often cannot discard sensory input. The sensory data accumulates until it overwhelms the nervous system, and the autistic person experiences a "sensory fragmentation," which might be a tantrum or violent behavior toward others or oneself—often extreme expressions of agitation or anxiety. In some cases, the autistic individual cannot recuperate from this "overload" except by exploding or withdrawing completely.

Our Horses, Ourselves

With Jacob, I have observed that often he is better at taking care of his need for recuperation in these scenarios than his primary caregivers: When he is overwhelmed, he "corner dives," lying on his belly, closing his eyes, arm over his head, his head nestled into the closest corner, withdrawing from all contact.

At these times, the best strategy has been to find my own corner in the room, sit down, and quietly breathe with him, listening to the sounds he is making and the sounds around us. Trying to engage Jacob at these moments only deepens his need to withdraw. At times this reminds me of Amadeo "corner diving" in his stall when he is feeling fearful or does not want to be caught.

With both Jacob and Amadeo, these patterns of avoidance or withdrawal are fairly hard-wired habits. The worst thing to do in these moments is to raise the level of pressure—someone will likely get hurt. By *removing* the pressure, allowing some time to pass, and then beginning again in a different way, eventually Amadeo is able to come out of the corner and make a connection. The same thing is true with Jacob: after some time "away," there will be a sound or a movement that engages his curiosity, and out he comes. We begin again. The important thing with both is to be soft, steady, and have an "isn't that interesting" curious attitude toward whatever behavior is happening. No big deal, nothing personal. Neither Jacob nor Amadeo are being disobedient or "bad." Both are responding to fear or overwhelm *as visceral body-mind states* and are handling their nervous systems as best they can in the moment. If, in response, we become activated, frustrated, or angry the outcome is unlikely to be a good one.

We all share a desire for safety and connection. Feeling safe is a bodily response to what we are experiencing in our sensory environment at the moment. When we feel connected to those we love and trust, that amplifies our sense of safety.

As I reached New York City and began to walk from my train through the tunnels and big halls of Grand Central Station, I felt as if I had almost slipped into the chaotic sensory world of the autistic—by the time I caught the subway to Union Square I was completely overwhelmed. The scream of trains, the rivers of people, the clutter of sight and sound felt painful. There was no discernable pattern, and the only way I could cope was to basically shut down. A lot of people around me seemed to be doing that as well. We were "corner diving," in a way but without behavioral outbursts and in essentially socially acceptable ways. I began to think about cycles of exertion and recuperation in the non-autistic population, and how our failure to consciously integrate stillness and consciously recuperative moments into our daily activities can lead to fragmentation and overwhelm. As I came out of the subway, I stopped to take a breath.

Bringing consciousness to transitional moments like these creates something that I like to call *interstitial awareness*—a focus on the spaces *in between*. We often think of moving from one "destination" to another, without much consciousness about our transitions or the journey from here to there, or where and how we might relax along the way. Moving from one block of activity to another can actually be an opportunity for opening awareness and deepening attention.

Learning to Pause, Integrating Recuperation

Many of us tend to harden into our activities, using momentum and drive to get from one place or activity to another. We are "on." There may be physical tension, absence of breathing, and tightness in the jaw or buttocks. Relaxing doesn't have to be a vacation in the Caribbean, a nap, or a drink after work. We don't have to collapse from exhaustion or succumb to overwhelm. There are the other, more subtle ways to rest.

Rudolf Laban, the choreographer and movement theorist, discovered that factory workers engaged in repetitive motion labor were more efficient, less fatigued, and happier in their work when small, apparently random, and seemingly unrelated recuperative movements were "salted in" amongst their repeated work patterns. For example, as you are working at your computer, taking a breath, leaning back, stretching your arms or legs, and allowing the eyes to meander and

TRY THIS

EXERTION, RECUPERATION

 ALL DAY

PURPOSE: Incorporating intentional, conscious recuperative moments as we transition from one activity to another helps to refocus mind and body. These small recuperations are deeply restorative, and practicing them over time has a lasting, calming effect on the nervous system. The more balanced and easeful we become, the more those qualities transmit to our horses.

1. Just before you begin a transition from one activity to another, *pause*. The transition may be getting out of your car, getting up from your desk, getting out of bed, standing up from a meal, getting on or off your horse—any shift of a body-mind state.

2. Take a focused breath. Slow your movement and notice the details: the shift in the position of your body, the feeling of your foot in the stirrup, the change of visual focus. Maintain a soft awareness throughout the transition, pausing along the way. If you find yourself losing focus, pause, breathe, and then continue.

orient to the space around you can expand not just your field of vision, but soften the body and create a feeling of reconnection to the world beyond the screen. It is a way of awakening and rebooting. This "intentional pause" is a way of refreshing ourselves when we begin to feel activated, fatigued, or overwhelmed. According to Dr. Stephen Porges, "Our body functions very much like a polygraph...continuously

PAUSING, AWAKENING

 5 MINUTES

PURPOSE: Learning to just stop—fully suspending whatever it is that you are doing and coming to stillness—is an opportunity to "wake up" to the present moment. When you integrate stillness into your horse time, you are including your horse in these deeply restorative and "rebooting" moments, and shifting the dynamic of your relationship to one that includes attentive *non-doing*—just being.

1. Stop whatever you are doing and settle into stillness. Notice the details of the stillness: where your body is in space, the quality of your breathing, what you are seeing and hearing, and any sensations in the body.

2. Begin moving again, resuming your activity (typing, reading, walking, riding).

3. Pause again. Let your whole body come fully into stillness—a complete, momentary release of the activity before you resume. Let the pause be a true moment of breathing stillness, not just a breathless "wait." Take the time to listen and bring mindfulness into each pause.

4. Now try the following, surprising yourself with where and when you pause:

   - Pause while chewing.
   - Pause in the middle of getting up.
   - Pause as you put on your coat.
   - Pause in the middle of sentence.
   - Pause as you are dialing a number or writing text.
   - Pause as you get into or out of your car.
   - Pause while grooming, tacking up, or mounting your horse.

PAUSING WHILE RIDING

🕐 ANY TIME

PURPOSE: Pausing and coming to stillness during a ride gives us an opportunity to recalibrate what we are doing. This is a powerful tool for breaking up unconscious habits and patterns than can accumulate when we are "working." In meditation, there is the instruction, "Begin again," meaning that if you find your mind wandering, simply bring your focus back to the breath, and start fresh. The intentional pause gives us that opportunity.

1. While you walk down the long side of the arena or down the trail, pause. Take one or two conscious breaths. As you do this, feel your seat and legs yielding and softening into the back and flanks of the horse. Let your hands, arms, and shoulders soften. Consciously lengthen down into your stirrups and upward through the top of the head. Notice what is around you, including sounds.

2. Walk on again and after several moments pause again. Imagine the inside of your body connecting with the inside of your horse's body in this stillness. As you begin moving again, consciously focus on that connection. Leave nothing out: hooves/feet, head/tail, inside/outside.

responding to people and places. We need to learn more about how to read our body's responses. We have to know that when we feel uncomfortable, there's a reason our body is feeling uncomfortable and we need to adapt and adjust to that."[64]

Conscious, intentional pausing is adaptive and deeply recuperative, bringing us back into the present moment. It is about *being* as we are *doing*. Consciously slowing our activities, getting up from the desk to walk outside for a moment, taking a focused breath, drinking a glass of water, petting the cat—these are all restorative and can bring us back into a more balanced, expansive state. Sometimes a pause may be momentary, other times longer. Each time you pause, let your sensory awareness open out, remembering to breathe.

While I am riding, I use the intentional pause to soften and center. The simple act of pausing interrupts automaticity, awakens awareness, and creates the space for more harmony between me and my horse. Several times during the ride, I ask my horse to *flow forward into a halt*—softly inviting him to stop without bracing—and then drop the reins (loose contact, on the buckle). Then I just stand

3. Pause again, this time noticing any tension or bracing that you feel in your body as you stop: Scan your hands, shoulders, legs, buttocks, lower back, face, jaw, feet, and ankles. Consciously send a flow of breath to any parts of the body that feel tense, and at the same time, visualize a spacious, warming relaxation spreading through your body and the body of the horse. Walk on again.

4. Pause again and soften your focus, like you are looking out of your eyes from the back of your skull as if it were a large empty room. Scan the space around you with relaxed, receptive eyes and a global focus, at the same time noticing where your horse is looking. Begin moving again, keeping the feeling of an easy, expansive focus.

5. As you alternate between stillness and moving, be aware of both the container and the contents of your body and your horse's body. Can you imagine the support of the organs, the fluids, and the fascia in both the movement and the stillness?

6. Bring the relaxed, attentive quality of stillness into your riding so that you can flow seamlessly from stillness into movement without losing feeling or awareness.

(sometimes with eyes closed, depending on what else is going on in the ring) and focus on feeling the inside of my body connect with the inside of my horse's body. I am looking for the feeling that all my cells and all his cells are humming on the same frequency. My breath is the portal and the anchor. I am waiting for the horse to drop his head, take a big breath and for both of us to lose any sense of needing to move, settling into a shared relaxation and openness to each other and everything around us. When we begin moving again, I find it easier to offer a soft connection, and to feel both of our bodies as a harmonic whole.

FINDING FEELING AND RESONANCE

Much of my work with Amadeo is about slowing, listening, and sensing *the right moment*. For example, when I want to put the halter on him, I don't necessarily go directly to that goal. I take my time, noticing his responses, my own feelings (calm, anxious, hurried, steady) and track how that is expressing outwardly. This

SLOWING, STOPPING, GOING

🕐 15 MINUTES

PURPOSE: *Slowing*, like pausing, is a way to find and feel yourself more deeply and reliably. Slowing allows your brain to gather more information about whatever it is that you are doing. When we move quickly, we miss many steps along the way. Slowing is an elegant way of expanding and softening the movement conversation between you and your horse.

1. Begin walking with your horse, keeping an open, soft hand on the lead rope. Walk with an intention of inviting him to join you with a relaxed, rhythmic, and steady stride. Be aware of the synchronous pattern of your footfalls with those of your horse. Feel grounded through your legs and pelvis with an easy expansiveness in your upper body. Be sure that your body is expressing the feeling and intention of moving forward together.

2. As you walk, notice your breathing and any changes in tension in your body or mind. Is your horse with you? Are you visualizing what you want? Is your body expressing this intention and connection or do you have a thought that he will balk or spook? Just notice whatever "script" you are writing mentally.

3. Gradually slow your walk, so that you are taking one conscious step at a time. Communicate this intentional slowing through your body (and

"tracking practice"—of him and myself—helps me sense the moment when to take the next step. Each step of the process has its own timing, its own rhythm: pick up the halter and lead rope, approach him, let him touch the items in my hand, touch him with them, put the lead rope over his back, put the halter on. This whole process means asking the question and then waiting—pausing—to feel the response. Sometimes it is instantaneous, and all of these steps happen smoothly and easily. Other times, there is a longer wait. Sometimes it is about not *doing* anything, but just *being* in the present moment. Amadeo has taught me this more clearly than anyone, horse or human.

Amadeo's serious spooks have also helped me to find new ways of attuning. Walking with him, I intentionally sync my steps with his in a quiet, settled way. Almost immediately, he joins me, and within moments we can stop, move forward or backward, and turn together. I am not demanding or pushing, just listening for the voice if necessary), rather than pulling on the lead line to slow your horse. You are inviting him to pay attention as well. Come to a halt with a gradated, slowing, "3–2–1" rhythm, like the feeling of blowing out a candle. This allows time for the image and the message to be transmitted to the horse. Look for a feeling of orchestration between your movement and the horse's.

4. As you begin walking, prepare inwardly with a "1–2–3–Go" so that you are not just setting off without including your horse. *Look* at your horse as you begin to shift your weight forward. Feel inwardly the invitation and forward intention in your body, your heart, and the hand holding the lead rope. If your horse is not shifting with you, try again, this time visualizing moving forward together as a single body.

5. Repeat this slowing, stopping, and going pattern several times, noticing how conscious slowing allows you become more aware of all of the little details of this movement. Are there any gaps or momentary disruptions in the flow of the movement or your connection? Slow even more and see if they fill in and smooth out.

6. Now, can you let go of being the leader in this slowing, stopping, and going? Can you picture it as an unfolding duet between you and your horse?

right moment, for an opening or a softening in the contact between us. This elegant dance dissolves the fear and the resistance (in both of us), and creates the smooth orchestration and friendly cooperation that is, I believe, what we both want.

THE GLASSBLOWER'S BREATH

The "glassblower's breath" means cultivating an improvisational, spontaneous and playful attitude toward *whatever* we are doing—even the most mundane activities: taking the laundry from the dryer, making tea, cleaning tack, hand-grazing your horse. In dance, music, and theater, *improvisation* is an in-the-moment, continually unfolding bodily experience—one without a fixed path or destination. It is, according to Stephen Nachmanovitch in *Free Play: Improvisation in Life and Art* (GP Putnam's Sons, 1991), "the expression of organic, immanent, self-creating structure," what he calls "intuition in action." When we are *improvising*, we are traveling through time and space without a map, following the wild and ragged heart of the body, allowing ourselves to access the deep wells of creative impulse and inspiration. Improvising is a way to step out of the rote, the habitual, and the known. Oliveros says that what makes improvisation wonderful is "the unpredictable turns of chance permutation, the meatiness, the warmth, the simple, profound, humanity of beings that brings presence and wonder to music." Improvising is a listening practice. We wait to be moved by an impulse, and then follow that until another arises. Because it is an organic, inwardly attuned process, it is also like Jane Hirshfield's "Horse Zen," a practice of heart, body, and mind.

Sometime today take five minutes to lie down in a quiet spot and let your body soften and move in any way that it wants. Little, big, fast, slow—it doesn't matter. No editor, no instructor, no judge. Listen to the body and let it speak. At the barn, in your office, change your routine and improvise your way through some part of your day. When you are grooming, try different strokes, holding the brush with your non-dominant hand or doing things in a different order. Vary the rhythms of your touch and imagine that as you brush the horse, you are playing music—not a familiar melody, but an unspooling improvisatory piece played by your hands and the horse's body. At work, intentionally change the timing of an activity: type very slowly, or pause then resume, noticing how even that small change brings you more consciously into your body. Let your eyes take in the whole landscape: up, down, both sides, far and near, small and large. Let whatever you are doing be delicious, sensuous, irresistible—improvisational.

I think now of standing in the arena with my horse Sanne, preparing to ride. I do not have a plan; I am waiting to see where this particular day will take us. Each day before our ride, Sanne gently pushes his nose into the hollow in the front of my shoulder and rests there. Feeling him nuzzle, the warmth of his breath, I fall into the present moment like a stone dropped into water. We stand like this for what seems like a very long time. Sanne is the glassblower, faithfully reminding me why I am here with him: to slow down, to connect, and to savor this very moment, the only one we truly have.

CHAPTER SIX

THE FLIGHT:
FINDING EARTH AND SKY

One Heart

Look at the birds. Even flying
is born

out of nothing. The first sky
is inside you, open

at either end of day.
The work of wings
was always freedom, fastening
one heart to every falling thing.

Li-Young Lee
"One Heart" from *Book of My Nights*.
Copyright © 2001 by Li-Young Lee.
Reprinted with the permission of
The Permissions Company, Inc.,
on behalf of BOA Editions, Ltd.

Riding a swimming horse feels like flying. Once on a trail ride with friends on Martha's Vineyard, we rode to Sepiessa Point in West Tisbury. At the tip of the land, the view opens out to the pond and the sea beyond. We walked into the water with the horses, small waves lapping at their legs, the salt air enveloping us, and the soaring swallows diving and spinning like aerial calligraphers. I was riding Mia, an elderly Lipizzaner mare. I remember my anticipation as she stepped deeper and deeper into the water, feeling her hooves soften into the sandy mud of the pond, watching the water climb her legs and waiting for her to begin swimming. Then suddenly we were flying—buoyant, aloft—her legs stretching through the water, no longer earthbound. A photographer captured my bliss that day, grinning ear to ear—a fool in love with the sea, the horse, and the moment.

Playful bursts of flight are instinctual for horses; it's just part of their exuberant movement language. Trainer Sarah Hollis says of her black Andalusian stallion Regaliz, "He loves his body and the power that comes from it. His favorite activity when he wants to show off is bouncing up and down from levade[65] to a low crouch, then leaping back up and down again."

For the rider, the body of the horse is a conduit between sky and earth. On a horse we feel ourselves to be faster, more powerful. As the horse's feet leave the ground, we are lifted into flight with the earth of the horse's back beneath us. The rhythmic movement of the horse is transmitted through the rider's body, head reaching skyward as hips and legs reach downward.

FLYING WITH HORSES

Working with aerialists in my dances with horses gave me some surprising insights into our dynamic, bodily relationship with qualities of groundedness and balance. I discovered over time how like flying riding could be, and how the relationship between earth and sky, gravity and levity, is shared between horse and human.

My dreams of flight and horses began during rehearsals of the equestrian dance I created entitled *RIDE*. The dancers seemed so small next to the horses, so earthbound and predictably bipedal in their movement. I wanted a way to lift the dancers off the ground; to balance the size and power of the horses; to let them take flight like the riders. I asked an aerial equipment company to create six low-flying swing trapezes, which we mounted to the arena trusses. On the first day the dancers whooped and swung like children on a giant swing set. Initially they struggled for balance, but as they practiced, they found complicated, playful ways of mounting and dismounting as they careened through the air like equestrian vaulters. Standing on the bar of the trapeze, the arcing thrusts of their swinging reached nearly to the trusses of the arena. At one point one of the riders exclaimed as she watched, "That is exactly how I feel when I am riding!" Over time the dancers became adept swing-riders, discovering new ways of flying that evoked the wild beauty of birds and horses, their movement connecting earth and sky.

Goliath, Norman, and Roy Wind playing together in the arena.

On the back of the horse, we are lifted into flight. My horse Sanne ridden by Brandi Rivera.

Several years after working with the low-flying swings, I met aerialist, equestrian, and dancer Paola Styron, and that meeting sparked my desire to explore more deeply the possibilities of "flying" with horses. Styron had been a rider from childhood, and during her career as a dancer had become a preeminent aerialist in dance and theater performances, widely respected and sought after for her elegant work in the air and on the ground. Jamie Leonard, the head technician from the aerial company Flying by Foy,[66] says that Styron is simply the best aerialist he has ever worked with. Her skills in the air are unmatched.

Styron is an etheric being: a human bird, seemingly hollow-boned, quick and airy, as comfortable spinning upside down, twisting and spiraling through the air as she is on the ground. Her frequent collaborator Flying by Foy became a part of our experiment in flying with horses. The equipment was a huge metal truss with pulleys and cables that attached to a harness, which allowed Styron to fly through the air like Peter Pan.

For Styron, flying is not just about the harness, the pulleys, the winch, the track, and the truss. Watching her negotiate the equipment, I see how much finesse is required to create the illusion of effortlessness, and to manage the constraints and the challenges of dancing in the air without a stabilizing connection to the earth. Each turn, inversion, or twist requires her to thread her arms through the wires, rebalance herself in the harness to create a seamless flow that is actually a series of micro-interruptions and a complex, silent conversation between Styron and the handlers who control her height and speed of travel. The result is breathtaking.

Dancers Dillon Paul and Alissa Cardone on the swings in RIDE.

138

"When you are flying," she says, "the slightest physical change—the turn of the head, an arc of the arm, torque of the torso—will affect the whole trajectory down the line. With the slightest reach, gesture...you set a force in motion and you have to surrender to it—to that being out of control in order to pull back into balance. And that then affects when and how your partner—the horse and rider—will respond. The dance feels very much like verging on losing control, swimming in and out of momentary balance."

Styron's description of flying, to me, sounds much like riding—hovering at times on the edge of control, swimming in and out of balance, negotiating the continuous, dynamic shifts as we orchestrate changes of direction, balancing our bodies, the horse's body, with all of the minute and immediate adjustments that this requires.

Working with Styron in the air continued to surprise me with insights about working with horses on the ground. Horses do not expect to see a human in the air. Most danger approaches in stealth from the ground, but an airborne person is perhaps a giant predatory bird—a human pterodactyl. Styron found that flying with the Andalusian stallion Capprichio in the performance of *FLIGHT* was different from any other aerial experience. When her body first lifted off the ground, Capprichio—a veteran of many, many performances—was uneasy and unsettled. Styron realized that in order to dance in the air with this horse she had to "come into her center and her ground" even more deeply—that is, she had to find her physical and emotional balance point. Riders, too, must find this balancing center moment-by-moment on the moving body of the horse.

Rider and dancer "floating" with Capprichio in the performance of FLIGHT at Mistover Farm in Pawling, New York.

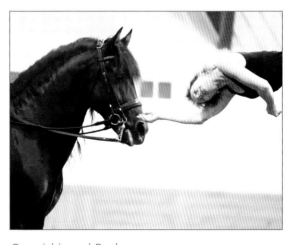

Capprichio and Paola.

"Capprichio required me to think from my physical center, rather than from my head," Styron says. "I feel the same way sometimes around certain people—they are so deeply embodied and grounded and evolved that they bring me into that place in myself."

As riders, we have to think from our emotional and physical centers like Styron. Our responses have to be intuitive and swift to be effective.

Balancing Between Two Worlds

Dancers Eiko and Koma use the word "trembling" to describe the physical sensation of hovering between two contradictory movement impulses in the body. During the Delicious Movement Workshop I described earlier in this book, we practiced "initiation," which is an exercise where we moved from two places in the body simultaneously. One point of initiation might be the tender skin of the inside of the left elbow and the other the lashes of the right eye. Each place had its own particular urgency and direction. We were instructed to move as slowly and seamlessly as possible, which exponentially increased the difficulty of the exercise. The resulting tension related to this physical puzzle created the sensation of trembling—hovering at the edge of control. How to continue moving without speeding up or collapsing is the body's mystery to unravel—the physical equivalent of a *Zen koan*, which is a riddle that unveils a greater truth.

In her aerial work, Styron is continually flying at the edge of that same "trembling," never resting in the resolution of a single direction or movement, but always dancing within a complexity of movement, weight, and momentum. Watching her gave me a new way of understanding this delicate life dance of losing and finding balance, both physical and emotional.

Riding can be like that. We think we are traveling in one direction down the long side of the arena, but really we are balancing, blending, co-creating—the ride unfolding improvisationally, mapping itself from countless possibilities. It is our work to feel for balance—emotional and physical—and allow ourselves to be

Paola, Capprichio, and Brandi in the performance of FLIGHT.

Our Horses, Ourselves

carried, shaping this dance with the horse (both on the ground and in the saddle) from within. Each action creates a series of reactions and corrections, our lives a continual fall and recovery, always at the edge, always "trembling." The problems arise—in both our riding and in our lives—when we seek too much stability, too much sameness or predictability, mistaking this for security.

TRY THIS

LOSING AND FINDING BALANCE

⏱ 10 MINUTES

PURPOSE: Balance is a continual, dynamic dance between gravity and levity, weightedness and lightness, stability and mobility. It is a three-dimensional, continually changing relationship between the earth and our bodies. Understanding balance as fluid rather than fixed helps us become more at ease and adaptable in our riding—less likely to brace or make big, destabilizing adjustments while on or with our horses.

1. Stand with your feet about 6 inches apart (aligned beneath your sit bones), knees straight but relaxed. Close your eyes and notice the small swaying movements that happen as your body balances in relationship to gravity. Are you swaying more forward and back or side to side or do you detect a small figure eight pattern? Your *center* is the place in your body that is poised between front and back, side to side, up and down. Because we are *moving beings*, our center moves when we move.

2. Be aware of any tension in your feet, ankles, legs, buttocks, or jaw as you sway. Are you breathing? Can you feel how balance is not static, but dynamic—always shifting and adjusting?

3. Open your eyes, and allow yourself to sway forward until you have to catch yourself by stepping forward, then let your body find its balance again. Now lean back until you feel yourself losing balance, then again bring yourself back to balance. Make these adjustments as best you can without engaging the big extrinsic or superficial musculature. Can you imagine the smaller, deeper, intrinsic muscles helping you to balance? These are not necessarily muscles under your direct control, but you can "bring them

CONTINUED ▶

CONTINUED FROM PAGE 141

on line" by using visualization, or performing specific movements that recruit them. For example: the fibers of the deep lumbar multifidus muscles become active in certain bending and rotational activities that involve the spine, even though we cannot engage and isolate them the way we can with the large muscles of the legs, hips, arms, and shoulders.

4. Now sway to the right until you must step sideways to catch yourself. Try the same thing to the left. What does it require for you to find balance after losing it? Does your sense of balance feel different? Look for a more fluid and elastic quality each time you rebalance.

5. Next time you are riding, pay attention to the moments when you feel out of balance. Sometimes this is a dramatic shift that disrupts your seat; other times it is more like a progressive erosion of your center. In the latter case, muscles gradually tighten, one side of the ribcage may collapse, your sternum may drop, and you can find yourself riding tight and breathless. Instead of correcting the imbalance abruptly or roughly, breathe consciously as you make more subtle, gradual adjustments. This will allow you to feel more clearly where your (moving) center is and its relationship to your horse's (moving) center. You will feel center as the *stillpoint* where there is no muscular effort required to hold you in a vertical alignment. Remember that balance is shared, elastic and flexible, rather than static or fixed. Breath is the key!

"Although we've lately come to associate gravity with heaviness, and to think of it as having a strictly downward vector, nonetheless something rises up into us from the solid earth whenever we're in contact with it. We give ourselves precious little chance to taste this nourishment that springs up into us whenever we touch ground, and so it's hardly surprising that we've forgotten the erotic nature of gravity and the enlivening pleasure of earthly contact."

David Abram
Being Animal: An Earthly Cosmology
(Pantheon, 2010)

Our Horses, Ourselves

Pony in his "airs above the ground."

GRAVITY AND LEVITY

Gravity and *levity* are part of our daily dance, a continual and often unconscious shifting between earth and sky. *Breathing* is the baseline of that dance. Each inhale is an ascent, each exhale a descent. Every step we take is a departure from and a return to earth, each descent providing the support for the following ascent. When sitting on a horse, we are experiencing up and down with every step; hips and spine a conduit and for that rising and falling rhythm. Styron says of her experience of riding that, "It speaks to some deeply embedded human desire to be reconnected with our own wild grace; to be grounded in our flesh: to feel the rhythm and reverberation of footfalls moving up through the bones, lifting us up and forward toward lightness and flow, releasing back down toward the earth again and again."

Paola taking flight with Capprichio.

FINDING EARTH AND SKY

🕐 10 MINUTES

PURPOSE: Becoming more conscious of and comfortable with our dance with gravity can help us to become more buoyant and grounded both physically and emotionally. As we ride, this dance with gravity is amplified by the horse's movement. Noticing the natural buoyancy of our bodies helps to diminish any heaviness or stiffness that disrupts the full functioning and expressivity of our movement, as well as our relationship to the horse.

1. Stand with your feet slightly apart and knees relaxed. Jiggle the body (picture a dog coming out of the water), loosening the big muscles of the legs, buttocks, torso and arms. Now, come back to stillness, looking for the *stillpoint* in your balance—the place where the body does not require muscular tension to stand.

2. Breathe through the whole vertical column of your body. Notice any tightness, and take a few minutes to let the filling and emptying rhythm of the breath dissolve those tensions. Feel the internal support of the breath in every part of your body, as if your body were a series of interconnected passageways: veins, nerves, bones, fascia.

3. Begin a small, buoyant bouncing movement, softly flexing and extending the knees, ankles, and hip joints, keeping the feet flat on the floor and the joints fluid. Feel that up-and-down bounce connecting you through the vertical channels of the body, from the bottoms of your feet to the top of your head. Imagine that as you bounce you are sending little ripples through the fluids of your body, focusing especially on the joints.

4. Gradually let the bounce subside, as if you were watching ripples diminish on a pond after throwing in a stone.

5. Breathe out, curve your neck forward, and soften downward through the spine, letting your knees bend more deeply, softening the hip and ankle joints as your arms release down, surrendering to gravity.

6. Breathe in and slowly roll up through the spine, so that the head is the last thing to uncurl. Let your arms rise slowly toward the ceiling, and then float down to settle at your sides.

7. At your own pace, alternate between curling and uncurling your spine, sinking and rising through your legs and arms, feeling a deep heaviness on the one hand and a feathery lightness on the other.

8. During the day, take one-minute breaks from work to stand up, feeling the whole length of your body from the soles of your feet to the top of your head—sky above, earth below. Do a minute or so of soft bouncing to wake up the body, then lift and lengthen your arms upward as you reach downward through your legs and feet, feeling yourself as a conduit between earth and sky.

Slow, weighted curling forward can help you find gravity.

BALANCING FROM WITHIN

🕐 5–10 MINUTES

PURPOSE: The purpose of our big extrinsic muscles is to support action and mobility when we need to fight or flee or perform some other athletic activity. Those muscles are voluntary and under our conscious control. For the most part, riding requires more subtlety and *only as much effort as is actually required*. Many aspects of riding involve fine motor control, which is the ability to use finesse, and to add or diminish strength in a highly nuanced, gradated way.

1. In the rising trot, the pelvic floor can be a powerful source of support for the up-and-down movement of your whole body. Imagine the movement of the pelvic floor like the fluid pumping of the jellyfish. Activating the pelvic floor through awareness and imagery, rather than muscular effort, creates an energetic relationship between your head and your feet—an elastic, buoyant counter-tension, between up and down.

2. The bony landmarks of the pelvic floor are the *pubic symphysis* in front, the *coccyx* in back, and the sit bones (*ischial tuberosities*) on either side. As you rise in the trot, there is a narrowing of the pelvic quadrants (front to back and side to side). As you sit, that same space between sit bones, coccyx, and pubis widens and opens.

When I walk my horse Amadeo, I can feel when he is getting distracted, starting to tense, getting ready to spook. Amadeo is a flight expert. Walking with him from the barn to the arena can be an aerial adventure. He has taught me to ground myself in an immediate and necessary way. To learn to feel my own tension: my hand closing on the lead rope, my body getting ready for the worst. Inside my riding boots, my feet feel like potato chips—brittle and curled. When this happens, I breathe, connecting myself downward, consciously softening and opening my feet inside my boots, feeling as though I am sinking into soft mud, each step making a deeper connection with the earth. Doing that, I feel him relax, his head dropping, his eyes and ears coming back to me, his body and brain settling back into harmony.

ALIGNMENT AND FINDING CENTER

Horses are generous, kind, patient, tolerating our imbalances, roughness, and distractions with more equanimity than most humans. What can we do for them

3. As you rise in the trot, ascend through your head and simultaneously descend through the feet with an elastic feeling, at the same time feeling the subtle condensing, or drawing together, of the space between the bony landmarks of the pelvic floor. Soften and widen the pelvic floor in a supported way each time you sit, still feeling that active, elastic, counter-tension between head and feet.

4. It is important *not* to make this an overtly muscular action. Simply bringing your awareness and a quality of aliveness to the pelvic floor is supportive of both up and down movements. Finding a more centered balance through the supple resilience of the pelvic floor helps you to be more subtle and feeling about the way you are using your hands and legs, allowing your horse to move more freely and in better balance.

5. Now visualize the energetic, glandular centers of the body like a column of lights from your tailbone to the top of your head. As you ride, imagine those lights becoming brighter and clearer with each rise and sit. Picture those same centers like illuminated runway lights along the spine of the horse beneath you.

besides providing the best care we can afford? We can begin by paying attention to the ways that we fall out of alignment—physically and emotionally—and make realigning and rebalancing our responsibility and an important part of our daily practice. I don't mean standing up straight with our shoulders back. What I am suggesting is something more fluid and subtle: a way of undoing old patterns and opening to new ways of feeling ourselves that is revelatory and vulnerable. As we just discussed, balance and alignment are never static, but dynamic and fluid, a continual recalibration in response to the *moving* situation. I have learned again and again that horses can help me in those subtle and not-so-subtle body-mind recoveries of balance and alignment, precisely because they offer so many opportunities for me to fall *out* of balance.

Bonnie Bainbridge Cohen's work with the endocrine glands is one way of helping us find our *midline* or *center*. While the glands are physical bodies, they are also energy hubs, corresponding to the chakras, and play an important role in the neurochemistry that governs our emotions. Engaging the specific conscious-

Brandi Rivera riding Sanne: I see a beautiful alignment, as if their energy centers are open, illuminated, and engaged.

Mariah MacGregor and Djuma.

ness and movement in each of these centers can have a profound effect on the body-mind as a whole.

At a workshop, Bainbridge Cohen was on hands and knees, demonstrating how tucking the pelvis, or attempting to straighten the lower back by "curling your tail" under, closes off and deadens the energetic centers at the coccyx and perineum. I realized I often felt this effect when I rode (or sat at the computer)—I unconsciously did a subtle version of this tucking or bracing in a mistaken, habitual effort to protect my lower back from discomfort or fatigue. I also noticed that when riding, I was *not* clearly feeling the connection between my head and my feet. I could sense how too much muscular engagement of the big, superficial muscles in my hips, back, legs, and belly had closed off that connection.

By bringing more weight and sensitivity into my feet, I felt a deeper, "spongier" connection with the stirrups, which immediately set up a clear vertical link between my head and feet. The surprising result was that it also greatly increased the stability in my seat and hands *without* bracing or gripping, and it brought me more clearly into my *midline*—that is, it allowed me to sense the vertical channel

Our Horses, Ourselves

of my spine. I learned to more effectively align my body by visualizing the energetic centers of the endocrine glands/chakras from tailbone to crown, I felt an even stronger and more stable balance.

I consciously integrated all these actions with my lovely, patient horse Sanne. The result was astonishing. His trot took on a buoyant, floating quality that I had never felt so clearly before. I realized that because his trot was so big and athletic, I had unconsciously been holding my hips in a slightly braced, protective position, even as I tried to loosen and release them. I could not open fully to his movement. Bringing awareness to the pelvic floor shifted me away from a "doing," muscular effort into a more subtle alignment of my body. I also felt how each pelvic half is actually a part of the leg, with the sacrum—a part of the spine—floating between. This gave me a greater feeling of both balance and freedom in the walk, the trot, and the canter, allowing me to join more fully with Sanne's big movement.

THE WEIGHT OF THE BODY

The way of love
is not a subtle argument.

The door there
is devastation.

Birds make great sky-circles
of their freedom.
How do they learn it?

They fall, and falling,
they're given wings.

Rumi
The Essential Rumi (Harper One, 2004),
translated by Coleman Barks,
used by permission of Coleman Barks.

Equestrian Mariah MacGregor was just fifteen years old when I gave her my beloved Djuma, a horse she had known and loved for seven years. Djuma was stunningly beautiful—a dark bay off-the-track Thoroughbred that my friend Susan Fieldsmith had rescued from a neighbor's backyard barn. He came into my life through pure chance. One evening when I arrived at Susan's barn, Djuma was standing on the crossties in the barn aisle as Susan and Mariah were trying to determine the cause of his lameness. As Susan lifted his hind leg, he swayed and looked as if he would fall. Mariah pushed on his side to keep him up. Susan

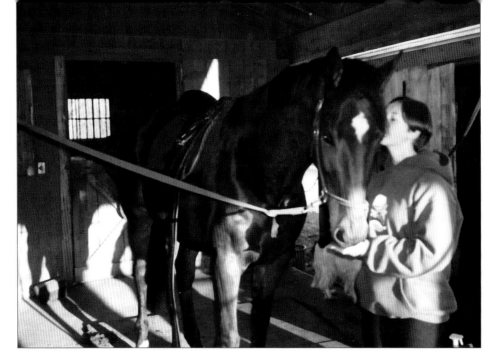

Beautiful Djuma—the embodiment of flight. "It's like being in love with a rocket."

With Djuma.

removed his blanket. I was stunned by the muscles of his chest, the architecture of that beautiful face, the slender legs, and the gleam of his dark coat. And the moment Djuma looked at me, the sensation was like lightning: electric, riveting, and brilliant. I felt that he was speaking *into* me, asking for my help. I was undone by the presence of this horse—the most beautiful creature I had ever seen. Susan, it happened, was looking for someone to take over his care, to be his person.

"Yes, of course," I said without hesitating. "Of course."

He was a big horse—17 hands—and I had to overcome my fear and my inexperience. I spent hours grooming him, hanging out with him in the paddock, learning how to lead him, loving this beautiful, wounded horse.

Wind Horse

To feel his muscles bunch and stretch
in unison with mine is feeling the
earth turn with your head in the clouds
and the last light of the falling sun
drenching your eyes with awe.
We dream together, by the sea I see him wet eyes
taking the sea into that deep and windy chest
turning I wish into
I can
fly.

How can I sense such dangerous devotion?
It's like being in love with a rocket
whose fuse is lighted and sparking
It's nights lying in bed
watching phosphorescence on my ceiling,
could I be at sea?

My recipe of childhood
and its regression into adulthood starts with this:
Mornings of gray slanted sun piercing the skin
of what we think we know.

A dark horse comes.
He comes again and again,
He comes only because we need to be taught
why he comes again and again.

A dark horse brings the dawn on his back
holds the earth in his hooves,
the oceans are the tides of muscle in his neck.
Captain of his own mysterious vessel,
he calls for us.

Mariah MacGregor

He recovered, and I wanted to ride him, but found that he was too spooky, too big, too much for a timid, novice rider with damaged hips. So Mariah rode him, and I watched my beautiful horse go round and round the arena, occasionally exploding sideways in a spook or straight up in a buck. It could be a falling leaf, or a passing car, or the flutter of a bird—Djuma was the embodiment of flight.

Djuma was the horse that grounded Mariah in her physical self. She says, "Our horses become a living prosthesis, an extension of our own body. That connection takes time to build, and once built can be damaged. A lifelong equestrian, I took this gift for granted until I developed an eating disorder as a teenager. As I systematically rejected the physical me, so did my horse Djuma. Suddenly he would not allow me to ride him. He embodied the disassociation I felt. The day a trainer told me that he was too dangerous to ride was one of the first days I admitted that I was losing myself."

Djuma's flights—the spooks, bucks, and bolts—were his way of helping Mariah to feel how she had "lost the ground," or the reliable, earthy stability of her own body. Mariah's fall out of harmony with both herself and Djuma ultimately brought her back to a deep appreciation of her own physicality.

"When you are riding," says Mariah, "you are transported to this liminal zone between the earth and sky, between the physical and the mystical. The contradiction of the horse's weight and his speed is a part of this magical state. You are at once light and heavy; both in control and at the mercy of nature. It's a contradiction that can serve as a metaphor for how we live our lives. Somewhere between the purely physical and the spiritual: between thought and action. Now riding reminds me of the pure joy of being alive and the access to the sacred we get when truly connected to the physical."

Each moment of our waking lives is a negotiation and reconciliation of our physical experience of up and down, of flying and falling. Walking itself is a negotiation of balance and imbalance, each step a little suspension and fall, a surrender to forward momentum, caught and lifted by the step that follows. All of our movement—conscious and unconscious—is a part of this bodily dance between earth and sky.

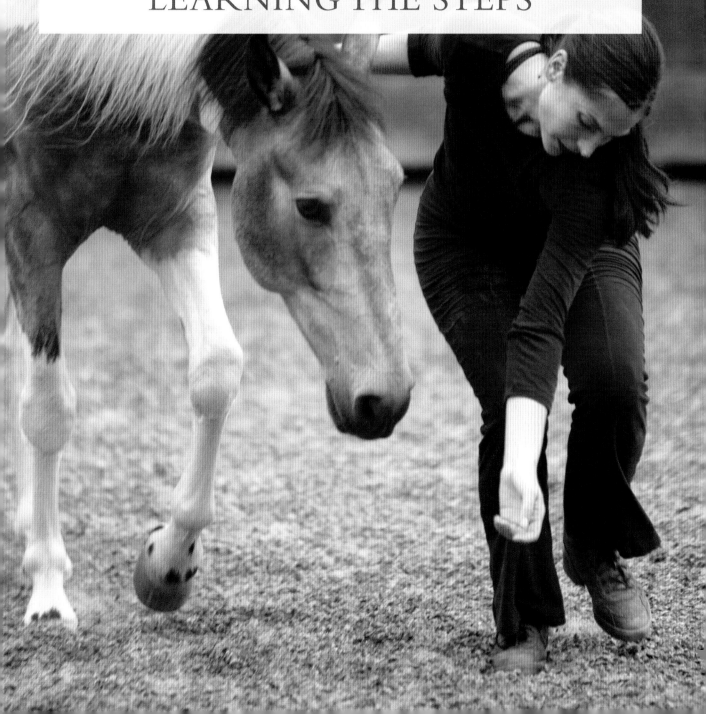

CHAPTER SEVEN

THE THIRD WALK:
BREAKING IT DOWN, LEARNING THE STEPS

Keep walking, though there's no place to get to.
Don't try to see through the distances.
That's not for human beings.
Move within, but don't move the way fear makes you move.

Rumi

Illuminated Rumi
(Crown Publishing, 1997),
translated by Coleman Barks,
used by permission of
Coleman Barks.

LEARNING THE STEPS

In a rehearsal for a dance I was choreographing, I asked the dancers to improvise their movement using two images: a passionate tango danced on all fours, and a languid, slightly tipsy ballet adagio, as if they had a long heavy dinosaur tail. The dancers played with these images, changing level, movement dynamics, and shape. As the rehearsal progressed, we developed their explorations into set phrases. One of the dancers was a master improviser, but when we began setting the placement and precise quality and timing of the movement, she struggled with its complexity and length. So we slowed down, splitting the movement into parts, breaking the steps into smaller and smaller segments, re-infusing them with the "juice" of the imagery. Gradually she became more and more confident and was ultimately able to perform the movement sequence effortlessly.

This way of learning movement is similar to the "Third Walk," a technique formerly used by the Spanish Riding School in Vienna to train their Lipizzaner stallions. Instead of a normal walking rhythm, the horse was asked to slowly lift and place each foot, a challenge to both balance and brain. Doing this helped the horses feel more clearly *when* and *where* they were placing their feet. It taught both *attention* and *feeling*, similar to the Buddhist practice of walking meditation. It was a way of connecting the outer act of walking with inner awareness.

When my family adopted Misha, our first greyhound, he was unable to climb stairs. Racing greyhounds live on one level, going from the kennel to the track and back, so they never encounter steps up or down. Confronted with a strange mountain inside a house, Misha was terrified, frozen. So with one of us behind him and the other in front, we helped him up the stairs, lifting one leg at a time—pausing, then moving forward. By the end of the week, he had grasped the sequence and rhythm, and going up and down the stairs became quick and effortless because he had understood that it was just one step at a time.

Our Horses, Ourselves

THE THIRD WALK

🕐 10 MINUTES

PURPOSE: As humans, walking is our primary gait but is often performed with little awareness. Becoming more deliberate and conscious about each phase of our walk helps us practice a mindfulness that can inform all our activities, from making tea to tacking up, from driving a car to riding a horse.

1. Begin walking in a rhythm that feels normal and comfortable to you. Notice the various sensations in your feet, legs, spine, shoulders, and head, and how you feel the movement connecting through your body, and any areas of tightness or relaxation, ease or imbalance.

2. Gradually slow your walk until you are lifting and placing each foot with care. Feel the texture of the floor, the softness or firmness of the sole of your foot on the floor. Notice if the sensations in other parts of your body become more detailed and clear. Does your breathing change? Is there any sense of your balance being more precarious?

3. Now slow the walk down even more, differentiating between the lift of each part of the foot—heel, ball, toe—and the placement of each part of your foot back onto the floor. Can you feel the skin on the undersides of your toes, the bones beneath the flesh, and the way in which each step transmits through your legs, hips, spine, arms, neck, and head? Be curious about this slowed-down dance between stability and mobility, including any emotional responses you may have to moving this slowly.

4. As you gradually increase your speed, notice if the quality of your walk has changed in any way. Can you imagine continuing to pay as much attention to the quality of your walk as you do to your horse's?

Chunking Down

When Clicker trainer Alexandra Kurland speaks of "chunking down" a desired behavior or movement, she is talking about breaking the learning process into smaller and smaller steps, similar to titration (see p. 111). In doing that, the separate elements become comprehensible to the horse: more doable and less overwhelming.

"Breaking the behavior down into small steps lets the handler explain each small unit of the behavior," Kurland says. "It lets the handler really listen to the horse so if he is worried or frightened the handler can adjust the lesson. Ideally every step in the training should feel like just a small step beyond what the horse is already successfully doing. If you taught a behavior in its finished form, it would be very difficult. But when you chunk it down into small steps, each training step seems very doable."

She observes that as humans we tend to be "lumpers" instead of "splitters." We ask for too much too fast, trying to build duration too quickly and seeing desired behaviors or training goals in too big a chunk—a little like trying to eat an entire meal in one bite. We do this not just with our horses, but also with our children, our spouses, and ourselves. Kurland believes that in order to be successful with our horses we have to introduce our ideas and intentions gradually, building understanding and success step by step, and learning to work in "horse time." In her experience, "When there is resistance, bracing, or stiffness, when the gaits (walk, trot, canter) lack expression, it is usually because people have asked too much too soon—they have seen a complex training goal as a single element...by learning how to teach in steps, when something goes wrong you can see in which layer of the process the horse lost his balance (mental or physical), and then structure a lesson around that specific element."

Kurland specialized in animal behavior at Cornell University and then went on to study with Linda Tellington-Jones, dressage trainer Bettina Drummond, and horseman John Lyons. In the early 1990s she was discussing animal training with a friend who bred and trained Irish Wolfhounds, and her friend said, "But of course you've read *Don't Shoot the Dog*,[67] haven't you?" This well-known book by Karen Pryor translates the principles of operant conditioning into practical training terms, and as Kurland read it, she thought, "This is something that the horse world needs to know." She saw Pryor's ideas as a way of filling in some of the great holes in understanding of why horse training works the way it does, and why horses respond the way they do.

"Most horse training is punishment-based," notes Kurland. "Novice horse owners are told they need to 'get tougher' with their horses. They are shown how to use crops to make their horses do what they demand of them. Punishment is so all-pervasive we don't even recognize that's what we're doing. Nor do we understand the consequences both to our horses and ourselves. We don't understand the emotional fallout that punishment has. And we don't recognize what a clumsy training tool it is.... *Don't Shoot the Dog* both made a great case for avoiding the use of punishment, and it gave us something to put in its place—Clicker Training."

This type of training is now commonplace in the positive reinforcement world of modern dog training, and certainly more prevalent in horse training, but in the early 1990s it was totally different from anything Kurland had ever seen or been a part of.

"At that time the usual training technique was the 'jerk and pull' correction-based training with people barking commands," she says. "This was so different I was absolutely intrigued."

Kurland's own horse was a beautiful mare whose spinal cord had been damaged in an accident, and as a result, she slowly lost the ability to control her hindquarters. Veterinarians told Kurland that she would never be able to ride her mare, that her lack of balance would make it too dangerous, and that eventually Kurland would be faced with the decision of having to put her horse down because the mare would no longer be able to walk without falling, or get up when she fell.

"Part of what she taught me was how important it is to chunk things down into very, very small steps. Basically you stop thinking about the big ultimate goals of riding or showing and you just look at what you are dealing with today with your horse," Kurland says. "Where are you today? What can the horse do and what can't she do? That's where you start."

Kurland explains chunking down by explaining her mare's difficulty walking: The horse had trouble walking out of her stall because it had a little sill, one of those boards at the bottom to keep the sawdust in. She couldn't walk over a ground pole; Kurland replaced a round pole with a flat board, and when that was too much, with a lead rope. Finally, she simply made a line in the dirt for her mare to walk over.

"In your training," she says, "you just keep chunking things down and chunking things down until you find the step where your horse can be successful. For me, that formed the heart of Clicker Training. By finding the small piece where my mare could be successful, I was able to rebuild her balance, her gaits, to ride her, and ultimately, she was the first horse that taught me *piaffe*.[68] That is astounding!"

For humans, chunking down the steps to a task or a goal, whether it is learning to post or to tango, creates an opportunity to change habits and build new connections and understanding along the way. By making the parts of the task smaller, simpler, and therefore more easily digestible, we can let go of the anxious push for speed and perfection. We learn to do the task step by step, being in *this* moment, breathing just *this* breath.

Taking It Apart

In a Clicker Training workshop with Kurland she taught us to balance and ground ourselves with a Tai Chi warm-up before we were allowed to work with our horses. She felt that in order for us to understand what we were asking for in the horse's balance, we had to understand it in our own bodies.

Settling into a wide, deep stance, we shifted our weight in a scooping motion from side to side—down-up, down-up—bending our knees, and using rhythmic breathing to create more fluidity and effortlessness. Next we faced our partners, one person shifting back, the other shifting forward, then reversing direction, in a wide, diagonal stance, knees bent to create a smooth, wave-like motion.

BREAKING IT DOWN

🕐 15 MINUTES

PURPOSE: When we physically experience (*embody*) a practice with our own bodies, it helps us to better understand what we are asking of our horses. This exercise is a good way to teach yourself to move with greater fluidity and awareness as you transition from standing to lying down back to standing. This titrated approach to movement is a good preparation for riding in that it teaches us to move more mindfully from one action to another.

One of the most challenging movements for many people is getting down to the floor and getting back up. If there are physical issues (knees, hips, shoulders) this becomes even more difficult. Usually the solution is the "jerk and pull" to get up or "squat and flop" to get down. The habit of just trying to get down or get up can create a rushed and even painful experience. Breaking the movement into slower, smaller steps can make it easier and more fluid.

As you do this exercise, repeat each part until you feel just that piece is flowing, and then connect it to the next part of the movement. You may want to practice this movement on a rug or yoga mat with a blanket for cushioning.

1. Begin standing in an open area. Without moving, visualize flowing effortlessly down to the floor in a single fluid movement. Then picture rising from the floor with a feeling of floating ease.

2. Exhale, slowly curving the spine forward and letting the head curl toward the floor. When you reach the end of your curling movement, soften and bend the knees so that your fingers can touch the floor.

3. Inhale and slowly curl back up, lengthening your spine. Your head is the last thing to come back to vertical.

4. Now breathe out and curl forward again, softening your knees as you bend your spine. This time, pay attention to the relationship between your head and your tailbone or coccyx. Feel how, as you curve your spine with bent knees, your head and tailbone come toward each other. Curl back up in a flowing, unspooling of the spine. The head and tail lengthen away from each other.

5. Repeat the curl forward, and continue to curve over and bend your knees until your palms touch the floor and you can gently lower yourself into a kneeling position. Adjust your arms so that your hands are aligned under your shoulders and your knees under your hips.

6. Keeping your hands where they are, but allowing the bend in your elbows to support you, pivot your hips to lower your right hip to the ground. You are in a slight twist. Take your time. Look for a "melting" quality, especially in your joints. As you lower to the floor, let the soft tissue of muscle contact the floor, rather than the boney landmarks of knees, hips, and elbows. Yield your whole body into the floor. Rest there for several moments, feeling its support.

7. Using your hands, arms, and breath, bring your body back to a kneeling position, feeling how the deep abdominal and back muscles support this movement without effort.

8. Repeat the twisting, sinking movement, softly lowering the fleshy part of your right hip to the floor with a pouring, fluid quality, using your arms and breath for support as you lower yourself gently to the floor.

Pivoting the hips down to the floor and sliding out with the support of the arms.

9. Let your body extend and fully settle onto the floor with a yielding feeling.

10. To come back up, reverse the movement. Exhale and roll *softly and slowly* onto your side, curving your spine so that the head and tail come toward each other.

CONTINUED ▶

Curling head and tail toward each other while lying on one side.

11. Using your arms and hands, exhale and press up so that your arms are partially extended and your weight is resting on your hip. Breathe out and softly pivot your hips over your knees. Remember to transition into this position through your soft tissue of the muscles rather than your bones.

12. Tuck your toes under and walk your hands back toward your knees, shifting the weight into the balls of your feet. Your head and neck are curved, and your knees are bent.

13. Shift back toward your feet until they are flat on the floor, knees still bent, head lengthening toward the floor. Release your hands from the floor, shifting the weight fully over your feet and slowly roll up to standing.

14. Repeat this sequence slowly several times, modifying it as needed for your body. Slowing down allows you to feel each part of the movement more clearly and keeps you from skipping important steps. Breathe throughout each of the transitions from up to down and down to up. Be interested in each step while finding a flowing continuity throughout the sequence. Look for a feeling of connectedness through the whole body. Can you let go of any urgency to just get through the movement or do it perfectly?

The purpose of these exercises was to develop responsiveness and sensitivity to our partners' changes of direction and weight, and to relax into an attuned, harmonious relationship. These were lessons that were integral to the work we would later do with our horses.

Kurland helped us get a feel for handling a lead rope, asking us to "play horse," with one person as the horse and the other as the handler. I held the clip with both hands in front of me, positioned just in front of my chest, as my "handler" picked up the other end of the lead. The sensation in my hands was immediate. I could feel the sway of the rope, the tension or relaxation in my partner's hands and body. Kurland said that the way we picked up the lead rope would set the tone for everything that followed, and our attention to this first connection with the horse was essential.

Next, using the lead rope, we learned how to cue our human partners to turn and walk forward or back, using a light "pressure and release" signal with our hands. It was not about forcing our partners to move by pushing or pulling, but gauging what was the *least* amount of pressure required to achieve the desired response. We took each step of the process apart and then put it back together to be clear about the details. By the end of the exercise, I could feel that if the first movement was soft and clear, then all the subsequent movements, including riding, would be improved. Over the next half-hour, my whole body began to relax and open.

This way of working was a revelation. I had watched many hours of video and attended demonstrations by various "horse whisperers" who would shake the rope, using the rope and their movement to establish dominance and "respect." The result was often a confused, frightened horse—head up, body tense. This sympathetic fight or flight reaction is a non-learning state for both horses and humans. A calm mind is a mind that can learn. An agitated mind or body is an obstacle to communication and is focused on survival.

"I had a participant who worked in New York City at a very high-powered job: a very intense energy," says Kurland. "She spent her weekends in a country house with her horses: a totally different energy. She really struggled to make the shift from that intense, driving New York City business world energy to 'horse time.' She did not have her own horse in the clinic—we were using sweet, very people-oriented, easygoing horses appropriate for first-time Clicker trainers. She went into the stall with one horse and tried targeting, and came back glowing, saying, 'Oh, I just love this horse, he is so smart, I just love him.' She came back the next session (we were doing five-minute sessions) saying, 'Oh, I'm not so sure, he's really grumpy and making threatening faces.' So I went over to watch them. She was driving him crazy with her energy. She had no focus, her intensity, her busyness—clicking for this and clicking for that, and all of the excess movement—was creating mayhem. He was just saying, 'Please get her out of here!' Learning to distill your energy down and to focus is one of the great first lessons."

In her book *The Long Quiet Highway* (Bantam, 1994), writer and Zen practitioner Natalie Goldberg says that when we are thinking about our *life purpose*— what we are supposed to be doing in life—and standing back from our experience and analyzing, it's as if we are putting a horse on top of a horse and then trying to ride.[69] One way to practice the Third Walk is to be sure that you focus on just this moment, not the horse-upon-horse story of what happened before or what might happen next.

THE CHICKEN AND THE CHOREOGRAPHER

I first saw choreographer Ann Carlson dance in her work *Animals*, where she performed with two goats, a service dog, a goldfish, and a kitten. She has also danced with horses and cows, and presented a work in which she embodied an elephant. According to an article in *Gender News* at Stanford University, "Carlson admits she likes the 'unpredictable layer' that animals bring to live performance, but she also highlights that these unconventional performers push us to explore the 'permeable membrane' between artifice and reality. Rather than worry that the dog might upstage the actress, Carlson invites the spectator to 'notice how we notice'—to become aware of our biases and become conscious that we may be giving greater attention to the dog, perhaps expecting it to run off-stage."[70]

In 2007 Carlson created *Chicken*, a political performance art piece about our relationship to animals as product. In it she danced in a clear, money-stuffed raincoat alongside a chicken.

I had seen the striking life-sized images of *Chicken* in a gallery at Harvard University where Carlson was a fellow at the Radcliffe Institute for Advanced Studies. Carlson says that the chicken connected her to her childhood, when she first began to decode the meaning of animals in her life.

"I remembered that we had a chicken!" she says. "Her name was Chuckles, and she would bang on the back door for a corn on the cob. We lived in the Chicago

---

TRY THIS

ONE MORE TIME

 5 MINUTES

PURPOSE: When we ask a horse to repeat a movement, we do not want him to do it in a mechanical way. Rather, we want the horse to approach the movement with a fresh mind and fluent body. As riders, we also want to approach that movement with an open mind and body, rather than a collection of habits and preconceived ideas. Pauline Oliveros called this practicing the "unique strategy." In other words, experiencing each breath, each moment, each movement anew. Practicing simple movements off the horse in a non-habitual, attentive way can help us gain greater awareness and insight in the saddle.

1. Pick up an empty glass or cup. Hold it for a few seconds. Put it down.

2. Pick up the glass again, copying exactly the timing and quality of the first movement.

Our Horses, Ourselves

Ann Carlson and her avian dance partner in Chicken.

suburbs and my folks had this funny willingness to have these animals that most people I knew didn't have. We had a wonderfully ambivalent relationship with Chuckles, because you would walk outside and slip in her poo-poo in the backyard."

When Carlson began working with the chicken for her performance piece, she did not have high expectations for a meaningful relationship. She thought, "Oh, chickens are all brainstem, they can't really learn anything." During the shoot the chicken would fly around the studio, and every so often she would lay an egg,

3. Pick up the glass again, and this time put it down as slowly as you can.

4. Repeat the movement as precisely as you can.

5. Now pick up and put down the glass three times, as fast as you can. What changes do you notice in the rest of your body and your breathing?

6. Pick up the glass at a normal speed while looking away from your hand and the glass.

7. Pick up the glass and put it down again with your eyes closed.

8. Pick up the glass and put it down again while standing and lifting one foot off the floor.

9. Each repetition and variation requires slightly different circuitry or organization in the brain. What changes do you notice in your body and breathing? Repeat the exercise with the other hand.

and then turn around and eat it! Carlson called the chicken's owner, who said, "Oh, *she's* the one. Thank you for figuring that out."

"After awhile we had this system where the chicken would be handed to me, and I would hold her and sort of meditate, and then I would put her down and she would rush off," Carlson remembers. "After maybe six or seven times— particularly on the second day—it was clear that she was beginning to know the routine. I would put her down and she would stay there, hang out with me, and move around, looking curious and beautifully chicken-like. So, I kept thinking about adaptability, learned behavior, the intelligence or lack thereof of a chicken— but the chicken really did seem to learn what was expected of her!"

Through repetition, the chicken was learning a behavior and a relationship. Repetition is one of the ways we learn something new—another aspect of chunking down. By repeating, we integrate the experience, becoming familiar with its shape and demands. Then by adding subtle variation or a non-habitual movement element to the repeated behavior, we gain flexibility and adaptability.

HOW LESS CAN BE MORE

"Awareness—knowing, and knowing that you know—is the opposite of automaticity and compulsion. Awareness means that you are in the here and now, living in the present. Awareness is a skill that we need to grow and evolve throughout life it we are to enjoy freedom and true choice. With awareness, we can have a brighter, more cheerful, joyful and alert life."

Anat Baniel

Anat Baniel is a petite woman with a quick smile and a vivacious presence. She mixes playful humor and fierce seriousness in her teaching. She is the originator of the Anat Baniel Method[71], a therapeutic movement practice that integrates neuroscience and the work of her mentor, Dr. Moshe Feldenkrais, author of *Awareness Through Movement* (HarperOne, 2009).

At a workshop at the Kripalu Center in Lenox, Massachusetts, we learned the "nine essentials" of movement outlined in her own book *Move into Life* (Harmony, 2009). What struck me immediately was the connection between the principles of her teaching and the practice of riding a horse. She observed that when we used more force in our movements, we lost differentiation—the ability to feel the finer nuances of our movement choices. She explained that when we look at the mind, *forceful thinking* is conclusion-based: narrow and inflexible. A forceful mind is one that works in broad strokes and lacks differentiation because it is compulsive. For her, this lack of nuance is what creates much of our physical and emo-

DANCING ACROSS THE MIDLINE

🕑 10 MINUTES

PURPOSE: This exercise challenges your brain and balance using non-habitual move-ment in a contralateral or diagonal pattern. Doing this sequence before riding brings a playful, alert quality into the body and mind. It also asks for lateral bend, rotation, quick weight shift, and oppositional coordination of the upper and lower body.

1. Standing in an open, flat area, touch your left foot with your right hand *in front of* your body. Switch, doing the same with your right foot and your left hand. Your eyes should follow the movement of the hand that is doing the touching.

2. Now, bring your left foot and your right hand together *behind* your body. Switch and touch your right foot with your left hand. Again, your eyes should follow the movement of the hand that is doing the touching, looking behind you.

3. Repeat this sequence, building up speed, being sure that you integrate your eyes into the movement. Vary the sequence by changing which side (right or left) you do first, or beginning with the back touches or facing a different direc-tion. Notice how quickly or slowly you accommodate to these changes.

Touching the left foot in front with the right hand, focusing on the hand and counterbalancing with the left arm. The right knee is slightly bent.

Touching the right foot behind with the left arm. The focus is down, back and to the left, and the right arm is counterbalancing.

tional suffering. Freedom, she said, comes with options. When performing her movement exercises, she told us that doing a movement bigger or with greater force actually freezes and desensitizes the parts we are moving. She urged us to become smaller and softer in our explorations; to see how subtle we could be and how much more we could feel.

My dressage trainer, Brandi Rivera, echoes these themes when I ride with her. "Be quicker and lighter," she tells me. She urges me to use fine rather than gross motor control. This means having:

- Soft hands able to flexibly restrain in one moment, and allow in the next.

- Legs that can quickly flick across the horse's flank and then drop into a soft draping position.

- Hips that soften and open to swing with the horse's motion, then momentarily hold to ask the horse to gather himself, then open and swing again to allow a renewal of energy to surge through the horse's body.

The modulation and blending of these elements in a sensitive, gradated way from one to the other, creates an effortless, conscious, and fluid orchestration in concert with the horse.

Many years ago, in a dance improvisation class, musician and choreographer Robert Ellis Dunn[72] taught an exercise he called "Body Part Melody." He asked us to create movement phrases by initiating from different parts of the body: a sharp flick of an elbow, the soft glide of the eyes, a jittery rattle of knees, the waggling reach of the tailbone, and so on. Improvising this way gives voice to the various parts of the body. As we move fluidly from one part to another, we *stop* thinking and *start* feeling and assimilating the movement. I find this much like the orchestration of aids in riding, where one cue flows into the next in a continuous and intuitive process of response and recalibration.

FINDING FAITH

The Phyllis Kind Gallery in Soho was stark white and spacious when I visited, inhabited by the ghostly forms of artist Gillian Jagger's sculptures. On the left side of the room was *The Absence of Faith*, a startling suspension of plaster fragments of a horse's body. I had seen a photograph of the work in *The New York Times* and felt an immediate, visceral connection to the artist's story of the subject: the accidental death of her mare, Faith. In person, the plaster fragments appeared to be flying upward, almost dancing up a series of slatted wooden pieces that resembled fencing.

BODY PART MELODY

🕐 10 MINUTES

PURPOSE: By challenging yourself to perform movements that are unfamiliar or organized in an unusual order, you gain greater agility of body and mind. We have a responsibility to be as fully present, as awake and flexible as riders as we expect our horses to be. This practice helps us to playfully "wake up" to the unexpected. Don't think of this sequence as something to perfect, but rather an ongoing exploration with infinite possibilities for variation and discovery.

1. Standing in a relaxed position, begin this sequence of movements. Each should be light and quick, but relaxed.

2. Brush your left hand down your right thigh, as if flicking away a mosquito.

3. Turn your head slowly to the left.

4. Shrug and drop your right shoulder.

5. Bend knees and circle your hips.

6. Brush your left foot forward along the ground and bring it back.

7. Continue to repeat this sequence, alternating sides, and gradually increasing the speed. Can you make the movements more and more delicate, subtle, and connected in sequence? Can you do all the movements at once? Are you breathing?

8. Take a moment to breathe into the whole envelope of your skin, from the soles of the feet to the crown of the head. Feel the whole body as a long, soft column of breath. Now try the sequence again—or create your own!

There were two horses—two Faiths—in the piece, each one with five or six parts—a head, part of a hip, a leg and haunch, and a shoulder, each hung on rough, slender wires so they seemed to be caught in motion, trembling with suspended animation as if tangled in a terrible trap. The fence sections were also suspended, so the whole felt like a web, a Jacob's Ladder, a storm, in which two horses were running-flying, their relationship to each other and their wiry, wooden environment both beautiful and terrible. I walked around the sculpture for over an hour. I wanted to stand inside Faith's body, to lie down under her, to enter her and to weep. I had never felt a work of art to be so emotional, so nakedly inescapable.

The sculpture The Absence of Faith *by Gillian Jagger.*

The painting Faith's Head *by Gillian Jagger.*

A few days later I called Gillian Jagger and introduced myself. We talked for over an hour about art, life, and horses, and I learned the story of Faith firsthand.

Jagger told me that from the beginning, Faith was an extraordinary horse. She had been left out in a field with her mother, untouched, until as a yearling, her owners took her mother to an auction to be sold. They tried to get Faith on the horse trailer, too, but she wouldn't go. A year or two later after, Jagger happened by the farm and saw "the most beautiful horse I had ever seen—this gray, absolutely magnificent horse." Her owners didn't really know anything about riding or horses and were frightened of Faith. They asked Jagger to take her.

Faith was terrified of the trailer, but after several days they managed to lure her in with food and move her to Jagger's farm where she met other horses. She immediately took over the herd.

"They just adored her," Jagger said of her herd. "She'd tell them when to go out and when to come in. I needed another horse like a hole in the head, but she could not be given away... she knew she belonged here, and the other horses knew she did, too."

At the time of her accident, Faith was nineteen years old and had lived with Jagger and her partner Connie Mander on their farm in Kerhonkson, New York, since she was four. It was a winter morning and blustery cold. Jagger went out to feed the horses and found Faith in the barn. When Jagger put grain in her feeder, the mare didn't move, so Jagger went back outside where she saw a fence post broken at ground level...and blood.

When Jagger located the hole in Faith's body, she began to realize how terribly hurt her mare was. It seemed she had reared up and come down on the fence post. It had actually gone right through her, making a hole in one side, and come out the other. Her veterinarian warned her the situation was likely hopeless.

"I just stood there with her," Jagger told me. "She had lost so much blood—she kept putting her head on my chest.... The vet came and we couldn't even get a vein to put an injection in, and we couldn't get her to walk because there wasn't enough of her left, and so she had to go down in the stall. I had my arms around her and she was leaning against my chest, and she went down, and I went down with her. I could hear everybody's voices in the background saying, 'Get away from her!' And I had my eye next to her eye and my face totally on her face and I saw the light go out of her eye as she went down."

A friend of Jagger's offered to take Faith's body away with his flatbed, but he couldn't get up the driveway because the ground was frozen. Jagger looked at her horse, lying there and did not know what to do with the shock of the death and the screams of the other horses. She went to get plaster, maybe to cover Faith because it was so hard to look at her dead body. She began working instinctively, feverishly, first coating Faith with soap, and then beginning to smooth the warm plaster over her body. A friend of Jagger's showed up unexpectedly and joined in her work, mixing bowl after bowl of thick white plaster until by about five o'clock that evening, the horse was totally covered. When they tried to remove the plaster, the cold caused it to shatter, and it came off in fragments, which Jagger carried into the barn, piece by piece.

It was not until June or July that Jagger could look at the rubbled messes of shattered plaster. She got some clay and began painstakingly to put the many broken pieces together.

"It was like the cracked earth," she said, "like I was putting the clay together to bring back what must have been the shoulder, what must have been the neck. Some of it, like the face and the neck came out wonderfully detailed, even though it was made of ten or fifteen pieces. Even the cracks running down where I'd put the pieces together seemed to come out like fragments from the Parthenon or something—like she was coming through from history. In those weeks where I worked with the piece alone and put wires through it and hung it, it was almost like Faith came back to life in front of me...almost like she gave herself back to me in that barn studio of mine."

The story of Jagger and Faith is one of a literal breaking apart and reconstruction—in both life and art. Jagger's sculpture, growing from the shattered casts of her horse's body, became a transformed whole, much in the same way that you reassemble an experience or a memory, reweaving the past into some kind of negotiable, navigable whole that is your life. Creating The Absence of Faith was Jagger's way of rebuilding her experience, of examining the instability of the parts, of bringing Faith back into form despite the refusal of her materials to hold. Faith

A THOUSAND VOICES

🕐 20 MINUTES

Purpose: This exercise helps us feel both the whole and the parts of our bodies by breaking our awareness of the body into smaller and smaller segments. Doing this allows us to feel two things: 1) the distinct expressive quality in a particular body part; 2) and how the body can hold and express more than one feeling or sensation simultaneously—even sharply contradictory or contrasting qualities.

When we are riding or working with a horse on the ground, we are considering the many voices or parts of not one, but *two* bodies. There are moments when we experience the horse and ourselves as a homogenous whole, and other times when we are negotiating the separate articulations and expressive intention of the parts. This process demands our ability to differentiate in both attention and action.

Moving All at Once

In riding, or groundwork, moving with one voice is similar to when our intention is to have all the parts of the horse's body—and our own—aligned and balanced, moving as a harmonious, flowing whole.

1. Lie on your back on the floor. On an exhale, curl slowly onto your side, moving your *whole body* at once. Picture all the trillions of cells speaking/moving in unison. Be sure that every part of you leaves the first position (on your back) and arrives at the second position (on your side) all at once.

2. Now roll from your side onto your belly, again focusing on moving everything simultaneously.

3. Roll from your belly onto your other side, picturing the cells migrating all at once, leaving together, moving together, arriving together.

4. Try doing the same "all at once" change of position more quickly, and notice if it is easier or more challenging to move everything at once at this faster speed. Does any part of you get left out?

TWO VOICES: Moving the Halves

Sometimes we are particularly aware of the two sides of our bodies, or horses' bodies, as very different—each with its own habits, faults, or prowess. The Two Voices improvisation helps us to feel the contrasts and similarities more clearly, and then find ways to meet in the middle, to notice disparities and then find an accord.

1. Lying on your back, picture your body divided down the midline into two halves, right and left. Imagine that each half has its own distinct personality. For example, your right side is calm, reasonable, and a little stubborn. Your left side on the other hand, might be impatient and rushed.

2. Begin a "conversation" between these two halves, letting each side of the body or "voice" take a turn before the other "speaks." This may shift you to another position—sitting or standing. Concentrate on moving *the whole right side* at once and then *the whole left side*. See if you can maintain a sense of individuality in each of the two parts; be aware of those moments when they begin to blend "personalities." Notice when there is a disagreement, interruption, or loss of focus.

3. Moving playfully, explore all the possible elements of a conversation: question and answer, stillness, listening, simultaneous speaking.

4. Now set the intention for each side of the body to listen attentively and respectfully to the other. What can they learn from each other? What can they share?

5. Try this with your riding: Be curious about the dissimilarities between your right and left sides, and those of your horse. Where is the compromise? What can one side learn from the other? Make this investigation as much about expression as function. Often there is a tendency to look at the mechanics of riding, losing sight of the dramatic or lyrical qualities. The absence or presence of those expressive dimensions can reveal themselves as habitual musculo-skeletal imbalances and constriction. Remember, the mind is reflected in the body!

CONTINUED ▶

SIX VOICES: Limbs, Head, and Tail

The Six Voice and the Thousand Voices explorations that follow are related to the complex orchestration of our bodies in movement, as well as the coordination of the many parts of our riding, both physical and emotional.

1. For this exploration, you can be standing, sitting or on the floor. Imagine the body as *six distinct* voices: right arm/shoulder, left arm/shoulder, head, tailbone, right leg/hip, and left leg/hip. This is like a panel discussion, in which participants take turns speaking.

2. Move the head, then move another one of the six parts, then another, and so on, in any order. Alternate freely among them. Let go of planning and just see what happens, enjoying the distinct flavor of each "voice." Moving this way helps us open to a playful expressivity of body and mind, dissolving expectations and inhibitions, creating space for new movements to arise.

3. If the conversation grows heated the order may break down, with everyone speaking at once or body parts interrupting each other. To begin, however, move more slowly and keep the parts as distinct and separate as possible, letting each take a turn to express itself.

A THOUSAND VOICES

1. Now picture your body as the "rubbled bits" of Gillian Jagger's plaster casts of Faith. Imagine being able to move from each of these small, separate parts, for example the inner ear, a single toe, one eyelid, your right kidney, or the inside of your left elbow? In moving this way, from the thousand voices, we are asking for a consummate degree of differentiation among the parts of the body, requiring us to move in unfamiliar, even challenging ways, and to listen to what is being expressed by each.

2. Lie on the floor with your eyes closed and let your body speak in movement. What part of your body is asking to move? Allow that part to move, until another place in the body "speaks." Think of each body part as taking a little journey, moving out into the space around you. Perhaps two parts are moving simultaneously. What is their relationship in space? To the rest of your body? How are they alike or different? What changes in position or demand for support do they create in the rest of the body? Can you move your knee with the same clarity as your little finger?

Our Horses, Ourselves

became more powerful in this fractured, flying form—the pieces of her could not hold the whole of her spirit or the tragedy of her death.

"I think it's the fact that they [the pieces] hang on wires that are very thin," said Jagger, "and there's something about humans that understands that frailty, and that kind of two-sidedness, the fact that you could almost crawl inside her body, which is exactly what I did. I got inside of Faith and felt I was in her looking out through the hollow of the neck, of the head...the rear end. I saw people do that. I think horses have that wonderful way of being an enlargement of our bodies and ourselves."

REASSEMBLING THE WHOLE

Horses can help us learn to slow and "chunk down" what is difficult. When we break down what we are asking of our horses, both horse and human can feel and digest the experience more clearly. Doing that brings more awareness and feeling to our actions. When I am riding, if I am having difficulty with a movement—the shoulder-in (a lateral bending movement), for example—I break it into smaller pieces, a couple steps of the movement at a time, depending upon how soft and forward the horse and I feel. I keep "chunking down" until I can clearly feel where the missing pieces of our communication are: where I am out of balance or too braced in my hands, back, or legs, and the other subtle ways we are losing fluidity and connection.

On the ground, my Friesian Sanne is often reluctant to walk forward if we have stopped to put on a blanket or open a door. I like to see that as a cue to breathe and renew my friendly connection with him, and then ask again. If he is still "stuck," I look for the missing piece of my invitation to move forward with me—perhaps a gesture toward a hind leg that seems disconnected, or adding a gentle vocal cue, making eye contact, softening my hand on the reins or rope, or feeling more clearly the forward impulse in my own body, but *with him*.

By splitting tasks into smaller and smaller pieces, shifting our approach, or simplifying goals by seeing each one in stages, we support our own creativity, spontaneity, and effectiveness. "Chunking down" has compassion, playfulness, awareness, and patience built into its steps. It also allows us to grasp the whole cloth of our aspirations because we have taken the time to study the details. Becoming conscious of how we approach the parts of a project—or a relationship—helps us avoid the frustration of being, in Alexandra Kurland's words, a "lumper." And just as Gillian Jagger rebuilt Faith from the shattered bits of plaster cast, we can learn to assemble the whole—of a project, a relationship, a ride—one precious piece of the puzzle at a time.

CHAPTER EIGHT

THE MIRROR:
SEEING OURSELVES, SEEING
THE OTHER

We are the mirror as well as the face in it.
We are tasting the taste this minute
of eternity. We are pain
and what cures pain, both.

We are the sweet cold water
And the jar that pours.

Rumi
Illuminated Rumi
(Crown Publishing, 1997),
translated by Coleman Barks,
used by permission of
Coleman Barks.

THROUGH THE LOOKING GLASS

I watched Sally work on the ground with her big gray stallion Bianco. They walked together slowly, his steps matching hers precisely. She dropped into a crouching position, and he did a perfect pesade—a low rear with his forelegs curled. Sally burst into a run and Bianco exploded across the ring in the opposite direction, coming to a perfect stop the moment she stopped at the other end of the arena. As they improvised, their movements and phrasing were an intricate inter-species tango, each reflecting the energy and intensity of the other. This was one kind of *mirroring*—clear and explicit.

What do we see when we look at our horses? Often the answer is ourselves. This is because there are other, more subtle ways that horses mirror us: their behaviors and reactions reflect and amplify our inner emotional states and unconscious physical expressions. Horsewoman and writer Kim Carneal Cox calls horses "mindfulness mirrors," meaning that the way a horse responds to us reflects what we are unconsciously expressing, offering us the opportunity to become more aware of our underlying intentions and behaviors. Mirroring, or *empathetic resonance*, is one of the ways that we decode our relationships to each other and the world. It is bodily, ongoing, present-tense engagement that requires our full attention and a willingness to be vulnerable. As a social species, we are wired for connection, though it often feels that our ability to see and feel each other is eroded by the disembodied, isolating, electronic aspects of our environment and daily lives.

Embodying Empathy

Neuroscientists tell us that one way of mirroring is through an empathetic experience of what we observe. This happens when we flinch seeing another person touch something hot, or feel our bodies engage and our breathing change as we watch an Olympic high jumper. There are neurons that are specific to action and others that fire in response to touch. According to neuroscientist Vilayanur Ramachandran, "If somebody touches my hand, a neuron in the somatosensory cortex in the sensory region of the brain fires. But the same neuron, in some cases, will fire when I simply watch another person being touched. So, it's empathizing with the other person being touched."[73] So our bodies receive, reflect, and amplify what we are seeing and feeling in ways that are far more precise and differentiated than most of us consciously know.

In *Made for Each Other* (De Capo Press, 2010), Meg Daley Olmert writes that the hormone oxytocin begins to be released with pleasurable touch and skin contact: "These nerves relay pleasant touch sensations to the brain where they release oxytocin and produce a sense of calm and connection."[74] She says that equine behavior expert Claudia Feh, who has studied free-living horses for decades, observed that when horses groom each other's withers, it results in a lowering of the horse's heart rate, indicating an inhibition of the sympathetic nervous system, or the fight-or-flight response.

Becoming aware of these reflexive, innate, neurochemical responses is one way that empathy and reciprocity can become more conscious and embodied. This requires that we move away from thinking—the part of our brain that analyzes, interprets, catalogs—and enter what Eckhart Tolle calls, "space consciousness," a state of awareness where we are "conscious of being conscious."[75] Cultivating this ability to transcend thought and personality and enter the field of stillness and presence is the basis of a profound connection with ourselves—and all other sentient beings.

Seeing and Being Seen

In his essay, "Why Look at Animals" (*About Looking*, Pantheon, 1980), John Berger observes that up until the nineteenth century, "anthropomorphism was integral to the relationship between man and animal and was an expression of their proximity."[76] Technology and consumerism have pushed animals farther and farther to the periphery of our daily lives, their presence now reduced to the ownership of pets (including horses), and sanitized viewing in zoos and on televised nature programs. For humans as a species, the loss of this connection is profound, psychically, poetically, and tribally. "With their parallel lives, animals offer man a companionship which is different from any offered by human exchange. Different because it is a companionship offered to the loneliness of man as a species." This loneliness has to do with our ever-increasing isolation from one another, the disappearance of animals from our lives, and the loss of our ancient communion with the animal world. Berger identifies *seeing* and *being seen* as the primal dimension in that relationship.

"The eyes of an animal when they consider a man are attentive and wary," writes Berger. "The same animal may well look at other species in the same way. He does not reserve a special look for man. But by no other species except man will the

DeAnna and Pony sharing breath and attention.

animal's look be recognized as familiar. Other animals are held by the look. Man becomes aware of himself returning the look. And so when he is *being seen* by the animal, he is being seen as his surroundings are seen by him. His recognition of this is what makes the look of the animal familiar."[77]

Do we not, each of us, hunger to be seen? Can this *conscious and reciprocal* moment of recognition—of simultaneous seeing and being seen—be the moment of connection that opens the gates that separate us? When we look *into* each other, suspending thought, analysis, ownership, or *doing*, we are conjoined in embodied *being*, and any sense of the animal and you as separate dissolves into the limitlessness space of that shared witnessing.

So how can we let go and dive into that freedom?

The Dancing Mirror

Nelson, the Mustang, was a particularly sensitive mirror. When I was unclear or nervous, he mirrored that. When I breathed, slowed down and listened inwardly to my body, he would settle.

Walking with Nelson.

One day after doing some basic groundwork in his small catch pen, I opened the gate so that we could continue our work in the big field. Nelson did not like to be confined, so as soon as the gate swung open, he started to leave. I wasn't using a halter or lead rope, but I raised one hand—just a shadow of a gesture—and he curved his path around and came back to me. Then he did something surprising: he walked calmly from the catch pen, across the open field, and into the big round pen that stood about fifty

Our Horses, Ourselves

ENVISIONING, EMBODYING ATTUNEMENT

🕑 10 MINUTES

PURPOSE: Stillness is a foundation of awareness. Learning to cultivate stillness in ourselves, and shared stillness with another being, opens the way for us to attune to each other with greater clarity and kindness.

1. Sit in a comfortable chair in a quiet space, your head and spine balanced over your sit bones. Feel the connection of your hips and thighs with the chair, the weight of your feet on the floor and your hands resting in your lap. Close your eyes and rest this way until you feel that your body and mind have fully arrived and settled into this stillness. Can you bring a quality of kindness and receptivity to yourself?

2. Within that stillness, notice the way that each in-breath flows multi-dimensionally from the core outward to the periphery of the body, and how each outbreath settles from the edges inward toward the center.

3. Visualize yourself standing in front of your horse. Imagine that the breath and sensation in your body is inseparable from the breath and sensation in the body of your horse; that the two of you are joined in this quiet presence. Rest in that feeling of connection for several minutes.

4. Slowly open your eyes, bringing your focus outward while maintaining a clear awareness of your inner body. Can you allow inner and outer awareness to dissolve into each other?

5. With your horse, take a few minutes to stand quietly beside him and feel yourselves together as simply *breath* and *presence*. Notice how this conscious focusing of intention changes your feeling of connection with your horse, and then your training or riding time together.

6. On your horse, stand in an area free of distractions, with your eyes open or closed. Sit in stillness (feet in or out of the stirrups) until you feel that your body and mind have fully arrived in the saddle, releasing any sense of urgency, getting ready or planning your ride. Once you feel that soft, receptive, quiet focus, move out of stillness *in connection with your horse*, paying careful attention to how you make that transition. Don't just squeeze your leg and set off, but *consider the horse*, stroke him, or speak his name, and softly invite him to move off with you.

MIRRORING AND FEELING

🕐 10 MINUTES

PURPOSE: Often in social situations we are subconsciously mirroring each other in the tone of voice, the quickness or slowness of our movement or the emotional tone between us. It is a way that we attempt to create rapport by replicating another's bodily and behavioral signals. The same thing is true with our horses. If our movements and emotional state are calm, deliberate and gentle, that is what we are encouraging from our horse. Playing with this mirroring exercise helps bring more awareness to not only how we mirror, but how we can more effectively invite attunement and empathy with our horses.

1. Stand facing a partner, so you are about 4 feet apart. Soften your eyes so that seeing your partner is more expansive and receptive, including your peripheral vision. Instead of looking directly at her eyes, see/feel her whole body with your whole body.

2. Begin moving together slowly, mirroring each other as closely as you can. Make breathing a part of this dance.

3. As you move, see if you can exchange the role of "leader" and "follower" seamlessly, without using words. Then let those roles dissolve into a river of shared movement and breath.

4. Now, can you mirror not only the movement, but also its expressive quality? Pay attention to the sensual, internal qualities of the movement. How does the focus on moving from the *feeling* of the movement, not just its *form*, shift your awareness of and connection to your partner and yourself?

5. Now stand side by side and repeat the mirroring exercise, but without looking directly at each other and using predominantly your peripheral vision. Can you see without looking directly?

6. Experiment with this side-by-side mirroring practice with your horse as you are walking together. Use your body and your peripheral vision to playfully engage with him. How closely can you mirror each other?

7. In his paddock or field, stand some distance away and mirror what your horse is doing: grazing, looking off into the distance, walking—all his rhythms of both movement and stillness. As you do this, what changes in you? In your horse?

8. For fun, try mirroring practice on the floor with a toddler or infant who is rolling, sitting, and crawling—see what happens!

feet away. He stood quietly while I followed, closing the gate to the round pen behind me. After a moment, I signaled him to move around me in a walk, and then come toward me in the center of the round pen. My hand signals were subtle, light, curving whispers of movement, and he responded readily and smoothly.

For several minutes we went through a sequence where I asked him to move away, change direction, and come toward me, both at the walk and at the trot. With each repetition, I could feel the dance between his body and mine become clearer, settling into a quiet, friendly duet. I thought of Anat Baniel's words: "More force is the definition of less differentiation." I practiced making my hand signals lighter and slower and consciously breathing into each transition. Nelson responded by softening and relaxing, as if he were saying, "Yes, that is right. Less is more. I understand you perfectly. When I don't, I will show you."

PATTERNS IN THE SAND

Bonnie Bainbridge Cohen says, "The mind is like the wind and the body is like the sand; if you want to know how the wind is blowing, you have to look at the sand."[78]

> "When you call out asking what life is about and nothing comes back from the wind, I have discovered that by studying the wind itself, it makes a spiral, the river a meander, the trees branch, as does a lighting bolt, and the surface of the earth cracks. These are in fact the answers to my questions. They demonstrate to me our interconnectedness. We share the patterns."

> Gillian Jagger
> *The Art of Gillian Jagger*, (Gallery Catalog,
> Elvehjem Museum of Art, University of Wisconsin-Madison, 2003)

Noetic scientist Lynn McTaggart, author of *The Intention Experiment* (Atria Books, 2008), studies the ways that our experience mirrors our patterns of thought, and how we can affect change in the physical world by focusing our intention, both positively and negatively. Vietnamese Buddhist monk Thich Nhat Hanh has observed that the outer act of smiling creates an inner sense of peace and tranquility, and teaches a smiling and breathing meditation that helps his students to release worries and anxieties. Noticing how our bodies mirror our minds can help us soften the hard edges of habitual responses, and unravel the automaticity and reflexiveness of our reactions. The feeling of "I always do it this way," or "That's just how I am," keeps us gazing in the mirror of sameness and habit. When we untether from identification with a particular way of being or doing, we can see and feel ourselves more expansively. That is the purpose of each of the meditations and strategies in this book. By changing the body we can shift the mind. In opening the mind, we open the body.

One day after being with my godson Jacob in his playroom, I took a walk on the beach, and I found myself seeing repeating patterns in the sand, the waves, and the light. I realized that all day I had been doing that with Jacob—looking for little chains of movement, sequences, or signifiers that made sense of the seemingly indecipherable collage of his movement. The next day I mirrored him meticulously, in as much detail as I could: the dynamics of his movement, the tension in specific body parts, the sounds, the sequencing of his gestures, and the spatial direction and shaping of each movement and each stillness. As I moved with him, I felt oddly adrift, untethered from my usual ways of perceiving and understanding. His movement was towing me into deep, uncharted bodily waters. Jacob noticed the difference in what I was doing and guided me—sometimes taking me by the hand—through a series of what felt like little dances. There were patterns—not predictable or identical, but specific sequences with very clear dynamics, rhythms and phrasing. Then, without warning, he drifted away. Perhaps it was the exertion, or maybe he had found the end of the dance, and I did not recognize it.

It can be the same with our horses. By looking at the patterns of their behaviors, the ways that their bodies reflect the stresses of their work, we can better understand how to partner with them. Being with Jacob often reminds me of my experiences with Amadeo. With both of them, I am always looking for those patterns in the sand, for the smallest of cues that will help me to understand and support them.

THE WIND AND THE SAND

🕐 5 MINUTES

PURPOSE: Often riders bring a concentration to their practice that has the unintentional effect of constricting body and mind. Or we may bring the emotional residue of a work or family situation into our riding. When we are more conscious of how our habits and emotional states are carried in the body, we are able to more easily release them, which helps our horses and ourselves.

1. Sit or stand in a balanced, relaxed position, with your eyes closed.

2. Begin to frown, starting with the forehead, then let the frown spread to the eyes, mouth, and jaw. Let the frown sift through your whole body, hold it for a minute, and notice any changes in your breathing or body, including your emotional response. Can you deepen the "whole body feeling" of frowning even more?

3. Breathe in, and as you exhale, release the frown. Take a couple conscious breaths.

4. Now begin to smile—a soft smile that begins at the corners of the mouth, and then spreads to the eyes. As your smile widens, let the feeling of smiling percolate throughout your body, permeating every cell.

5. Breathe in, and as you exhale, release the smile. Again, take a couple conscious breaths.

6. Explore intentional frowning and smiling as you go through your day, noticing the expansive, opening feeling of a smile and the condensing, narrowing quality of the frown. What parts of your body habitually frown? What parts of your body often smile? What is the difference between a smiling "mask" and a whole-body, genuine smile?

7. Practice smiling while you are riding and see what changes in your body and in your connection with your horse.

BODY-MIND RIDING

"The art of touch and re-patterning begins with an experiential understanding of vibration and resonance. Vibration is the natural state of all matter. Each of our bodies' tissues has a different frequency, or vibration. When we embody a cell, tissue, or system, we are heightening our experience of its particular vibration."

Bonnie Bainbridge Cohen

During a Body-Mind Centering workshop with Bonnie Bainbridge Cohen, I learned how to breathe into each lobe of my right and left lungs. She invited those of us in the class to differentiate the parts of the lungs with movement, feeling a soft, sliding articulation between each lobe and the next. She then asked us to sense the connection of each lung to the brain hemisphere on the same side of the body, and then to that *whole half* of the body. Instead of the crossing over (a contralateral relationship of left brain to right side of body or right brain to left side of body) she instructed us to visualize the whole left side of the body, including the left half of the brain, and then the whole right side of the body and brain. Moving via the body half, or *homolaterally*, is an older, more primitive developmental pattern in the body.

The right side/left side relationship is a continuous negotiation between stability and mobility, whether you are on the ground, in the air, or in the saddle.

Our Horses, Ourselves

I was interested in how that awareness could help my riding. While on
Sanne, I first concentrated on feeling
that soft articulation of the lobes of the
lungs, imagining the same movement
between the lobes of *his* lungs. Then I
practiced feeling the whole right side
of my body—head/brain/lung/hand/
hip/leg/foot—and then the whole
left side. That awareness gave me a
very clear feeling of the sameness and
differences between my left side and
right side. When I put the two halves
together, I found that sensing the
distinct body-halves simultaneously as
I rode was wonderfully stabilizing to
my body. I could feel Sanne becoming
more and more balanced beneath me.

*Brandi Rivera and Sanne together in
beautiful balance.*

At the same time, I was aware of
Sanne's lungs, horizontal where mine
are vertical—widening and narrowing as I rode. I could feel his breath and the lateral swing of his ribcage as an integral part of his movement. Most researchers feel
that dolphins and whales breathe consciously: each ascent to the surface for breath
is a decision and each breath taken is a voluntary act. Sensing the lungs as you ride
is another way of rising to the surface of the busy mind. As the lungs become more
mobile, the body gains stability and balance from their resilient support.

Riding is a complex and dynamic choreography, its elements and organization changing every moment. Each half of the body has its own voice, but they
must be singing in harmony, seeking balance, rather than one side taking over or
falling asleep. Riding with a "two-voices," body-half awareness is another way of
creating a more conscious, dynamically balanced body.

In that same workshop, Bainbridge Cohen also spoke of how the lungs "cra-
dle" the heart, an idea I introduced earlier in this book. As the lungs expand and
condense, they are massaging and enfolding the heart, with a counter-rotational
movement around its axis. This means that as we breathe, we are nourishing the
heart not just with newly oxygenated blood, but also with the movement of the
lungs. She noted that most heart disease today affects the coronary arteries—the
vessels that feed the heart itself. She suggested that perhaps this is because we
are so outwardly focused that we have become poor at nourishing ourselves and
our inner lives. As you ride, visualize your lungs and those of your horse cradling
and nourishing the heart. This awareness supports a more compassionate, connected relationship with yourself and your horse.

BODY-HALF MIRRORING

🕐 10 MINUTES

PURPOSE: Developing homolateral or body-half awareness as we ride helps to improve whole-body organization for both you and your horse. This is similar to the "two voices" strategy from the *Thousand Voices* exercise in the previous chapter, and the *Finding Connection, Feeling the Pathways* meditation from chapter 1. In this meditation, however, we are looking for how the sides of the body mirror each other, and whether that mirroring is helpful or detrimental. What can one side of the body learn from the other?

1. At the halt, walk, trot, and canter, visualize the two halves of your body mirroring each other along the midline of your spine. Be curious about the differences, as well as the similarities, between the two sides (including the container of muscle and skin, and the contents of bone, organ, fluids, glands), observing for tension or relaxation, texture (stiffness or elasticity), symmetry and asymmetry. Does one side feel stronger, more open, or braced and disconnected?

2. In which gait do you feel the most balance between the halves? In which gait does the mirror between the two sides "break"? When you are turning at the end of the arena or riding a circle, what changes in the relationship between the two halves?

3. Do you feel yourself bracing to maintain symmetry? Can you use visualization and breath to soften that tension and find a more elastic, communicating quality between right and left?

4. Notice how the two halves of your horse's body reflect each other. How are they alike? How are they dissimilar? Go beyond stiffness or suppleness in your observations—consider the emotional qualities of what is being expressed. How does your right or left side reflect the right or left side of your horse? Does feeling the homolateral relationships in your body help you to better feel them in the body of your horse?

5. Use body-half mirroring as a way of "setting an intention" for balance, in and out of the saddle, aware that each day that balance will be subtly different, both in your own body and the body of your horse. Be interested in those differences and open to change.

THE FLUID BODY

Body-Mind Centering focuses on an experiential understanding of the fluids within the body through movement and touch, initiating movement from each, and identifying individual psychophysical characteristics of the fluids and their various combinations.[79]

> *"The fluids are the transportation system of the body. They underlie presence and transformation, set the ground for basic communication, and mediate the dynamics of flow between rest and activity, tension and relaxation. The characteristics of each fluid relate to a different quality of movement, touch, voice, and state of mind. These relationships can be approached from the aspects of movement, mind states, or from anatomical and physiological functioning."*[80]

Bainbridge Cohen describes *cellular fluid*—the fluid within each cell—as having a quality of simple presence, a feeling of being "home," the fluid held within the container of the membrane, where everything comes into a state of rest. To experience this quality, lie down quietly, letting the body soften and yield into the floor, feeling the body and its fluids settling into place. This is similar to the savasana or corpse pose in yoga, where we let go of moving from one place to another, withdrawing our focus from the outer world, and settle deeply within.

Transitional fluids move between and in and out of the cells, mirroring the feeling of moving from the quiet, resting parasympathetic state of the cellular fluid into action *without* a sympathetic activation. We experience this when we slowly rise from a resting state into activity without any feeling of hurry or tension.

Extracellular fluid is any fluid that is outside the cell membrane and has a quality of moving in a single direction, like the flow of blood (arterial blood leaving the heart, venous blood returning) or lymphatic fluid (which always flows from the extremities inward). Think of riding or walking in any single direction—that is the feeling of these extracellular fluids.

I became curious about how the quality of these fluids is expressed in riding, so I investigated with Amadeo. At the halt, I looked for a state of deep rest, stillness, and presence—all qualities of cellular fluid. Then, instead of coming abruptly out of that stillness into forward movement, I looked for a more subtle, transitional feeling (in my own body) of fluid beginning to "stream" into motion. Then I added the light touch of my leg to move us into going forward, but without any "startle" or sympathetic activation.

The difference I felt in Amadeo's body was profound. He was softer and more settled as he transitioned from the halt into the walk and then the trot. There wasn't bracing or resistance—something I often feel as I ask him to move from halt to walk or trot. Halting again, I looked for a gradual, slowing down feeling of "coming home to rest"—the quality of cellular fluid. In the trot, I looked for

the steady, pumping pulse of the arterial blood, and in the canter, the smoother, streaming, and continuous feel of the venous blood. When riding Amadeo "from the fluids," I felt a more harmonious and refined quality in our connection.

Amadeo resting in the halt.

THE INTENTIONAL MIRROR

"Thought is like a mirror. One looking at it sees his image and thinks that there are two images, but the two are really one."

The Essential Kabbalah
Translated by Daniel C. Matt (HarperOne, 2009)

Dr. Allen Schoen believes passionately that animals have feelings and emotions, and that humans and all creatures can mutually benefit from heightened awareness and respect. An integrative veterinarian who uses acupuncture, chiropractic, and other complementary approaches with horses and other companion animals, he observes that sometimes horses may elicit people's darker side, the under-layers of their fears and their need for control. In his books, *Kindred Spirits* (Broadway Books, 2002) and *The Compassionate Equestrian* (Trafalgar Square Books, 2015), he expresses hope for the qualities of love and connectedness, as well as a more spiritual dimension, in the human-animal bond. He feels that horses in particular can show us the need for balance and the ways we have fallen out of harmony.

"I feel like part of my own personal healing journey is the ability to be aware of the human-animal bond, the mirroring and awakening of our own consciousness to who we are," Dr. Schoen says, "and letting go of the destructive emotions and patterns that we hold in order to have a deeper, more loving connection with our horse friends."

From his years of practice, Dr. Schoen has seen that animals are sensitive and conscious beings easily influenced by the people around them; that they are not so different from us in that their thoughts, emotions and actions are influenced by hormones, biology and previous experiences. He sees that they communicate

Our Horses, Ourselves

THE FLUID BODY

🕐 10 MINUTES

PURPOSE: Connecting with our fluid body can help us become more attuned to the basic flow of communication within our bodies, and the more subtle ways in which we move in and out of action. This water meditation helps to support a more receptive and settled state of body and mind.

1. Lie on your back either with your legs extended or with a pillow supporting your knees, feet flat on the ground. Bring your attention to your lower back—or anywhere that you feel tension or discomfort.

2. Breathe in, imagining that you are lying in the warm sand, the tide coming in with soft waves starting at your feet and gradually moving up your legs, lapping at your coccyx and gently moving up toward your sacrum. With each inhale and exhale, visualize those gentle waves flowing further upward over the lower back, the ribcage, the upper back and shoulders, neck and head softening and opening everything they touch.

3. Imagine that your body can expand infinitely in all directions, and that as the gentle waves pour through all the channels of your body, you become part of the water, the boundary of your skin like the permeable membrane of the cell body. Visualize the warm ocean bathing and dissolving any resistance or discomfort.

4. Now imagine the tide going out, leaving your watery body resting on the sand. Sense all of the fluids within the body coming into a deep quiet calm. Rest and breathe in this stillness.

5. When riding, experiment with shifting your consciousness from a muscular quality to a more liquid, buoyant, wave-like one. Imagine the fluids of your body joining with the fluids of your horse's body, becoming a single, exuberant sea of motion.

at many levels, and that it is most often humans who block the communication. In his experience, when people try to enforce their intentions, desires, and wishes without respect for the horse's consciousness, it creates an adversarial relationship, and that the more we can drop our ego and our controlling intentions, the more open and available our horses can become.

The Mirror: Seeing Ourselves, Seeing the Other

When asked why horses are uniquely able to help us become more conscious, he replies, "Size! They are big powerful animals! If you are distracted, angry, or tense, they become your mirror—a very big, powerful mirror." Because of their size, horses amplify everything: our tensions, our insecurities—but also our effectiveness and ease. In his own work he notes that if he is not attentive his equine patients will be resistant...a form of instant biofeedback that brings him back into a focused state.

"The flip side," says Dr. Schoen, "is that if we come to them with love and compassion then they are a mirror of *that* consciousness, so they provide an opportunity for 'waking up.'"

Often the battleground between horse and human is the body of the horse. Issues of power and control are never far from the surface.

"I have seen this over and over again," Dr. Schoen says. "There is a horse that people say is difficult and so the human says, 'I'll show him,' and then it becomes a battle. Someone gets injured, and so the belief is now that this is a dangerous horse, but in fact, the *person* was more dangerous."

Dr. Schoen often tells a story about a client who asked him to evaluate her horse because he was dangerous and no one could get near him.

"Everyone was scared of the horse. I could see in his eyes that he was angry. He was saying, 'Don't come near me,' with ears back and wild eyes. The regular vet had been treating him for pneumonia and colic, and the trainer kept on trying to get the horse to do dressage. And now he was totally unmanageable by anyone...everyone was trying to be dominant...the trainer thought it was all in the horse's head. No one was looking at the horse as a being that was in pain. I thought he was in pain and trying to defend himself. But no one was listening; they all had their own agendas and perception of what was happening."

Othering

Dr. Schoen's story is an example of the human habit of "othering." When we "other," we make something or someone alien or undesirable so that we can distance ourselves from them. Paleontologist and evolutionary biologist Stephen Jay Gould refers to this practice as *dichotomization*—our human need to divide things into their opposites: good/bad, human/animal, dark/light, me/not me, and so on. With physical pain or illness, we may *other* a painful body part or our bodies as a whole, splitting off and creating a body-mind fragmentation. Children may exclude or bully another child they have chosen as a scapegoat. We may *other* our horses and companion animals as a way of excusing and justifying our treatment of them. But because our horses mirror our inner feelings so precisely, when we *other* them, we are actually separating from ourselves—and the parts of us that we find unacceptable or unmanageable.

Dr. Schoen treated the horse for stomach ulcers and Lyme disease, and ultimately, the owner moved the horse to a different barn where he dramatically improved.

"He still had old memories, like a person with PTSD," Dr. Schoen says, "but at the new barn he got to trust the trainer and the groom and got better because he was not being punished or challenged."

Dr. Schoen believes that the horse reflects the whole ecology of his environment and history, including the humans with whom he interacts, and in this way, the horse creates opportunities for us to become more sensitive, attuned, and connected to our own bodies.

"If you are on a horse and not feeling, you will get thrown off," he says. "You have to feel how your legs are on a horse, how your hands are holding the reins. He gives you an opportunity, if you are conscious and awake, to feel that when your legs are around this horse and you are tight, he gets tight. If my hands are tight and I am pulling and yanking out of tension and fear, the horse gets tense and fearful. If you are conscious and awake the horse acts as a biofeedback instrument. You have to relax and breathe into the horse. Ideally, he forces you to be embodied, for your own sake and the horse's sake."

Dr. Schoen sees riding as a unique opportunity to feel your body interacting with another living being, and to become aware of how your thoughts, emotions, and physical self impact that being. He tells another story of a client who wanted him to examine her horse because he was always bucking her off. Everyone told her the horse was badly behaved and mean, and that she had to learn to control him. He looked the horse over, but "when I saw the person—how nervous and tense she was, how she jammed into the horse. I told her, 'I am not finding enough physical issues for your horse to want to buck you off. Try breathing, relaxing, being quiet for ten or fifteen minutes before you get on. Be calm, think good happy thoughts.' And the horse stopped bucking her off."

Alexandra Kurland echoes Dr. Schoen's experience: "If someone walks into a room shouting and upset, we will probably feel wary and on edge. If the same person enters the room calmly with a smile, our feeling will be entirely different. The horse, whose entire psyche is attuned to movement and feeling, is a perfect mirror for our inner state, and for any incongruity between what we are feeling and how we are behaving."

OUR HORSES, OURSELVES

Author Susan Richards says that at one point, she saw that each of her horses reflected an aspect of her personality—something that she did not think was always a good thing. She had a horse named Tempo who was very anxious. He was the leader of the herd, but very nervous when it came to human interaction.

"If I wore a different color or a flappy shirt, he couldn't handle it," Richards relates. "If there was a plastic bag in the pasture, it was like Armageddon. That's sort of how I was—a very anxious person."

CALMING THE STORM WITH A HEART HUG

🕐 3 MINUTES

PURPOSE: The Heart Hug from Linda Tellington-Jones' book *Dressage with Mind, Body & Soul* (Trafalgar Square Books, 2013) is a mindful way to prepare for a more open and loving relationship with your horse or another being. It is also a wonderful way to come back into emotional alignment when things have fallen apart.[81]

1. Place your left hand over your heart, and your right hand over your left. Let your hands yield softly onto your chest and each other.

2. Picture a clock on your chest under your hands, with six o'clock at the bottom of the circle. Beginning at six o'clock, very slowly and gently circle the hands, softly moving the skin over your heart around the clock for a circle-and-a-quarter. As you circle, allow the palms to "breathe" slowly, in and out.

3. At the end of the circle-and-a-quarter, keeping your hands on your chest, inhale and gently lift them toward twelve o'clock, then let them settle back toward six o'clock as you exhale. This movement creates a gentle tractioning of the skin on the chest wall.

4. Repeat the Heart Hug several times, breathing in, breathing out.

Hot Shot was a Quarter Horse gelding who had been abused somewhere in his distant past, so he knew that to survive he had to just go along, never make a false move, and keep it safe.

"I felt there was a lot of me in that," says Richards. "God forbid I should not be a team player. I would never complain, was always doing what I was told."

Then there was Georgia, "this big, bold, saucy, funny, charismatic, totally independent mare. She didn't care what anybody thought about anything. Georgia was just very confident and fun, and yeah, and I wanted to be that, so she was sort of my role model."

Richards attended a literary festival in Wales sponsored by the British version of *GQ (Gentleman's Quarterly)*. It was at a house owned by an aristocrat, and she thought it would be a lark, but once at the party, Richards felt that everyone there was prettier and smarter and richer and better.

"I slid back into that icky mire—thinking I don't belong here...I was Hot Shot, trying not to put a foot wrong."

Now she feels that at sixty-plus years old she is finally growing up and coming out of her shell, perhaps lingering for longer periods in Georgia's territory, although shadows of Hot Shot and Tempo can appear.

BEDLAM FARM

There is a way of breathing
that's a shame and a suffocation.
And there's another way of expiring, a love breath
that lets you open infinitely.

Rumi

Illuminated Rumi (Crown Publishing, 1997), translated by
Coleman Barks, used by permission of Coleman Barks.

Jon Katz has the look of a gentleman farmer: blue jeans, red suspenders, and a blue denim shirt. But Katz is *not* an ordinary farmer. He is a transplant from the urban world of New York City. He and his wife, artist Maria Wulf, gradually migrated upstate as they found that more and more parts of their life together were planting themselves deep into the soil of a place called Bedlam Farm. Cambridge, New York, is dotted with family-owned farms—bucolic canopies of corn, alfalfa, hay, and dairy cows, spread across the lush hills of the upper Hudson valley. Home to both animals and artists—Katz and Wulf

Jon Katz and with the donkey Simon.

have dogs, barn cats, sheep, and donkeys—Bedlam Farm is both practical and poetic; a laboratory for Katz's ongoing investigations into his questions about the human-animal bond, and the creative space that enables him to write many bestselling books about it.

Katz told me, "I am drawn to the idea of animals helping to heal people who are disconnected from themselves and from the earth and as creative stimulation. Part of what I have learned from them is acceptance. They don't see the world in terms of suffering—they live in the moment. They don't complain. We complain about everything and they just go through it."

MULTI-DIMENSIONAL BREATHING

🕐 10-20 MINUTES

Purpose: I believe that even without knowing our histories, our horses see and perceive us in all of our complexity. Breathing into all three dimensions of the body can help us feel the multi-dimensional fullness of ourselves, in the saddle and on the ground. As you do this exercise, can you imagine letting the mind reflect the multi-dimensionality of the body and the breath?

Length

1. Stand in a clear and quiet space. Feel your breathing connecting you vertically from the soles of your feet up through the top of your head. Become a long, fluid column of breath. As you do that, visualize the breath creating longitudinal space between and within the organs.

Depth

2. Now feel your breath in the sagittal (forward/backward) dimension, connecting the front and back of your body—not just the torso, but also the pelvis, face and head, and the fronts and backs of your arms and legs. Pay particular attention to the unseen and often unfelt back body, from heels to head, and how it, like the front surface of your body, expands and condenses. Can you sense the lungs and digestive organs expanding forward and back with the breath?

Width

3. Let your breath open horizontally, connecting the right and left sides of your body: legs, arms, lungs, ribs, shoulders, hips, head, feet—widening as you inhale and narrowing as you exhale. Which organs do you envision widening and narrowing with the breath?

Three Dimensions

4. Now breathe into all three dimensions—length, depth, and width—simultaneously, without pushing or any feeling of urgency. Just let the breath flow outward in all directions and settle inward toward the center.

With the Horse

5. Practice multi-dimensional breathing with your horse. With each of these dimensions, include the contents of the body in your sensing and feeling.

Imagine the voluptuous fullness of the organs (including the fluid structures of the fascia) providing support for the whole body.

6. At the walk, feel your breath and movement undulating along the vertical axis of your body, from the soles of your feet through the top of your head.

7. Next, notice the forward/back dimension, feeling the relationship between the front and rear surfaces of the body as you walk. Lastly, feel the side-to-side, horizontal oscillation moving through the body as your weight shifts, including the mobile support of the organs.

8. Finally, as you walk, notice the "container" and "contents" of your body and your horse's body, breathing and moving in all three dimensions.

Rose in a Storm (Random House, 2011) was my introduction to Katz and his work. It is the story of a farmer and his valiant Border Collie Rose, overwhelmed as they confront a devastating blizzard. I swallowed the book whole when I was housebound by a fierce Nor'easter, the wind howling and snow banking on the doors and windows all around me. I went on to read more of his work, relishing the frank, spare quality of his writing and the thoughtful nature of his relationships with animals. I subscribed to his daily blog, *Bedlam Farm Journal*, and loved the intimacy and depth of his posts and their accompanying photographs.

Simon, an abandoned and abused donkey, appeared suddenly on Katz's blog when he and Wulf had brought him to Bedlam Farm. There were heartbreaking photos of the emaciated animal and detailed descriptions of his slow rehabilitation. Katz was troubled by the question of "rescue"—an issue he saw as fraught with complex questions about our relationships to animals and each other.

"Animal rescue is a remarkable cultural phenomenon in America," he told me, "and it goes hand in hand with differing ideas about human beings, about salvation, anger, righteousness, emotion, and obligation."

In the unfolding story of Simon, I felt a deepening physicality in Katz's writing, and when I had the opportunity to meet with him in person at an author event in Salisbury, Connecticut, I asked him what his experience with the animals was teaching him about living in a human body. How was the language of movement and his senses shaping that journey for him? Our conversation eventually led to my visiting Bedlam Farm.

"It's probably something about a donkey's placid look, their slumbering lenteur, their infectious slowness and drooping presence that grips people's attention, that brightens up your day, that creates softness and affection."

Andy Merrifield
The Wisdom of Donkeys (Walker Books, 2009)

Katz is first of all a dog person. He loves the rituals of throwing, catching, walking, and herding. He understands their various temperaments and the specific and particular rhythms of their individual care. He knows how his body moves with the dogs and the dance of herding sheep. Donkeys, too, have been a part of his life for many years. His first experience of what he calls "donkeyness" was an obstinate, opinionated female named Carol that he called The Lonely Donkey. Katz says that Carol was incredibly idiosyncratic and grumpy, that she had been alone for sixteen years with a farmer who never fed her or gave her water, so she had been living on rainwater and bark. He adopted Carol, and says that far from being grateful for her salvation, she was "feisty, demanding, obstreperous." But because she was lonely, he acquired little Fanny, a miniature donkey with soulful eyes who withstood Carol's abuse and was soon joined by Lulu.

Donkeys do not have an exalted, glamorous history. They have often been mistreated, overworked, and treated as machines. He says that they, like dogs, have a genetic knowledge of human beings.

"It's very rich. I also feel that donkeys love you directly. The way you get a donkey to love you is to sit still....If you sit down, they will come to you and they present

Simon with MacKenzie, the daughter of the animal control officer. "She was hanging off his back, you know, with the bugs and everything. She just loves him. And I thought, 'He kind of wants to live, he wants to live.' You could see him responding to that affection."

196

themselves and press against you. That's where there's this exchange."

As Andy Merrifield says in *The Wisdom of Donkeys*, "Time slows down amid donkeys. In their company things happen quietly and methodically. It's a calm that instills calm. We move slowly when we want to listen to ourselves, to others, and to the world around us. We move slowly when we want to confront ourselves." [82]

For Katz, it was Simon who helped him confront himself and brought him most deeply into his own body. One day they received a call from the animal control officer about a donkey that had been removed from a neighboring farm. Would they consider taking him? When they went to see him, what they saw shocked them both. Simon was horribly emaciated—"a dead spirit"—when he and his wife took him in.

"His ribs were so exposed that they were wings," remembers Katz. "His hooves were splayed on his ankles. He had red sores and lice and rain rot. He was just about on the edge of life. I could see he was right on the cusp of deciding whether or not to live...and that was very, very shocking to me. I thought he would just be skinny, but he was right on the edge of life...I've seen a lot of dogs in distress, but I've never seen anything like that."

Katz felt something wrenching and powerful pass between himself and Simon in that moment—an almost mystical sense of a direct communication between man and donkey. He describes Simon looking him directly in the eye, and felt as if the donkey

Jon Katz with Simon. "I am so moved by his struggle to live. It takes him a long and painful time to stand up, but he always does. His bones stick out all over his body, and his spindly legs struggle to carry even his slight weight. He follows me everywhere."

"The minute I saw Simon, he touched many parts of me—anger, fear, grief—powerful emotions I have often suppressed."

"Simon, an animal in need, was the perfect storm for my own notions of rescue: abandoned, ignored, neglected, in pain and suffering. I related to that."

was speaking to him—a wordless, perfectly clear communication—asking him for help.

What followed were anxious weeks filled with the slow and loving care of Simon. They had no idea if he would live, but each day was filled with stroking and brushing, watching him eat grass...Katz felt that each time he approached the donkey, Simon got stronger.

"It was amazing to see this minute by minute. He just began to return to life. He started to fill out. He started to heal. His skin started to grow in. And I saw his eyes. As a photographer, I paid a lot of attention to his eyes. They began to come to life and sparkle, and that was very rewarding."

"Animals are a test of our humanity," Katz said when I visited with him. "Animals teach me to be patient. To swallow my frustration. To subordinate my ego in the life and needs of another creature. To give voice to a voiceless being."

He feels that each animal comes to us to help us connect with and heal a particular part of what he calls our "frayed soul." For Katz, Simon was a mirror of the bruised and battered part of himself.

Katz admits that it is difficult to show himself in photographs and videos on his blog, exposing his body and his emotions in such a public way. But there is one he has posted—a video where he holds the camera as Wulf brushes Simon. Her strokes are soft and long, smoothing the surfaces of Simon's new coat, stroking along the curves of his long ears. Then Wulf takes the camera and we see Katz, his body curved forward as he massages Simon deeply. They are face to face; Simon tilts his head upward. Katz's mouth is slightly pursed and he touches his lips to Simon's soft nose. I feel that I am witnessing a holy unraveling of this man. Simon is letting him all the way in. He is letting Simon all the way in.

"I think I've spent more time seeking to open up in the past few years than almost anything else except writing and taking photos," Katz says. "The process of opening up is essential to any notion of a spiritual life. You open and open and open again. And then you open again. To love. To friendship. To teachers and

Our Horses, Ourselves

learning. To safety. To new experience. To growth and to change. To the reality of your life and your place in the world. To changing the story of your life, if necessary. To trust. To faith. To intimacy. To responsibility. Opening of the hearts, human and animal.

"I think I've never felt very good about my body or thought about it very much. I had a lot of trauma issues about my body as a kid, abuse and other things. I was a bed wetter until I was fourteen or fifteen, and so I always had a really terrible sense of my body...I think I absolutely related to the state in which Simon appeared, this degraded, abused state."

Katz laughed when he told me how a friend had given him a gift of a massage, recalling how frightening it was to be touched.

Maria Wulf with Simon.

"So it's funny that I'm in a rather physical relationship with a donkey who I'm always touching, and he's always pressing his head against me, always coming up to me—I'm always touching him, hugging him, scratching him. There is a dance with Simon."

Katz feels that donkeys connect more deeply with women because women are more open emotionally. He sees that his wife is much more intuitive about this physical relationship than he is.

Maria Wulf with Simon, Lulu, and Fanny.

"I think that connection forces you either to be more nurturing, or open and more self-aware. All of those things relate to your body. Simon's arrival has changed me. I am more open. It's odd, but I feel healthier, more alert, more energy. I believe I am moving differently, more fluidly. I am more connected to my body and mind in some way I don't fully understand.

"The reason I love photographing Maria and the donkeys is that the photographs speak of opening—opening of the hearts, both human and animal. I looked at one of these pictures one day and I saw this shocking thing: I saw Maria kneeling down and each of the donkeys with a head on her shoulder, and she was just speaking to them so softly...and they were listening to her. Maria was touching one of them and their eyes were almost closing, and there's this rapturous, beautiful thing. There it was and I caught it. I could actually see it. I have lived with the donkeys for a number of years, but I'd never before seen anything like that opening up of Maria to Lulu and Fanny, and their opening in return."

Watching Wulf with the donkeys, I witnessed a beautiful, effortless connection—a dance of stillness and attention. Wulf said she had never been around horses, but that connecting with the donkeys required her to be quiet and still. She likened that stillness to the negative space that she became aware of in watching a dance performance.

I thought then about the "doing somethingness" of my relationship with horses: the training, tacking up, and riding, with its specific exercises and goals. I recognize in Wulf's relationship with her donkeys something that I discovered with Diego: something more quiet and open-hearted, rooted in stillness and connection. The difference was that there was more *being* with Diego than *doing something with him*. I was not getting him ready for a life under saddle, or competition, or any other human "use." With him, I learned how to allow things to unfold in a nonlinear, unrushed way. Horse time is biologic, sometimes even

geologic: it doesn't have to do with any human form of time measurement, but with listening and with waiting. I got to be very good at waiting.

One day when I went to see Nelson, he would not let me come anywhere near him. So I sat leaning against the fence for about two hours until he finally came close enough to get a treat. I had a lot of time that day to feel my impatience and frustration and to just wait, allowing all of that to dissolve into simply *being there*. When Nelson felt that softening in me, he appeared.

"My experience with the donkeys taught me to listen with my heart

"I found myself having a conversation with someone where my intention was to listen with my heart not my head," says Wulf. "The idea came to me when I was meditating, but it was only after doing it with a person, that I realized that is what I had been doing with the donkeys all along."

instead of my head," Wulf wrote on her blog (www.fullmoonfiberart.com). "When I sit with the donkeys, I am still and quiet. I open my heart and they place their bodies next to mine and the space between us becomes charged."

I took hundreds of photographs the day I spent with Wulf and Katz, and looking at them later, I saw in Wulf's movement a similarity to the way she describes moving with her work in her studio.

"My body is a part of my work," she says. "I lay my quilts out on the floor, constantly bending and straightening. I crawl around them rearranging pieces of fabric and pinning them together. I stand on my desk to get a different view.

TRY THIS

TOUCHING AND OPENING IN STILLNESS

🕐 15 MINUTES

PURPOSE: One way to connect is through listening touch. Not petting or grooming, but resting the hands with the intention of finding connection and supporting coherence—the feeling of your bodies settling into a balanced state. You can do this with your horse, or any animal or human companion.

1. Place your hands gently on the body of your horse or companion. You may wish to close your eyes. Let your hands settle, feeling the connection through your whole body.

2. Imagine that the cells in your hands and body are awakening and coming into harmonic attunement with the cells in the body of your companion. Listen for a feeling of reciprocity between your hands and the part of the body you are touching—that you are being touched as you are touching. This may feel like warmth or a subtle vibration.

3. Let your hands gently rest, then lift or slide them to another part of the body. Make this change from one place to the next slowly and mindfully. There should be no sense of needing to "fix" or change anything—just a simple *giving* and *receiving* that flows in both directions. Can you receive as much as you are giving?

4. Move your hands quietly and intuitively, transmitting and receiving appreciation and love from your heart through your hands. Can your touch mirror the qualities that you want to evoke: kindness, softness, openness, blending? Breathe in, breathe out.

LETTING GO

🕐 10 MINUTES

PURPOSE: This releasing practice, based on The Sedona Method[83], can help us let go of any old patterns that are not serving us. It is a process of self-inquiry that can dissolve habitual holding patterns, helping us discover a more settled state that reflects our positive intentions rather than our fears or habitual beliefs.

Releasing can help us with the horse that we are having difficulties with, the part of our riding that we struggle with, or any situation where we feel stuck.

1. Take a moment to focus on a situation that feels like a problem. Maybe it is an old injury, a relationship that feels stuck, or a project that has become uninspired. Maybe it is a recurring issue with your horse that is clouding your riding and your time together.

2. Read each question below, then close your eyes and take several moments to absorb each question and feel your response.

    • Can you simply welcome that injured body part, stuck relationship, or recurring issue with your horse? In other words, can you just *let it be there?* Breathe.

    • Can you also welcome anything that is connected to it, any memories or stories fears or ideas about it? Breathe.

    • Can you also welcome your desire to do something about it, figure it out, control it, or change it? Can you welcome the impulse to hold onto it or push it away? Any wanting to separate from it or be one with it? Breathe.

    • Finally, can you welcome any sense that it is personal, that it is about *you,* or that it somehow defines who you are? Breathe.

    • Now, can you just let all of that go—just drop it—even for a moment? Breathe.

Repeat the above questions and see if anything shifts in your responses the second time through. At the end of this exercise, notice if your relationship to the situation feels even a little softer or more relaxed.

Our Horses, Ourselves

I hang my quilt from the ceiling when tacking, walking from front to back to pull the yarn through and tie it. I circle it and lift it, walk around it and crawl under it. It drapes over my arms and I bunch it up in my hands. It's like a dance, an embrace."

That embracing dance, with its stillness, pleasure, and absorption is what is too often missing in our time with horses.

"They're not pets," I remembering hearing someone say to me brusquely at one barn.

Maybe not, but horses, donkeys, and other animals (and people) are our companions, and we can learn to be less business-like and more congenial, kind, and generous—even when they are also our business.

LETTING GO OF THE STORY

During an Aikido and Horsemanship clinic with Mark Rashid, someone started to tell a long story about how difficult her horse was. He looked at the woman and said, "Don't tell a story."

During the rest of the workshop, I noticed the stories. So many of the participants were tethered to the past, to fear or frustration, and to things that were probably going to go wrong because they had in the past. Rashid's point wasn't to deny the woman a voice or a chance to share her story, but to help us understand that when we tell these negative stories we are, inadvertently, intending or planning a negative outcome because our expectations—positive or negative—often shape our experience. When our conversations are grounded in our problems, focusing on what we actually want can feel counter-intuitive or even impossible.

When I am with my horse, a client, or a student, or alone settling in to work on a dance or a piece of writing, I consciously set an intention for softness, openness, and flexibility. While riding, if I find myself breathless, bracing, pulling, or losing mental or physical balance, I try to release that resistance as quickly as possible, focusing instead on the qualities that I would like the horse to reflect back to me. By softening, breathing, pausing, slowing, smiling, and listening, we can mirror what we love and appreciate, rather than what we fear.

CHAPTER NINE

THE DANCE:
IMPROVISING AND THE
LANGUAGE OF THE HERD

"Everything in the universe has a rhythm,
 everything dances."

Maya Angelou

THE DANCER AND THE DANCE

What does it mean to dance? At first I thought it was about the steps and codified movements, about becoming adept, achieving a level of technical mastery. After years of training, though, I found that way of moving to be too dry and ambitious, too disconnected from what it was in me that needed to move. It wasn't until I was fairly well steeped in what dancer and choreographer Merce Cunningham describes as "wanting to dance or having theories about dancing, trying to dance, or having within your body the memory of someone else's dance," that I realized I was not really dancing. I was moving, but could not *feel myself* in the dancing.

Studying Laban Movement Analysis gave me a detailed and precise language for feeling and observing the expressive dynamics, spatial forms, shaping, and anatomical underpinnings of movement. I dove deep into the study of Authentic Movement with Susan Schell and Carolyn Sadeh. From them I learned about letting the body "speak," waiting to be moved by a physical impulse, and how to follow the body's movement without judgment or analysis, rather than directing or formulating it with my mind. From dancers Eiko and Koma I learned the difference between *necessary* and *arbitrary* movement. From dancer, choreographer, and teacher Bessie Schonberg, I learned about obsession—taking movement out to its wildest, raw edges—letting myself be consumed and transformed by my own dancing.

I came to understand that a deeply felt and sensuous relationship with my own body had to happen before I could have any kind of relationship with an audience. My dancing and my dances became more grounded in what was delicious and fierce *in me*. Now, in the farthest reaches of what I insist is middle age, I am still exploring and discovering, still curious, hungry, and passionate. Dancing is a practice, not a goal. The practice *is* the goal.

Returning to horses as an adult, I felt almost immediately how very little my dancing prepared me for riding. It was a bit like expecting that fluency in French would allow me to speak Russian. I felt immediately that becoming a skillful rider and horsewoman would take time. One of my trainers, Beach Bennett, said that it takes two lifetimes to become a rider. I found this humbling, and at the same time, inviting—the prospect of endless learning, stretching out before me.

As a dancer, I was curious about the kind of communication I could have with the horse when both of us were standing on the ground, and what parts of my dancing language had any meaning to the horse. Riding and groundwork are, after all, a duet form. Could the horse and I communicate through movement in a way that reflected the structure of conversation: question, answer, suggestion, and response—an evolving, somatic relationship that was both improvisational and authentic?

"There are two ways of working with the body. One is when mind informs the body; the mind is telling you what to do. That's one way of working. The other is when the body itself informs the mind; your body impulses guide you and then you do these movements and suddenly they become your movement; it's part of your creative process and you're able, from that point of view, to have experiences that go beyond words; that go beyond your conscious thinking, but are part of you. That's the thrill of working with movement." [84]

Anna Halprin

I invited some dancers from my company to come to the farm on Martha's Vineyard, saying, "Let's just see what happens." It took only a few days and we found ourselves deep in a new world of "dancing with horses." There was a freshness and excitement in being out of the dance studio, dancing in the dirt. We absorbed the barn, the smells of wood and hay, the sounds of breathing, nickers, the touch of skin so unlike ours, and all the physical details of our new dance partners, nearly ten times our size. It was immediately clear that a new dance was emerging. We called it *RIDE,* because to *ride*—whether a horse, a bicycle, or a wave—means to be engaged, balanced, and fully present.

What is the vocabulary of equine movement? Besides the walk, trot, canter, there is the flicker of an ear, the movement of the eye, a sudden bracing through the body, a tail swish, a shiver of skin, a startle, the flare of nostrils. Because we were small and fragile, unfamiliar with our big partners, we had to be wide-awake and careful. We could turn on a dime, but not so the horses. They needed more time to change direction. We partnered with each other like humans in horse costume—one dancer as the front legs, the other the back—and awkwardly tried to coordinate our movements in the walk, trot, and canter as we circled, spiraled, backed up, and moved laterally in "four-legged" choreography.

Ingrid Schatz improvising with Norman in an early rehearsal of RIDE.

As the riders warmed up with their horses, we warmed up in another part of the arena. We improvised: walking, running, turning, falling—keeping a distance and making our movements slow and small so that we didn't startle the horses. We were careful not to direct our movements *at* the horses. We practiced breaking our dancing into smaller and smaller parts, building a language of trust. We began moving closer to them, introducing each new element slowly, as we deconstructed and then reconstructed our dancing alphabet with the horses.

Gradually we began incorporating touch—soft strokes, using our voices reassuringly. These touches grew into deeper presses, using physical connection to shift the direction of the horses' movement, feeling when they pushed back or yielded away. We tried various kinds of music: quiet and then louder. Big bass sounds were more alarming to the horses than higher-pitched sounds, like violins or wind instruments. We asked the riders to experiment with letting the horses respond to us, the dancers—letting them look at us and make decisions rather than just directing their movements in the language of formal dressage. Over time the horses relaxed with us, and we felt ourselves becoming more and more an inter-species herd.

In dancing with horses, we were seeking to blend our natures, merge our physicalities, to create what musician and author Stephen Nachmanovitch calls a "moiré."

"When [the artist] has to match the patterning outside him with the patterning he brings within his own organism," he writes, "the crossing or marriage of the two patterns results in something never before seen, which is nevertheless a natural outgrowth of the artist's original nature. A *moiré*, a crossing or marriage of two patterns becomes a third pattern that has a life of its own."[85]

Our Horses, Ourselves

Norman's Dance

This marriage of two patterns is exactly what we discovered when we began to improvise with Norman and his rider Lauren Withers. Norman was a five-year-old, 17-hand, dappled gray Dutch Warmblood—at once a gangly youngster and an old soul. Lauren had a dancer's feel in riding and she, Norman, and one of our dancers, Ingrid, formed an immediate bond. They began to improvise, Ingrid and Norman standing side-by-side, then Ingrid moving sideways to the right, her hand on Norman's neck.

He yielded away from her to the right, his long legs crossing. Ingrid shifted to move to the left, and, he followed. Ingrid leaned into him: sometimes he shifted away, other times he pressed deeply back into her. She broke into a run and he chased, a light loping canter, his eyes locked on her. Lauren allowed him to move, following his responses to Ingrid, who stopped, her arms encircling the big horse's neck. Ingrid arched her back and slid down to the ground in front of his hooves. As she rolled away he stepped carefully toward her, nuzzling her. Lauren leaned forward, her hands sliding down Norman's neck, and as Ingrid rose from the ground, their hands and arms brushing by each other.

Those improvisations eventually became *Norman's Dance*—the emotional center of *RIDE* because it expressed everything about the beauty and possibility of the human-horse bond. It was truly shaped by Norman's curiosity and his willingness, his desire to be with Ingrid.

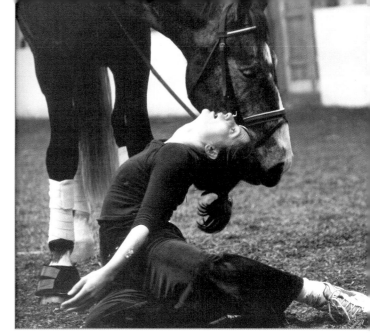

Ingrid and Norman in the performance of RIDE.

Improvising with Horses

Mia Keinanen, one of the dancers in *RIDE*, is a dance artist and academic. An avid improviser, Mia was a member of my dance company for over ten years, and has danced professionally in Europe and the United States for the past twenty. She holds masters and doctorate degrees from Harvard University in Human Development and Psychology, and currently divides her time among Moscow, Helsinki, Oslo, and Berlin, working as a research scholar, dancer, choreographer, and teacher. As a student of the neuroscience of movement, she learned that when we experience a life or death situation—falling from a height, for example—we feel a slowing of time and a sense of clarity and mental acuity. The belief is that in extreme situations our senses are quicker and that we notice more.

"It turns out they aren't," she says, "but the memory bank in our brains opens wide, and we may access all the little things that our brain usually discards as trivial, as well as remembering things that we had forgotten. I feel this when improvising, without having to jump off the roof."

She goes on to say that *improvising*—opening the mind and body to move without judgment or pre-planning—is freeing, something like *Alice in Wonderland* falling down the rabbit hole, tumbling into a world of unknown possibility. Those experiences mean that she shares connections with fellow dancers "because we share a history of bodies and brains meeting in a wholly different plane. There is no way back. I feel sad that many people go through their lives possibly never feeling that!"

Mia found dancing with horses as part of *RIDE* extraordinary. Being around big animals with brains and bodies tuned to different frequencies, she felt herself searching for new patterns.

"And when my antenna hit the horse frequency, it was a bit of an electric jolt," she says, "so strong and so delicious, once again, letting me feel different mental and bodily realities." Part of that exhilaration is the feeling of being included in the herd, feeling part of a different tribe, with the intuitive, improvisatory language of movement at its root.

Mia feels that her practice of improvisation has helped her "read people better, which makes navigating in the working world like a walk in a park. I most often know what to say to different people, and how to handle a situation so that they relax and open

Mia, Alissa, Ingrid, Dillon, Harriet, and DeAnna improvising with the Marwari mare Bijli and rider Francesca Kelly in RIDE.

up." It also opens options for her as a parent. "If I cannot get the kids in bed I try to get into an improvisational mind to find out what is needed in that particular situation. Laughter? Sternness? Calmness? I find I can get into the improvisational state easiest by manipulating my eyes: I think about the third eye, and wait for the information to come from my peripheral vision."

PLAYING WITH SENSUAL ATTENTION

 5-10 MINUTES

PURPOSE: Whether you sit at a desk all day or work in a barn, whether you are riding, gardening, cooking, or caring for a child, you can become more improvisational, sensual, and playful as you move through your day. Habits can be helpful—they prevent us from having to relearn certain activities every time we do them, like eating or walking up stairs. Habits can also be dulling and keep us from a wide-awake, experience of the moment.

When we consciously change the way that we habitually do things with our horses, incorporating variation and improvisation, and a more playful quality of connection, we help ourselves and our horses to stay fresh and curious about what we are doing together.

1. Let your feet play. Whether or not you are wearing shoes or riding boots, let the bottoms of your feet caress the floor, or snuggle into the insides of your socks. Slowly and gently flex your ankles and curl and uncurl your toes. If you have bare feet, let your feet explore and stroke each other. As you walk, let your feet soften and open to the floor like sponges.

2. When you next pick up something from the floor, slightly exaggerate and slow the action so that it becomes a whole-body movement, engaging every part of your body from head to foot. Make the movement luxurious and indulgent, dramatic even, intentionally taking more space and time.

3. Play with slowing down any movement or activity throughout your day, noticing how that changes the physical and emotional quality of what you are doing. For example, if you are folding laundry, do it more slowly than you think is possible and bring a sensuous quality to each part of the movement. Pick up, sip, and put down your cup of tea slowly and deliberately, noticing and enjoying each detail of that action.

CONTINUED ▶

4. With any activity, play with moving with either lightning-quick precision or sloth-like, with a slow, languid feeling. Notice any changes you feel as you experiment with these two extremes of time.

5. Improvise! Make a completely unnecessary gesture or movement that isn't about accomplishing a task or exercise. Let your body go! Maybe it is swaying your head from side to side or creating a shape in the air with your arm or drawing your initials with your foot. Notice how that changes your energy and perspective. Sprinkle playful, unnecessary movements throughout your day.

6. With your horse, try doing things in a different order. Start by taking him out for a walk or a graze, giving him a massage, or grooming slowly and attentively. Warm up by walking in meandering patterns around the field or arena. Let go of clock time and goals, and drop into the extravagant, pleasureable feeling of what you are doing.

Ingrid and Pony, improvising in the hay-filled round pen.

PONY DANCES

Sarah Hollis and Escorial (Pony) taught us a great deal about improvisation and the subtleties of equine body language within the herd. During our first visit to her farm, we watched her work with Pony. She held two long wands that acted as extensions of her arms. With a turn of her shoulders, a change in the angle of her hips, a shift in the direction of her focus, or a change in the tone of her voice, Pony performed curving turns, waltzing pirouettes, rearing and walking on his hind legs, and the Spanish Walk—an elegant, high, alternating extension of the front legs. Their relationship appeared both playful and serious: they were attuned to each other like a couple that has been dancing together

Our Horses, Ourselves

for years. Watching, I was reminded of horsewoman and philosopher Vicki Hearne, who says that good horse training "recognizes and engages with those things that are important to horse *being*: not only sensitivity to body language and touch, but the desire for balance, for rhythm and precision of movement."[86]

Sarah Hollis and Pony.

Sarah invited the dancers with me into the round pen. They approached Pony and patted him. She suggested that we start with some of the basic cues that Pony knew. They tried the first very simple movement—walking with him in a circle in the round pen. Pony looked at them with disinterest. After a few moments, he walked away to investigate the far end of the ring. At Hollis's cue, he rejoined them for a moment, and then took off at a gallop, head up, eyes anywhere but on the dancers. Hollis said he was confused and frustrated by the lack of clarity in the dancers' movement. Horses do not move for its own sake, she explained: their language is economical and specific to the situation.

Hollis taught us to watch Pony's eyes and the tilt of his ears, which indicated his focus and when he was

Ingrid, DeAnna and Pony trying to figure it out. (Pony has no idea what they are doing or what his response should be.)

"hooked in" with his attention. My dancers struggled with the timing and spacing of the movements, how to use their shoulders, arms, hips, and eyes to indicate subtle and specific cues for direction, speed, and distance.

Over time Pony became our master teacher, always insisting upon a meticulous degree of clarity and precision from our movements. We learned that a shoulder moving one way meant to him that he should approach, while another way meant he should bend his body in a curve with us. An extended arm and he kept his distance. The exact timing and spacing of the cue for a halt was necessary to facilitate a difficult movement like a rear or a leap forward. The language among horses in the herd is precise, a calibrated conversation with specific meanings. We dancers had to become confident bilingualists.

DeAnna and Pony listening to each other.

Ingrid and Pony sharing a moment of trust and connection.

I could see that Pony was often improvising—playfully and intentionally adjusting his movement, calibrating his steps based on his understanding of space and time, how big the movement should be, and how fast or slow. He seemed to love these games, and his mastery of this new material. I saw him judging his steps, slowing at the right moment, speeding to catch up, bending or stepping sideways to stay at a safe distance. Pony re-shaped his movement to integrate us into his herd, making spontaneous and strategic decisions about when and how to move.

> *"What is conscious improvisation? For that matter what is unconscious improvisation? The body knows what to do even if the small mind does not comprehend. The body 'dances' the music—the nerves fire and the mind notices slightly after it happens. Conscious improvisation involves strategy and responding strategically even when the outcome is unknown. A strategy of conscious improvisation might be: play only if you are listening or trust the body to respond. This melds of course the notion of conscious/unconscious improvisation."*
>
> Pauline Oliveros
> *Quantum Improvisation* (Deep Listening Publications, 1999)

Improvising and the Herd

Improvising with horses connects us powerfully to our own sense of "herd-ness." It helps us recognize and feel the rhythms and currents within our human tribe. Surprisingly, the way horses listen and respond to each other within the herd has striking similarities to the improvisational strategies used by musicians and dancers to create dynamic, attuned relationships on stage. Improvisation, whether with horses or on stage, opens us to the source of our creativity, and to ways of relating that are playful, spontaneous, and fully grounded in the present.

Dancers improvise in many ways. We may close our eyes and drop in to an inner world of image, memory, and sensation, or we may improvise with a score

Our Horses, Ourselves

of specific strategies that shape our choices during performance. For example, when working with Pony our initial score was: 1) consciously alternating movement and stillness; 2) using entrances and exits; 3) mirroring or contrasting what Pony was doing with our movement.

Strategic improvisation in music is the innovation of the composer Pauline Oliveros, whom I introduced on p. 28. Several of her Deep Listening improvisational strategies are based on the idea of listening to sounds all around you, then choosing when and how to respond to what you have heard. For example, upon hearing a sound you may respond to it *instantaneously*—as fast as possible—with either sound or movement. A second possibility is that you hear a sound or see a movement and choose to *delay* your response by a second, a minute, or any amount. (Imagine hearing a loud crash in the morning and responding to it later in the day—now that requires some sublime attention!) A third possibility is that you *anticipate* another person's sound or movement by moving or sounding just before they do. Playing with these strategies creates an electric quality of relationship and interaction with a partner or within a group. It is a time/space-based, intuitive, improvisatory, and embodied way of listening and responding to the world around us.

Watching horses respond to each other in a herd through the lens of these listening strategies was a revelatory way of more clearly translating what I was observing. It also gave me some fresh ideas about how to be with, and dance with, horses. The following strategies are a distillation and translation into movement of several of Oliveros' Deep Listening sound ideas.

Movement and Stillness

In the herd, movement happens against a palette of stillness. It is the same for humans—our movement arises from and dissolves back into stillness. For the horse, a prey animal, stillness is relative. What may look to us like "nothing happening" is actually a dense tapestry, holding cues for survival, safety, and pleasure. For the human animal living in the interactive, computer and car-bound urban world, stillness is also relative, difficult to locate in the thrum of activity and distracted busy-ness. Movement is valued over stillness, doing over being. But in fact, stillness is not desk-bound non-movement, but rather a profound, attentive immersion in listening inwardly and outwardly without moving. It is wide-awake and engaged. Cultivating an awareness of the alternation between stillness and movement, or sound and silence, helps us become more attuned to our bodies, our horses, our environment, and the present moment.

It is so easy to get caught up in the momentum of *doing*, efficiently finishing the job, and putting everything away. Intentional stillness uncouples us from mindless momentum, rushing from one thing to the next, and opens the door to *being*. Notice how finding stillness with your horse changes the quality of your time together, bringing you into simple, shared presence. How does it change you?

MOVEMENT AND STILLNESS

🕑 10 MINUTES

PURPOSE: Cultivating a movement and stillness practice helps to deepen our psychophysical awareness. Very often, we are only attuned to our moving, to activity, without attending to or valuing stillness. In my teaching, I have found that this foundational practice of alternating movement and stillness has the greatest potential for awakening awareness in dancers, riders, or clients.

Learning to rest in stillness with your horse, and to move in and out of stillness with mindfulness, is nourishing for your relationship, and profoundly settling for both horse and human. Recently my very wise horse Sanne has been asking for moments of complete stillness in our time together. Between moments of work, or at the end of a ride, we just stand together, me in the saddle, feet out of the stirrups, on the buckle, and I "fill up" with the beauty and quiet of simple presence. It is the consummate recuperation.

1. Lie down on the floor in a comfortable position. Let your body soften into the floor and notice how your breathing is part of that relationship. Let your body settle into a deep, pleasant stillness.

2. Roll slowly from your side onto your belly and again rest in stillness.

3. Slowly shift your body into a different position or shape. If your body is extended, curl or fold. Rest in stillness.

4. Continue to alternate movement with stillness, varying the duration of each. Try taking a longer, more circuitous path to change position, or move only a small amount before being still. As you practice, be aware of both how and when you move, and the deepening quality of your stillness.

5. With your horse, pay attention to the way your body shape changes as you move around him: bending, lengthening, folding, and unfolding. Feel your movement as a breathing dance. Now, intentionally integrate long moments of complete stillness into that dance. See what happens.

Instantaneous Response

Have you ever been standing next to your horse when you are both startled by a sudden loud sound or movement? Say, for example, a bale of hay falls from the loft overhead and lands with a thump just outside the stall.

Moving quickly and instinctively engages our fast-twitch muscles, activating body and brain through the sympathetic nervous system in preparation for flight or fight. Most of us can recall one of these moments—being startled by a sudden sound, a sneeze, or a terrifying moment in a movie. When we "jump out of our skins," that is an *instantaneous* response to a perceived threat, without delay or hesitation. It is a "gut reaction."

When a racer springs from the starting block at the sound of the gun or a cat pounces after a fly, there is a hot, playful "gotcha," quality to their movement. Can you think of a time when you had a lightning-quick response? Learning to intentionally respond instantaneously is a playful way of awakening the body's intuitive, dynamic responses.

In the Deep Listening workshop I took with Pauline Oliveros, thirty students stood in a circle holding hands. Oliveros instructed us to pass a hand squeeze around the circle as fast as we could. The first time around was sluggish; Oliveros urged us to let the movement impulse pass straight from hand to hand, without a detour through the thinking brain, which only slowed us down. After three or four times, the hand squeezes flew around the circle. Waking up our fast-twitch, quick-response muscles created an electric quality in our movement because we were not thinking about *what* movement to do, but only *when* to move in response to a stimulus.

The Instantaneous Response at work: As one Mustang stallion moves, the other responds immediately. This is very high-voltage movement—economic in the extreme because it may be life-or-death.

The Instantaneous Strategy helps us drop our self-consciousness and habits of choosing and editing *what* to do and *when* to do it, moving us into the world of instinctual response. Oliveros says, "The ideal attention state for the player is global, which would be characterized as readiness to move, or respond, without being committed to a particular response until the cue comes."[87]

Ingrid and DeAnna in The Stallion Tango, *part of the performance* FLIGHT. *The dance is based on images of the instantaneous responses of battling stallions.*

THE INSTANTANEOUS STRATEGY

🕐 10 MINUTES

PURPOSE: Sharpening our instantaneous responses is a good way to test how precisely we can respond to a movement cue. There are times when we do need to respond instantaneously with our horses, often when *they* are reacting instantaneously to something that has alarmed them. Practicing this strategy helps us to calibrate our response. We don't always need to have a *big* and forceful reaction—sometimes a very small, quick response is all that is needed.

1. Stand side-by-side with another person, about an arm's length apart. Look straight ahead but focus peripherally, seeing them at the edges of your vision without needing to look directly *at* them. Begin to tune into your partner: how is she standing, breathing, and what is the quality of tension or relaxation in her body?

2. Decide which of you will be the first to move. That person will move with a quick, sharp quality—like the darting movement of a frog's tongue capturing an insect. You are trying to surprise your partner, moving when she least expects it.

Our Horses, Ourselves

3. When your partner moves, move in response as quickly as you can, without hesitation or delay. Repeat this several times, without looking directly at your partner. See how precise your timing can be. The person who is initiating can vary the timing, playing with the element of surprise. The stillness *between* movements is important—can you feel the crackle of physical attention as you wait for the next cue? Think of a cat preparing to pounce, and the response of whatever it is pouncing on when it does. Notice how you feel as you play the game: any changes in energy, breathing, or emotion. This way of moving engages the sympathetic nervous system, and you may enter an exhilarated, intensely alert state. Remember, you are not thinking about making a movement that is interesting or beautiful. You are getting your mind out of the way so that you can respond instantaneously with any kind of movement.

4. After several minutes, exchange roles, continuing to refine your cues and responses.

5. With your horse, notice the times when you respond instantaneously to him. When does that happen? Is it always necessary? What I have found is that sometimes quick, reflexive movement is not needed at all but is just part of our habitual fear-based reaction to the sudden movement of a very big animal. We *do* need to be able to get out of the way or protect our horses or ourselves when the situation warrants. Skillful calibration of our responses is the key to more competent horsemanship. Observe your habits of reaction and how they define the physical and emotional relationship with your horse. Do you see those same patterns in other parts of your life?

Delayed Response

The telephone is ringing. You are in the midst of finishing an email, so you allow it to ring once, twice, and then move to answer the phone.

You are about to enter an intersection and wait for a break in the traffic before moving forward.

We may *delay* because we are evaluating when it's the right moment to act, because we are preoccupied or feel that we can "take a breath" before responding. In conversation, delaying may give the exchange a more deliberate, thoughtful, less reflexive or automatic quality. Or we may delay for effect—to create a moment of tension or drama before moving or speaking.

In the herd, a delayed response might look like this: The lead mare hears a sound, her ears twitch or her head comes up but she does not move from her spot. After several seconds, she trots to a point several yards away, looking alert. One by one the other horses move toward her, as her foal hurries to catch up.

THE DELAY STRATEGY

🕐 10 MINUTES

PURPOSE: With your horse, delaying your response to something that happens under saddle or on the ground can be a way of softening and assessing *before* acting. Obviously, this is not always possible because sometimes things have to happen quickly, for safety's sake. But our quick responses are often "on the muscle," using more force than necessary. Practicing the delay, even by a fraction of a second, creates space for a new pattern to arise in you, your horse, and your relationship.

1. Stand side-by-side with your partner, about an arm's length apart, focusing straight ahead, but seeing them peripherally.

2. Decide which of you will move first. When your partner makes a gesture, wait to respond. This delay could be a fraction of a second, several seconds, even a minute. This is not about what movement you do, but *when* you do it. For example, your partner may run her hand through her hair, and you wait several seconds before taking a step or shrugging your shoulders. *Feel* when you are moved to respond, rather than *thinking* or *reacting reflexively*.

3. Vary the length of time you delay—sometimes longer, sometime shorter—and enjoy the element of surprise! Practicing the delay strategy brings greater awareness to our habitual patterns of response, giving us more choices about how and when we react to an event or situation.

4. After several minutes, exchange roles.

Our Horses, Ourselves

In a football game we often see the quarterback delaying his release of the ball, waiting for the ideal positioning of his wide receiver. Similarly, with a delayed response, we are making an intentional, conscious choice about the timing of our reaction, allowing time to elapse—a second, several seconds, several minutes, or longer—rather than moving instantaneously. With our horses, sometimes we need to respond quickly. Other times, we may be able to soften and delay our response.

Anticipation

Sometimes we experience *anticipation* in conversation as an interruption, where one speaker jumps an idea into the mix just before another person speaks, or cuts in to get a thought out there first. Instead of waiting, we take the liberty of moving first. We frequently do this when we are driving as we prepare for a lane change or to access an exit on the highway. In sports, wrestlers circle each other, reading their opponents' body signals in order to anticipate their next move. In the kid's card game Slapjack, players try to anticipate which card will come up next so that they can slap it first in order to stay in the game.

In a performance, anticipation, like the instantaneous or delay strategies, can create tremendous tension and dramatic effect in the pause that precedes action.

These two stallions appear to be preparing to move (attack or flee) first by anticipating how and when the other will move. The horse on the right has a more forward-moving feeling, while the one on the left appears to be gathering himself in. Which will move first and how?

THE ANTICIPATION STRATEGY

🕑 5 MINUTES

PURPOSE: Anticipating can help us to avoid unsafe or frightening situations with our horses. When you can see your horse becoming anxious—say, on the crossties—while you may not yet be sure about the cause, you still change something about the scenario (moving your horse, speaking quietly and reassuringly, assessing what the trigger for his distress might be) to defuse any potential difficulty. Note: It is important to differentiate between *expecting* a problem and *anticipating* one. *Expecting* is like a little contract that you and your horse have (when "x" happens, he will do "y"). That is a *habit*, which is the opposite of the observational attentiveness and calibrated response that the strategies offer.

1. The next time that you are sitting at a table with a group of people, see if you can precede one person's action, such as reaching for the salt or taking a drink of water, by anticipating when she is going to move.

2. As you continue exploring anticipation, notice if your movements happen long before hers or if you can move just before she does. (The fun of this game is to anticipate without others noticing!)

3. Notice when you tend to anticipate and move first. Is anticipation more familiar than delay? Which of these strategies feels the most familiar?

Simultaneous Movement

A crowd of people is standing at a busy street corner in New York City at rush hour. When the light changes to green, they all set off at once—the whole group moving as a unit. That is a good example of the *simultaneous strategy*.

We see simultaneity when a cue sends a message through a whole group, and they move together instinctively, not pausing to sort out the information. Dancers prepare for unison or simultaneous movement either by counting into the music ("five, six, seven, eight") or by using their embodied listening skills to feel the exact moment to move together.

A "herd" of soccer players jumping simultaneously to deflect a ball from their team's net.

Dancer DeAnna Pellecchia and Pony feel the moment to move simultaneously.

THE SIMULTANEOUS STRATEGY

⏱ 10 MINUTES

PURPOSE: Both on the ground and in the saddle, practicing the simultaneous strategy is a very elegant way of "joining up." It is an embodied attunement through movement and breath. That means that listening to each other is not *what you think* or only *what you see*—it is a whole-body, present-centered relationship.

1. Stand next to your partner about 4 feet between you. Let your eyes take in the periphery, as well as what is directly in front of you.

2. Begin moving unhurriedly, each of you doing your own movement (as opposed to mirroring), going slowly enough that your bodies can dissolve into a single flow. See if you can move without one person being the leader. If you notice that one person is initiating, begin again, attuning to each other and sensing the moment to begin moving simultaneously.

3. Feel the moment to stop together at exactly the same time. Pause in stillness—for a short time or longer. Move together again, beginning at the same moment. Randomly change the direction you are facing, your speed, or level—each of you moving in your own way. As you move you are also trying to feel when the next simultaneous stop may come.

4. Again stop together at the exact same moment and pause. Can you begin to intuitively feel when to move and when to stop simultaneously? Continue this simultaneous moving and pausing dance for several minutes, becoming more attuned to each other as you go.

5. Now try it with your horse on the ground. When you are walking together, match each other's footfalls, as if you are one body. Halt together as a single being. Let the "stop" and the "go" that follows be a simultaneous, mutual decision. Can you let go of being the leader? Can the "go" and the "whoa" be a shared decision?

6. When riding, try moving simultaneously with your horse, not ahead of or after, but at the precise moment. Play with letting your halts and your "go" come from both of you, stopping and then moving off simultaneously, not you giving an aid and the horse responding (that would be you asking for an *instantaneous* response). Can you ride forward together from thought and breath? How much lightness and connection do you want? If you lose simultaneity, exhale and begin again.

Sarah Hollis, and Ingrid and DeAnna, with Pony. When your horse feels heard—when you are listening to him as much as he is listening to you—you will find that all forms of movement flow together.

EQUAL FOOTING

🕐 10 MINUTES

PURPOSE: So much of our time with horses is about goal-focused activity, with the human in the reliable role of director. In that uneven *doing* equation, the essential loving bond with the horse is often lost, along with the possibility for hearing what the horse may be expressing. What happens when we let go of all of that *doing* and just rest together in *being*?

1. Stand near your horse either in his stall or in his paddock (somewhere you feel safe but where you do not need to hold your horse or direct his movement). If you do need to hold a lead rope, let it loop and release any tension you feel in your body.

2. Let your feet find a deep, soft connection to the earth. Be aware of the dance of all the small muscles, bones, and joints in your feet and legs as they continually adjust their relationship with gravity. Feel the flow of your breath. Notice any sounds including your horse's breathing, belly sounds, and all of the sounds around you. Remember to let your eyes soften and absorb what is near, what is far, and what is in the periphery. If you have taken your horse out to graze, use this time to, as Eckhart Tolle says, "become friendly with the present moment," rather than space out or check your phone.

3. Staying aware of your own body, fully take in the presence of your horse, his balance, and his movement or stillness, and anything he may be expressing through his eyes, ears, body and mind. If he moves away from you or toward you, notice that without reacting, adjusting as needed. As you move in relation to your horse, feel a deep softness through your feet, legs, and hips, flowing upward through your whole body. Can you be two bodies *on equal footing*, just standing? Not an owner and her horse, not one who knows and one who does not, but just two standing bodies. Can you rest in the pleasure and appreciation of this connection? Could this become a part of your daily horse time?

PONY REDUX

After a two-year hiatus, DeAnna, Ingrid and I rejoin Sarah and Pony to rehearse for an upcoming performance. When we dance with him this time, DeAnna and Ingrid dance as one body, linking their arms around each other's waists and moving as a kind of lateral quadruped.

To our amazement, the cues are flawless, and we are able to improvise freely with Pony, sometimes using familiar patterns and other times just moving with him and allowing new movements to arise. It is almost as if we have all been attuning to each other in our imaginations during our time apart.

Ingrid, DeAnna, and Pony finding equal footing.

PUTTING THE PIECES TOGETHER

To see all of the strategies we've just discussed in play at once, observe a school of fish or a murmuration of starlings. Watch for moments of instantaneous or delayed response, anticipation, or simultaneity—all played out in a shimmering kaleidoscope of apparently choreographed but entirely improvised fluid motion.

You can also see them on a crowded street in the city, or a busy restaurant. The next time you are in a crowd of people, notice the rich weave of movement, stillness, sound, and silence around you. Become aware of when you join or separate from these ever-changing, sensual rhythms and textures. The world of movement we share is an intricate web of exchanges, starts, stops, interruptions, subtle phrasings, overlays, and emotional shadings. Becoming aware of this ongoing, improvisational matrix helps us to feel part of a larger, interactive whole, rather than like isolated, independent actors. We humans are animals—just one of an interconnected, interspecies tribe that is in a constant flux of adjustment, response, motion, and change. Attuning to the underscore of our movement interactions expands the choices of how we relate to each other, making it easier to feel our participation in the patterns that include and influence us. Observing our movement relationships through the lens of these listening strategies allows for more subtle differentiation and awareness about the ways that we are orchestrating our bodies and minds with others of all species, and the world around us.

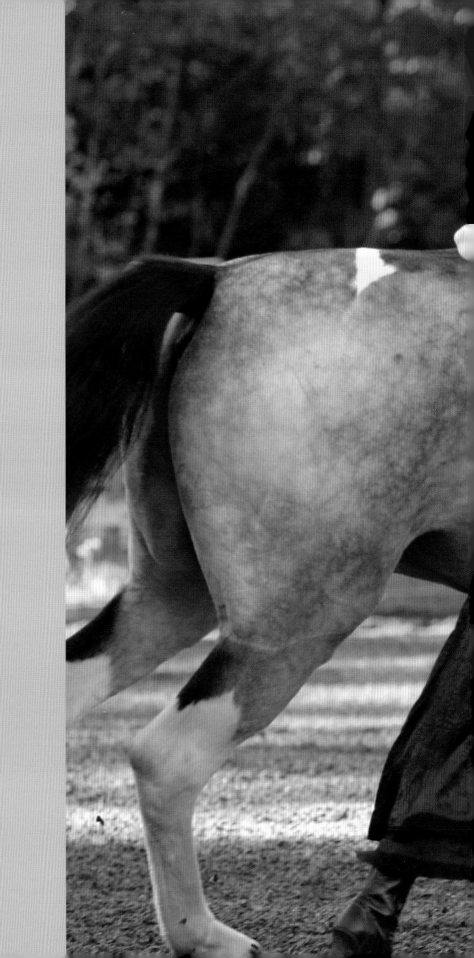

CHAPTER TEN

THE WILD ARENA:
TAMING THE BODY

Yet the earth contains
The horse as a remembrancer of wild
Arenas we avoid.

James Wright
"The Horse" from *Collected Poems*
© 1971 by James Wright and reprinted by
permission of Wesleyan University Press.

INTO THE WILD

The Bitterroot Ranch in Wyoming is 1,300 acres of mountains, high grassy meadows, gullies, and sage plains located in the Wind River Mountains near the Shoshone National Forest. My family spent one vacation there, every day riding out into the raw beauty on horses chosen for us, suited to our abilities and temperaments. Ranch owners Mel and Bayard Fox rode ahead of us, their horses big and rangy. I rode Three Dot, a Mustang mare named for the white markings on her face. Several years ago she appeared out of the wild at their ranch, badly wounded, and after many months of care, survived and flourished, becoming a favorite.

Fauve

Caw Caw, Caw Caw Caw.
To comprehend a crow
you must have a crow's mind.
To be the night rain,
silver, on black leaves,
you must live in the
shine and wet. Some people
drift in their lives:
green-gold plankton,
phosphorescent, in the sea.

Others slash: a knife
at a yellow window shade
tears open the light.
But to live digging deep
is to feel the blood
in you rage as rivers,
is to feel love and hatred
as fibers of rope,
is to catch the scent
of a wolf, and turn wild

Arthur Sze

"Fauve" from *The Redshifting Web: Poems 1970-1998*. Copyright © 1998 by Arthur Sze.
Reprinted with the permission of The Permissions Company, Inc., on behalf of
Copper Canyon Press, www.coppercanyonpress.org.

We made steep descents down banks of shuddering, skidding stones, our horses slipping and teetering with their human cargo. Suddenly, the landscape exploded open into sagebrush plains, and my stomach knotted when I saw the limitless expanse ahead. I could feel Three Dot gathering herself, ears pricked forward. Our guides moved their horses out, not just cantering, but almost galloping. The line of horses stretched out as our speed picked up—bits of dirt and stones flew up from the horse in front of me as we snaked through the narrow lanes of sage and up and over shallow hills. This was the wild arena: terrain unfolding in sheets of wonder, pages of unpredictability, astride a horse that knew only speed and forward and the surge of power and pleasure, all of us drinking the wind.

Several years ago, while wandering in the narrow streets of Stuttgart, Germany, I saw this painting in a shop window. It stopped me in my tracks. This was no tame portrait; the whole image was alive with motion, sound, and scent. The woman was naked, her horse a plunging stallion, great testicles and hind hooves pushing into the foreground of the painting, his eye white with fury or excitement, teeth bared. She held him with her bare thighs, laughing over her shoulder. I recognized the feeling of all that power and sass—horse and rider dancing, sweating, pushing into each other.

What I am seeking with horses is both that wild exhilaration and a deep communion. The horses are a way to enter the wild as an explorer, and to be, as composer John Cage

"Into the wild" with the Friesian gelding Mozart—painting by Pam White.

The wild ride—painting by an unknown Russian artist.

said, "unfamiliar with what you are doing." Mastering a skill should not tame us. Rather, it should take us out to the fierce edges of ourselves.

Try as we might to avoid it, the wild is all around us, constantly pushing at the edges of our tenuous sense of order. Our bodies are often the wildest arenas we *never* enter—unexplored sensual landscapes of unlimited possibility. The wild body is one that is allowed to dream, to move, to feel, and discover what it does not know. But too often our lives are spent taming the body, ignoring it, making it manageable, appropriate, and monitoring its borders. Often, it is only when the unexpected occurs—illness, injury, or trauma—that the body becomes feral, forcing us to enter a savage terrain of the unknown. These experiences can catapult us into a new awareness, shift our perspective, and necessitate a transformation of body and mind.

DANCING THE WILD AND THE TAME

*Dancing is not getting up painlessly like a speck of
dust blown around in the wind.
Dancing is where you rise above both worlds, tearing
your heart to pieces, and giving up your soul.*

Rumi

The Mathnavi, translated by R.A. Nicholson.
(Cambridge University Press, 1934)

One day after we had seen horses and cattle in some nearby fields, I watched as Eiko bent at the hips—spine stretched horizontal to the earth, hands and feet curved into hooves, neck elongated—and began to crop grass with her fingers. A perfect horse! Entranced, I joined her and others came as well until we had become a silent, wandering herd.

Our Horses, Ourselves

Surprisingly it is dancers—artists of the flesh—who often avoid the "wild body," packaging their physical experience in the armor of skill, perfection, and technique. I have experienced some of my most disembodied moments in technique classes, losing any sense of *why* I am moving and *what* is moving me. What I want is more heat and juice in my dancing, new ways of entering and experiencing the body and plumbing its depths, different maps for the uncharted landscapes of flesh and movement.

In a Delicious Movement workshop with dancers Eiko and Koma[88] at their home in the Catskills of New York, I found a beginning. The surprise was that it looked nothing like what I know of dance with its rich, luscious shapes and rhythms, complicated architectural phrases, unspooling across broad stretches of space. For Eiko and Koma, the wild is found in slowing movement to its geologic bones, until it becomes nearly imperceptible, revealing the body as an unfolding metamorphosis of image, sensuality, and mystery. I watched as Koma demonstrated a slow walk as he visualized carrying "a slender thread softly moved by the wind" while "a lotus bloomed from a pool of water in the hollow of his shoulder." Within a few days I felt the whole container of my dance training cracking open to reveal a sensuous world within: irresistible, dangerous, and breathtaking.

The workshop with Eiko and Koma was like spelunking in dim, violent caves, or falling in slow motion toward an unknown planet. At the end of the week, I could feel a world of sensation and possibility even in the smallest, slowest of movements.

Later on, with the horses, I could understand that riding was *not* about controlling my body or the horse's body, but *releasing* into a conjoined dance, surrendering to the tides of common movement. I felt how even in stillness, there were shared waves of breath and connection if I just let go and entered the water.

In one of my first Authentic Movement classes, I closed my eyes and fell into a vast stillness followed by an

move as fast as you can
    into a room
        into a shape
            into a sound.

now slow as grass growing
    as a sloth pulling
        limb after languorous limb
            across a canopy of time.

fast again, faster, fastest
    hand, arm, leg, hip
        everything at once.

slow, slower, slowest
    until you can
        hardly
            feel yourself
                moving
at
    all.

Paula Josa-Jones

UNTAMING THE BODY—THE QUICK AND THE SLOW

🕐 10 MINUTES

PURPOSE: Changing the speed of your movement is one way to wake up the wild mind and the wild body. When we play all the way out to the ends of the time spectrum we awaken to greater aliveness and expressivity of body and mind, and have more of our authentic, feeling selves to offer our horses.

1. Lying on the floor or sitting in a chair, rise to standing *as slowly as possible*. Feel your breathing all the way through this movement like a reliable river of support. Now return to sitting or lying down *as slowly as you can*, breathing all the way through.

2. Now come to standing, alternating moments of stillness with moments of extreme quickness—in other words, break the rise into small pieces. How fast can you move? Picture an animal that moves with lightning quickness, like a jumping spider or a leaping frog. Move *fast*, then still, move *very fast*, then still, all the way to standing and then back to sitting or lying down. How do you support this movement so that you are not just dropping to the floor, but controlling your descent? Breathe!

3. Now come to standing alternating moving with extreme sustainment or lightning quickness, and salting in moments of stillness. Don't plan the movement—let your body decide when to move slowly, when to move quickly, when to be still.

eruption, a commotion, a chaos of the body. It felt as if wild impulses were woven like ganglia between the cells, knitted into the muscles, streaming through the bones. Coming out of that experience, I wrote in my journal:

Movement like the capaill uisce—*the ferocious water horses in* The Scorpio Races[89]—*rising out of the depths to devour you whole; pulling you down to the floor of the sea and leaving you dismembered. Dances waiting to flood you when you close your eyes—irresistible and intoxicating. Entering the body this way is a leap of faith that you will survive the storms of your own movement.*

Our Horses, Ourselves

Riding can be like that—primordial and ecstatic. Like dance, it carries us out of the solemn, staid body and into the rambunctious, unpredictable terrain of the flesh. It can also be like a sitting in meditation, finding the solid banks of the river that hold the wild waters. With our horses, control isn't about bending the horse to your will, or suppressing his exuberance and curiosity. It is about learning to ride with a body that can be *both wild and still*, with a quiet, receptive mind, and a kind heart. That means being able to hold the contradictions and differences; opening to and exploring the entire expressive reach of ourselves in *all* parts of our lives.

THE HORSE ARTIST

My wife Pam has been drawing, painting, and photographing since she could hold a pencil. She grew up on the Missouri River surrounded by miles and miles of rolling hills, flatlands, bluffs, sink holes, and huge stretches of limestone banks with caves carved by the river's millennial movement. As a child, she would sit under a tree in the pasture, reading *Drinkers of the Wind* by Carl Reinhard Raswan, and dreaming of racing horses in the hot Moroccan desert. Her riding was a way to escape, to fly, to feel alive, to feel her body.

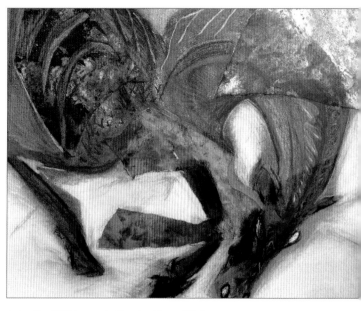

Into the Wild—painting by Pam White.

She says, "I have gone downhill and uphill, in the deep waters at my father's quarry. In and out of the gulches, the sink holes, the fields (many in cultivation with irate farmers shooting I think, over my head) and the dips, the country roads of my lime-stoned youth. All my life I have ridden to feel the wind in my ears, the horse under me, for it is where I can truly feel alive."

Pam finds the wild in her paints and in the horses that have captured her heart and her paintbrushes for the past twenty-five years. Not for her the quiet, elegant, tidiness of George Stubbs. Her horses explode across the canvas in surges of color and movement. They often push themselves up against the edges of the paper, as if they are urging the painter to go on painting them and their herds along the walls, like the horses of Lascaux in southwestern France, to which her paintings have been compared. Other paintings are like palimpsest, as if generation after generation of horses had lived on the canvas or paper. She mixes media like an alchemist.

"Some of the horses I paint are horses of ecstasy; I paint them predominantly with my right hand, not my dominant hand," she says. "Their movement comes first, and then their separate energies dictate the colors. Sometimes they are all of a piece, sometimes very individual. I feel I am receiving their dictation; that they are telling me who they are."

TRY THIS

ENTERING THE WILD ARENA OF THE BODY

🕑 15 MINUTES

PURPOSE: Listening to and moving from the body instead of directing movement from the mind is a way of entering the "wild arena" of the *now*—the rich source of our creativity and spontaneity. Feeling and responding to movement impulses arising from the body helps us better listen and respond to whatever arises moment to moment with our horses.

1. In a quiet space with room to move, lie down and close your eyes.

2. Wait to be moved. That means that instead of "I move," there is the feeling that "I am moved," without planning or directing. Your movement could be anything, from the whole body to the smallest shadow of a gesture in an extremity. If there is no movement, just wait and listen inwardly for an impulse to move.

3. When one movement subsides, wait for another impulse. Some may last a long time; others arise and subside more quickly.

4. After five or ten minutes, come back into stillness and slowly open your eyes, gradually letting your awareness move from an inner to a more outer focus.

5. As you go about your day, notice any movement impulses that arise from your body. They may be very small or bigger and more expansive. They may percolate up from the center of the body, the extremities, or even the face. Allow yourself to let those impulses out to explore and play, like little "movement children." Be curious and see what happens.

6. Now consider: How can this practice of listening to the body nourish the rest of your life? How can it open the gates to greater freedom of body and mind? How does it inform your relationship with your horse, your human family?

236

Grazing Horses

Sometimes the
green pasture
of the mind
tilts abruptly.
The grazing horses
struggle crazily
for purchase
on the frictionless
nearly vertical
surface. Their
furniture-fine
legs buckle
on the incline,
unhorsed by slant
they weren't
designed to climb
and can't.

Kay Ryan
Say Uncle: Poems (Grove Press, 2000)

Paintings by Pam White:
Top: Across the Plains
Middle: Horse with Orange Mane
Bottom: In the Sunset

The Precipice of the Unknown

When she was little, our adopted daughter Bimala was afraid. Her early child-hood had been filled with trauma. Everything seemed to paralyze her with fear. She was withdrawn, remote, quiet, a "good girl." We tried everything, but nothing could convince her that she was safe.

Then one day she came to us with a picture she had drawn in pencil. In it, an ornately patterned, winged cat was leaping down through the clouded air, paws outstretched. At the tips of its paws was a ball, and inside the ball was a tiny figure, arms waving. Beyond that were three more balls, each with a tiny figure inside. Under the picture, she had written, "Throw the fear ball away." That was the moment of realization—of her learning to intentionally toss away her fears, one ball at a time.

Sometimes the wild is a state of mind. It can appear as an unwelcome visitor—a death, a loss, an accident of some kind. At those times it can feel like we are struggling for balance, skidding down a slippery and dangerous slope. What I learned from the Mustang stallion Nelson is that when that fearful state of mind is chronic, our responses become reflexive, unthinking, and hard-wired in the body.

For a long time Nelson would not let anyone stand on the left side of his body. That side was where he had been freeze-branded by the Bureau of Land Manage-ment after his capture...perhaps something else had happened there, as well. For Nelson, his left was like the dark side of the moon—his wild side.

Many horses seem to have a "wild side" and a "tame side." We've all been on a horse that can walk by an object in one direction without flinching, and then walk back by it in the other direction and spook. I often imagine that humans are more like this than they know: that we have one side that is pretty mellow and can handle what comes along, while the other side is spooky and weird. Not exactly Jekyll and Hyde, but disconcerting nonetheless. "I'm fine." "I'm going to die." Ricocheting in our brains, back and forth, back and forth.

Over time Nelson let me move to his wild side, usually by walking around his tail and moving calmly toward his head, or turning my body and walking backward from his right to his left side. I was trying to understand his reactions by varying my approaches and movement patterns. But every time I would do it, he was nervous, as if it were the first time and my showing up on that side was a nasty surprise. His skin jumped and he spooked off, as if a bogeyman had popped out of the ground. I would touch him again, and he was still nervous, but allowed it.

One day, when it had been several weeks since I'd seen him, we went through the usual touch-and-spook dance, and then as I went to touch him again, a curi-ous thing happened. I unexpectedly felt myself drop into what I can only describe as a warm lake of calm.

"What's this?" I thought. Nelson dropped his head, exhaling. I realized that I had relaxed and let go of my expectations for him to react, and he felt that immediately.

With Nelson, standing on the "tame side," hand on the "wild side."

After my calm-warm-lake moment I could touch him all over. We were both breathing. I felt these huge blooms of love for him. For horses and humans, love is the thing that shortens and smoothes the journey from the dark side into the light.

The next time I visited Nelson it had been snowing, so things looked and felt different. Nelson was spookier than he had been for a long time. The snow was falling off the trees onto the hood of my car, making this random timpani sound, which we both found alarming. The light was refracting differently, and the footing was sloppy and icy. He allowed me to take the giant snowballs off his feet, and then we went to work. I was asking him to move on cue into a circle going left so that his wild side was the one facing me. When he circled to the right, his body was a smooth curve and he moved comfortably—either close in to me or farther out, depending on how I had asked. When he went left, his body was straight as a plank, he didn't want to look at me, and he was clearly tense and worried. It was as if he could not feel himself, or me, on that side.

The lovely thing was that after a few times around, he got quieter and calmer. That was when I hit a patch of slippery slush and made a shockingly disorganized predator movement, nearly falling, arms flung out for balance. Nelson took off. But, after a few moments, he came back and we went on. Nelson was not the momentary spook and I was not a discombobulated slip on the ice. We were both more than that. Nelson's curiosity was now bigger than his fear, and his desire for connection, maybe even his trust, was greater than his need to run. For a prey animal with PTSD, this was a huge breakthrough—his opening and realization, like the drawing my daughter had done. He had found his way out of a momentary disruption and whatever memories that might have triggered, into the *now*. Eckhart Tolle says, "The whole essence of Zen consists in walking along the razor's edge of Now—to be so utterly, so completely present that no problem, no suffering, nothing that is not *who you are* in your essence, can survive in you. In the Now, in the absence of time, all your problems dissolve."[90]

One way to become more fully aware of the present moment is to notice our transitions. As we transition from one activity to another, we may become unconscious, or "turn off" in that gap, not noticing that we are, in fact, shifting a state of both body and mind. It is helpful to see each transition as a path from one state of consciousness into another. When Nelson and I had our spooky moment, a path opened. We moved together from that moment of disorganization across a threshold into a more settled body-mind. When you are driving to the stable and get out of your car to walk to the barn, you are entering a new activity segment.[91] Noticing that and setting a conscious intention to be fully present in that shift creates the opportunity to "wake up to that moment." Setting a *conscious intention* is simply a decision to pay attention, and then getting quiet enough inside to notice what is happening in body and mind. Instead of moving unconsciously from the car to the barn, move slowly and feel your body, the anticipation of being with your horse, and orient by looking around. Entering the stable is another transition, from an outside to an inside space. Notice that change. Bringing your horse out to be groomed is another transition. Walking from the barn to the arena, beginning your ride, alternating cycles of work and rest within your ride—with each of these is an opportunity for awakening and opening, focusing on just this one and only wild moment.

THE WILD RIDE

Ann Carlson, the choreographer and performer I introduced in chapter 7, takes a broad view of dance as "any movement in time and space," and uses her choreography to challenge stereotypes and cultural assumptions. Transformation—being open to the physicality of the chicken, the cow, the dog, the goat, the whale, or the horse—is deeply woven into Carlson's way of approaching her subjects. Much of her work with animals seems to exist in a different reality, as if the audience had been ushered into an alternate, more elemental, interconnected and feeling world. Her dance *Bird* was inspired by morning television host Joan Lunden, who would do things like drive a tank, bungee jump, or be a Las Vegas show dancer in front of the camera. Carlson remembers, in particular, Lunden's awkward vulnerability and her awareness of being in an aging body attempting the role of a show dancer.

ENTERING EACH NOW

🕑 10 MINUTES

PURPOSE: Mindfully transitioning from one activity to the next, noticing the details, is a way to connect the fragments of our experience into a whole cloth of awareness. As we practice that steadiness of presence when we are with our horses, we are not unintentionally dropping out of connection, but staying present as we move from one part of our time with them to another. That makes us more reliable; they can sense that we are really there *all the time*, not mentally or physically coming and going, appearing and disappearing.

As you are sitting and reading this, perhaps you notice that you are thirsty or hungry. Maybe you want a cup of tea. Try the following and see how it changes your experience.

1. Put the book down and as you stand, be aware of the transition from one position to another. Pause. Set the intention to be aware of each part of getting your glass of water or making your tea. Do only that. Be aware of all the sensual details of the coolness of the water, the shape of the glass, or the warmth of the cup, the scent of the tea, the anticipation of the taste.

2. When you come back to reading, clearly feel each part of that transition. Set the intention to stay present in your body and aware of your breathing as you are reading. Feel the weight of the book and appreciate the details of its shape and design.

3. With your horse, set the intention to be fully aware of each part of your time together, particularly the transitions from one activity to another. If you become distracted, notice that and refocus your awareness.

4. As you transition from one part of your horse time to another, let the transition cue you to savor the physical details of your horse: the scent of his breath, the softness of his eyes, the smoothness of his coat, and the architecture of his face and body. Feel his body in your body. Let your eyes and ears take in what is around you. Be profligate with time. Rest in the moment.

"She allowed herself to be filmed learning the routines, trying to look younger, but she couldn't get the routines right and didn't have the stamina for it," says Carlson.

In *Bird*, Carlson played a part-bird, part-human dancer, exploring the human body as an animal, and then imitating an animal. It is funny, then pitiful. In her words, the bird dance was like "diving into the wreck" of being a performer who did not really want to perform any more, along with all her complex feelings about that.

Carlson and I became friends when we both were living on Martha's Vineyard with our families. One evening as we shared the things we were passionate about, she said she had always had a double-edged set of feelings for the horse: total desire and total fear. As a pre-pubescent girl she had a lot of horse longing. She lived in a city and wasn't around horses, so it was more of a perennial fantasy connected to the American West and her yearning for a more rural, wilderness environment. She and her father shared this, talking about horses and making trips to Nebraska where she could spend time on horses, hanging around with kids who thought riding was no big deal and would gallop around bareback. She told me of an association between the Western landscape and the horse's back that connected her to a deep feeling of the earth:

> *"I remember just lying back on the horse's back for a very long time with my face to the sky.... Every time I find myself drawn to an animal as an adult and want to be in the presence of that animal, I don't think, 'Oh that's from my childhood.' I'm following something that I think it is about the earth, and the earth as another being. There is some bridge there with the animal that is movement and breath from the ground."*

John Killacky, who was the performing arts curator at the Walker Art Center in Minneapolis at the time, invited Carlson to do a residency at the museum. He asked her what she would like to do. She thought about it and wondered what would it be like to spend a lot of time on horseback and what she would learn. She asked if she could find someone to teach her barrel racing, which she wanted to ultimately treat as metaphor for something else. The trick was to perform it well enough that she wouldn't make a fool of herself (or make the audience nervous for her lack of ability).

That summer she worked with Maren Luedemann, Miss Rodeo Minnesota. Luedemann agreed to work with Carlson every day for four to six hours over the course of nine weeks. As Carlson entered the subculture of rodeo, she found it weird, fascinating, and awful all at once.

"The truth of the matter was that it was very hard, and scared the shit out of me," she says. "I felt often that I was facing something very foundational about my own existence. It became about death to me. I was partnering with this horse, and entering into this agreement with this person who couldn't be further from my experience.... Even the superstitions that were woven through the culture—I didn't know that I had stepped over them until I did. 'Don't put your hat on the ground. Never lay your hat on a bed.' I loved all that. It was like being a foreign journalist."

Learning to barrel race reminded Carlson of early dance training, which can be ruthless because it goes against one's own grain. When you haven't done it before, you are continually putting your body into new positions. Luedemann even taped her heels down, "so you can see how it feels."

Carlson learned on Risky, a sixteen-year-old Quarter Horse mare that had run barrels all her life. She was completely consistent and could be trusted; Carlson didn't have to know too much because Risky knew everything.

"I just needed to know where my body was," she says, "which became harder and harder in that context. It was disorienting not to know."

Carlson built her performance primarily based on things she did during lessons with Luedemann and Risky. It was very improvised and framed as a riding lesson, with Luedemann coaching her throughout. In fact, Carlson felt afraid to do anything without her, afraid to be in the arena without her—the performance, over time, became more and more about fear and death. There were moments where she adored her horse, and at the same time she remembers thinking, "I am really dealing with my own death. Something about longing that I associated with freedom and aspiration and the earth itself. My connection to all of that translated into death. I guess I was really surprised."

Carlson and Risky ran the barrels three times during the course of the performance. A spotlight followed them around and the sound system was booming.

"I've never had an experience like that—it was so exhilarating—almost to the point that I could have just disappeared. And then I had that moment where I just fell off."

Carlson and Risky had run the last barrel and were running "home" when she had a momentary ambivalence: should she go around the arena one more time? At that moment, Risky, reading her thoughts, veered right immediately. Carlson stayed in the air, then hit the ground hard and rolled.

Ann Carlson riding Risky in Rodemeover at the Minnesota State Fair.

Risky stopped immediately, and walked over to her and just stood. There was a low "Oooooohhhhhhh!" from the audience, and then an eerie silence.

"I just stayed on all fours for a minute, the whole place was spinning, and I had no idea which way was vertical. Finally, I stood up and got back on Risky and went around the arena once, waving. I dismounted and said over the loudspeaker (because I was still wearing a microphone), 'I don't know where I am.'"

A neurologist happened to be in the audience, and immediately rushed to Carlson backstage. She says that even as the doctor was asking her name, she thought, "My name could be anything." She had these existential moments where she would think, "Who am I? What is the basis of identity? Where does it exist? Where does it exist neurologically? Where am I?" With those questions came quickly the thought that the soul is not connected to any particular information like name, place, or time, that we have an existence that is not tied to any of those familiar anchors and yet she felt very rooted in "this body that was having this confusion."

"I remember thinking, 'Where's Risky? How is she doing?' I wanted them to let me hook up with this animal that I had this experience with, and let me get some information from her," Carlson says. "I realized then that as unable [to ride] as I was, and as inexpert as I felt, I had been getting so much information from Risky...earthbound information that I was always looking for, that connection of the ground and the earth and this other way of being."

Looking back on it, Carlson now feels that in some ways the fall was inevitable, inextricably woven into the making and performing of this particular work. She feels grateful to have had the experience, and grateful not to have been injured except for the concussion and the resulting temporary amnesia.

"Whenever I tell the story there's not a moment that I don't say, 'Thank God that I can savor that experience.' There could have been other outcomes. Once I did fall off I felt a lot less afraid. It was like an old version of myself had died. The death was really the fear."

A year or so later, a museum in Los Angeles wanted Carlson to perform *Rodemeover*, and when they asked her what she needed for the performance, she responded simply, "The horse." Once Risky had been purchased and made the trip to California, not only could Carlson ride every day, but there was also delicious "hanging-out" time. She could spend whole days lying down near Risky, just being with her. In some ways, it felt like the only thing she *could* do.

"That was my wanting to trust and be trusted, wanting her to acclimate to me not as a rider, but just as another animal," Carlson says.

She felt that lying down with Risky was perhaps a kind of reenactment of the fall—a kind of bowing or supplication or a shift of power, like when a dog rolls on its belly. Sometimes Risky would ignore her, and at other times she would come and sniff her, and still others she seemed bored. Carlson found herself wanting to say to her, "Risky, can we enter into this experience together, not you as the 'barrel horse' and me as the 'choreographer,' but just these two beings.

"I loved her body—it was very compact...very muscular in the front, very 'Classic Quarter Horse'.... She had this kind of 'house pet' feeling for me sometimes: very tame, soft—surprising for something so big. [But] she would sort of quiver just at the sight of a standing barrel.

"I realized that in making up an idea, I have a relationship with that idea—a desire and longing and delight around the idea of the horse. But then when the opportunity arose to work with this one particular horse, of course her presence and personality and way of being *pushed out* the idea.... Taking that step into the real with the actual horse transformed the original idea."

Eventually Risky went back to Minnesota to a young girl who had been riding her before Carlson bought her. The girl's father called and asked if she could be persuaded to sell. It was so hard to let her go, something so deep and earthbound, but finally Carlson said yes.

"Every turn in my relationship with her was unexpected," she says now. "The depth was unexpected, my unwillingness to take power, my fear, my delight and exuberance when I rode her. It was all so deep."

THE ROGUE WAVE

Carlson's story is one of passion, curiosity, obsession even, and then a fall and the lessons learned. Several years ago I experienced a great loss—an abrupt and inexplicable tearing away of something precious and irreplaceable. For many months I could not function, and entered a deep state of shock and depression. It was as if I had fallen down the rabbit hole, into a dark, frozen world of grief and confusion. Several things happened as a result. I began to study somatic trauma healing practices, seeking a path to recovery that included the body. Another result was that it birthed a new solo called *The Traveler*. That dance asks what it means to be lost, and to find oneself in *terra incognita*, not once or twice, but throughout our lives. How do we re-map ourselves in the face of events completely out of our control? Making and performing that dance was one part of how I navigated out of the depths and found a way to move forward.

Sometimes we seek the wild. We intentionally enter the big surf with its rush of terror and thrill. Other times the wild ambushes us—like a rogue wave—and we are caught up in a maelstrom of events that can reshape our psyches, change our bodies, and disrupt our sense of self in relation to the world. We can't always choose; we may have to ride the next wave, whatever it is. Consider this though: the wildest moment may be this very one, with its fierce stillness and the steady rhythm of our own breathing.

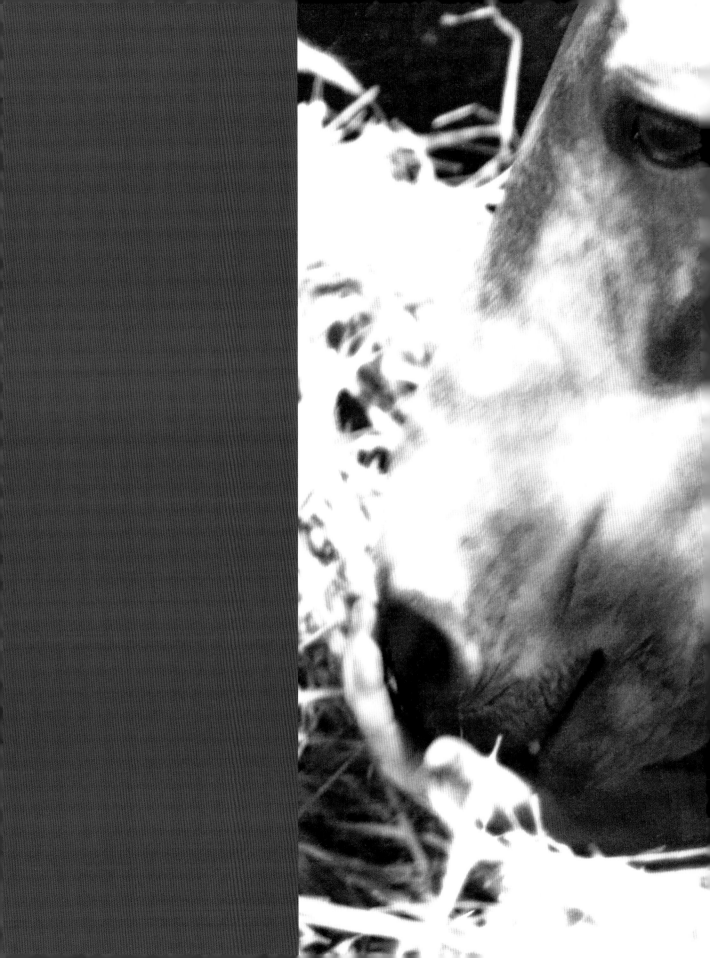

CHAPTER ELEVEN

THE LANDSCAPE OF DELIGHT: SAVORING THE BODY

My horse with a mane made of short rainbows.
My horse with ears of round corn.
My horse with eyes made of big stars.
My horse with a head made of mixed waters.
My horse with teeth made of white shell.

Anonymous

The Navajo Horse Story, Translated by Louis Watchman.
The Poetry of Horses by Olwen Way (J.A. Allen, 1995).

THE RAPTUROUS BODY

Francesca Kelly breeds and raises Marwari horses—a desert breed from the Rajasthan region of India. The horses are small, delicate, and impossibly fast with ears that curl in toward each other like lyres. In India they are used for racing, "dancing," and a sport called "tent pegging," where riders race at full tilt and attempt to spear a tent peg as they gallop past.

One day we were riding out together on Chappaquiddick: I was on a black and white Marwari stallion and she was riding her favorite mare. As we approached the beach, the horses began to prance, pulling themselves up, as if they were preparing for flight. I was nervous. I had never ridden on the beach. Francesca said that we would race. I had never raced either.

We reached the long beach and she gave her horse a nudge with her heels; the mare was off and my stallion surged. Galloping is very different from cantering. You are up in the stirrups, arched over all that thrusting power beneath you. There is the storm of flying legs below, and the wild, windy flight above. I could not believe how fast we were going. Sand was spraying. There was speed, the delicious terror of all the motion and beyond, the sea and all its power. I was grinning and my stallion was gaining. I was flying wide-awake, ecstatic. Suddenly, I wanted to win.

The body hungers for rapture, for delight. When we speak of "jumping for joy" or "bursting with excitement," we mean a joyful union of body and spirit. Perhaps though, our daily expectation for any of these states is low, and that we rarely awaken with a goal of experiencing bliss. Is this why we are drawn to horses?

Rapture is found in these moments of high intensity "peak experience," but even *more* in the sea of detail. The finer and more nuanced our perceptions become, the deeper and more nourishing our experience. Embodiment—meaning a deep sensual experiencing of our bodies—occurs in microtones and an incremental sifting into our bodies of feeling and awareness. Are joy, appreciation, and delight only destinations, or can they be the way we journey through life? Teaching the body to bloom into slow, sensuous feeling gives us access to a more reliable elation.

Our yearning to connect the landscape of our bodies to the landscapes around us is elemental, essential. One day while living on Martha's Vineyard, I walked down to the ocean, into the water and let wave after cold wave wash over me. The sea felt anesthetic, cleansing, alchemical. I wanted to *be* the water, to dissolve, to feel myself as an ocean in an ocean. The body is like a mollusk, opening and closing with the tides of sensation, emotion, and experience. Little particles of information drift across the tender and the hard parts of us, entering the secret, dark caverns, as well as settling on the worn surfaces.

DeAnna savoring the landscape of Pony's body.

As a dancer, I have no shortage of movement, but horses have moved me into the landscape of my own body in delicious and unexpected ways, and into the actual landscape as well, carrying me over fields, beaches, into the forest, and home again. Riding and spending time with horses can dissolve our imagined, habitual separateness, because we are joining the terrain of our bodies and minds with that of another being.

THE BLESSING OF THE BODY

I first heard James Wright's "A Blessing" when I was invited to participate in a "my favorite poem" program at Boston University organized by poet Robert Pinsky in preparation for the publication of his book *Americans' Favorite Poems* (W.W. Norton and Company, 2000). On the evening that I attended, an eighteen-year-old student named Iris Moon sat next to me. When it was her turn, she rose and began reading in a soft voice. I had just begun to ride again after many years, and this poem, with its confluence of horse, human, and earth, captured all of what I was feeling.

MAPPING THE BODY

🕐 10 MINUTES

PURPOSE: *Landscaping* is what dancer and choreographer Pamela Newell calls the practice of mapping the body with movement, using the floor for feedback to feel into its contours and underlying structures. With her movement, she is "mapping the body" as if it were an unknown topography of anatomy and sensation.

We can use this idea of landscaping with our horses, using our hands and body to "map" the landscape of the horse's body. What is important about this exercise is not limiting our exploration to the hands and arms, but taking the whole body into action as we touch. This is best done either in the stall or outside with someone holding the lead rope so the horse can move in response to your movement.

1. Begin by standing next to your horse, attuning with his breath. Place your hands on his body and let them settle. Be aware of any response.

2. Begin to slowly move your hands over his body with a soft, fluid touch. Imagine that you are connecting through the hair to the skin layers beneath.

3. Moving slowly, expand the size of your movements so that you are engaging your arms, shoulders, and spine, extending out into your far-reach space over his whole body. Notice his reactions to your movement.

4. As you do this, start to move your feet, stepping intentionally and rhythmically as you move around your horse. Include *your* whole body in mapping *his* whole body: legs, belly, tail, mane, and all of the familiar and unfamiliar places. Be an explorer, discovering new terrain.

5. Track his responses. Does he move away or seem nervous about what you are doing? Slow down and reduce the size of both your touches and your steps. Be sure that you are breathing.

6. From time to time, pause and lean into him, giving your weight in a way that allows him to press back toward you. Come out of that weight-sharing in a gradual way so that you and he can rebalance yourselves.

7. When you are with your horse, on the ground or in the saddle, can you feel yourselves as two interconnected, continuously moving landscapes of skin, muscle, bone, nerve, organs, fascia, and fluid?

A Blessing

Just off the highway to Rochester, Minnesota,
Twilight bounds softly forth on the grass.
And the eyes of those two Indian ponies
Darken with kindness.
They have come gladly out of the willows
To welcome my friend and me.
We step over the barbed wire into the pasture
Where they have been grazing all day, alone.
They ripple tensely, they can hardly contain their happiness
That we have come.
They bow shyly as wet swans. They love each other.
There is no loneliness like theirs.
At home once more,
They begin munching the young tufts of spring in the darkness.
I would like to hold the slenderer one in my arms,
For she has walked over to me
And nuzzled my left hand.
She is black and white,
Her mane falls wild on her forehead,
And the light breeze moves me to caress her long ear
That is delicate as the skin over a girl's wrist.
Suddenly I realize
That if I stepped out of my body I would break
Into blossom.

James Wright
From *Collected Poems* © 1971 by James Wright
and reprinted by permission of Wesleyan University Press.

In her notes to the poem Moon said, "The poem leaps at you, something moves inside—metamorphosis. It's not just a poem."[92] Zander Sulauf, a professor of English, wrote: "This is the poem that changed my life forever. Nothing compares to the excruciating beauty of this poem."[93]

"Breaking into blossom" means letting yourself be ravished by the moment, in Wright's case, experiencing an ecstasy of connection. For me at the time, the bodily, irresistibly sensuous quality of the poem and the idea of blossoming—from joy, connection, or love—was revelatory. According to Rumi translator and writer Coleman Barks: "Rumi says that merely being in a body and sentient is a state of pure rapture. Form is ecstatic."[94] Wright's poem is the perfect expression of what Barks describes as "living right at the point of contact, the nailhead of attention and spontaneity."[95]

Several years ago, my friend, the playwright and actress Laurie Carlos, walked with me onto Lucy Vincent beach on Martha's Vineyard. She stood rapt in the waning evening light, the rounding waves glistening, the air full of the rustle of sea and sand. She exhaled and said, "I cannot contain this much beauty." I did not understand until I heard "A Blessing" that I too could give myself permission to be swallowed whole by the moment.

FAR AND NEAR, FOREGROUND AND BACKGROUND

🕐 10 MINUTES

PURPOSE: Our appreciation of the landscapes that surround us is found in both the broad sweep of distant hills and the intricate, close-up details of a tattered leaf or the shining stones in the bed of a stream. Often we have a tendency to flatten our vision, seeing only into the distance, and missing what is very close to us. How does this way of perceiving foreground and background reflect your mind? Your body?

When you walk out with your horse, are you scanning the distances or are you drawn into the close up detail or both? Do you have a preference? How do imagine your horse is experiencing this landscape? Is he always focused in the distance looking for danger, or is his attention on what is near?

1. Stand outside and close your eyes. As you open them, notice what is in the foreground and the background of what you are seeing, what is near and what is far. Let your attention move from distance to close up.

2. Close your eyes and turn to face a different direction. Open your eyes and see what draws your attention—both the whole and the details.

3. When you ride out with your horse, are you always scanning the distance or focusing on what is near you? Try something different: focus intently on the details or scan the whole field of vision in all directions.

HORSES AND THE LANDSCAPE

Alice Walker titled her book of poems *Horses Make a Landscape Look More Beautiful,* a line borrowed from the Lakota holy man Lame Deer, known as the Seeker of Visions. He said, "We had no word for the strange animal we got from the white man—the horse. So we called it *sunka wakan,* 'holy dog.' For bringing us the horse we could almost forgive you for bringing us whiskey. Horses make a landscape look more beautiful."[96]

> *Look at the slight valley of the horse between haunch and shoulder,*
> *recalling its rider and the low hills between. Form never forgets.*
> *Though they are free to be real horses not obscured by work,*
> *not pull anything, they must think hard to do nothing but remember*
> *their lovers to run the low hills and dream and eat up green landscape.*

Allan Peterson
"Lasting Impressions," *All the Lavish in Common*
(University of Massachusetts Press, 2006)

Poet Allan Peterson says that the shape of the horse both invites human/ridership/participation and suggests a relationship to wildness and landscape. Of his bodily experience of the horse he says, "A bird may be a symbol for soul, but horses are sheer earthly physicality. To be on a horse, or merely to be next to them, is to experience that potent physicality as our own. Unlike animals whose anatomy is obscured, a horse's muscularity, power, and grace are directly visible."

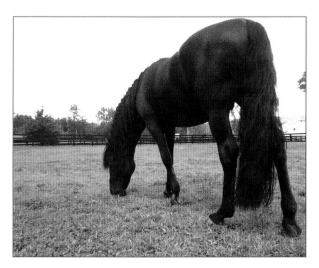

Capprichio the Andalusian stallion in the landscape.

The landscape of my stallion Capprichio's body, held by the landscapes that surround him.

LANDSCAPES INSIDE, OUTSIDE:
THE CONTAINER AND THE CONTENTS

🕐 10 MINUTES

PURPOSE: Bonnie Bainbridge Cohen states that, "Whereas our external skeletal-muscular system guides our external movement through space, organs occupy our inner space and therefore guide our internal movement. Muscles provide the visible forces for the mobility of our bones; organs provide the internal patterning that contributes to the organization and patterning of muscular coordination."[98]

Learning to feel the deep support of the organs as we ride or work with our horses on the ground helps us balance our reliance on more superficial structures. Differentiating through moving and perceiving between the "container" and "contents" of the body gives us more clarity about the source and support of our movement. Whenever we bring greater articulation and awareness to our bodies, it is expressed outwardly, and we have more of ourselves to give to our work, our families, our horses.

As you do this exercise, picture both the container and the contents—the vessel of the skin, the structure of muscles and bones *and* what it holds. Imagine your breath creating space between your organs and among your cells, and in the infinite space of your mind. Then bring that awareness to the time you spend with your horse. If it is helpful, you can refer back to the Dimensional Breathing exercise in chapter 8 (see p. 194).

1. Lie down on your back on a blanket or yoga mat. Place a folded blanket under your head.

2. Gently bring your attention to the *outer* contours of your head, slowly turning it from side to side, noticing the smoothness or bumpiness of your skull, the texture of your hair. See how detailed your awareness can become.

3. Now focus on the space inside your head, picturing the *inner* surfaces of the skull, the folds of the brain, sinus chambers, the orbits of the eyes. As you turn your head slowly from side to side, imagine that you are initiating the movement from the backs of the eye sockets or the frontal lobe of the brain.

4. Come back to stillness. Can you feel both the outer and inner structures of your head—the container and its contents? Can you feel both at once?

5. Come to standing, with your feet about 6 inches apart, knees relaxed. Turn your torso to the right, initiating from the bony structure of the shoulder girdle. Do the same movement to the left, paying attention to the outer framework of the shoulders, scapulae, sternum and ribs. Come back to center.

6. Now rotate to the right initiating from the lungs and kidneys. Let the ribs, scapulae and sternum "ride" on the movement of the organs. Rotate to the left from the lungs and kidneys, and then return to center. What do you notice about the difference between moving from the container and the contents?

7. Now consider these questions that Bainbridge Cohen asks: What is the relationship between the external movement of your body through space, the internal movement through your tissues and the movement of your mind? How are these patterns manifested in your relationships with others and with the environment?[99]

8. The next time you are riding, be conscious of your organs, letting the outer structures of muscle and bone "ride" on that internal support. As you turn or make a circle, let that movement initiate from the lungs and kidneys and notice how you feel.

Mysoke poet Joy Harjo says, "Horses, like the rest of us, can transform and be transformed. A horse could be a streak of sunrise, a body of sand, a moment of ecstasy. A horse could be all of this at the same time. Or a horse might be nothing at all, but the imagination of the wind. Or a herd of horses galloping from one song to the next could become a book of poetry."[97] In the introduction to her book *She Had Some Horses*, Harjo connects the living bodies of horses to the body of the earth. For Harjo the horse is a shape-shifter that reveals our possibility for transformation and the inseparability of our bodies from the body of the earth, what David Abram, in *Becoming Animal* (Vintage, 2011), calls, "the felt encounter between the sensate body and the animate earth."

In Joy Harjo's iconic poem "She Had Some Horses," she describes horses whose bodies "were skins of ocean water" or "bodies of sand" or "splintered red cliff." When I first met Nelson the Mustang, he was that "splintered red cliff" in Harjo's poem. Being with him at first, I felt how at times my body reflected the fractured landscape of fear and withdrawn indifference that he embodied; how we mirrored each other's uncertainties and nervousness. Over time that fearful terrain softened into new contours. After many months I noticed that the texture of my body changed when I was with him. I felt that I had been homogenized—as if my body was expressing a single harmonious tone, instead of a hundred nervous, little notes; as if my cells were aligned and humming together like the deep resonance of a meditation bell. I could feel our bodies finding each other, skin-to-skin, cell-to-cell, bone-to-bone. Later on, when Nelson would seem nervous, instead of reacting, I would settle into my body and wait. Eventually he would join me there, in the shared landscape of breath and stillness.

"Energy vibrates and forms patterns in nature.
The same patterns appear at all levels of existence.
Patterns that exist in the world outside the body
also exist in the world inside the body."

Bonnie Bainbridge Cohen

ENTERING THE BODY, ENTERING THE LANDSCAPE

As a child, friends and relatives would find Gillian Jagger in the hunt area toddling off underneath the horses, with everybody having a fit. "That's the picture of security to me, being underneath the horse looking up." Born in London, the daughter of noted sculptor, Charles Sargeant Jagger, her passion for horses goes back as far as she can remember. At the age of seven, her family moved to the country and she remembers the huge farm horses coming to cut the hay and occasionally getting to sit on a plump carthorse.

Jagger says that horses were always in her work, and that the very first drawings she made were trying to get the hang of a horse's face. She remembers being about three years old when her aunt corrected her drawings so that the neck and head didn't become all one thing. The first adult artwork that she did of horses was in the 1950s, when she was jumping horses and looking down on their necks and ears. For her the horse was a landscape, and her early horse paintings—long before her horse Faith and the project that followed her devastating death— focused in on the intricacies of a whorl on the horse's forehead, or the way in which the hairs at the crest became the mane. Painting was Jagger's way of trying to get close to and hold what she was seeing and feeling. She painted parts of horses, exaggerating them, blowing them up so that the withers would be seven feet high, six feet wide.

"Blowing up the horse's hair... It was all to make it 'feel-touching' even 'feel-hugging'...to have art for what I feel it is," Jagger says, "getting inside something where your brain, your touch, your emotion is integrated. When we create from love we're not as self-conscious intellectually about what are doing."

When I asked Jagger about the similarities of some of her paintings to her earlier sculptural works—vast expanses of cracked and rolling metal resembling ancient lava fields, she says that there is clearly a relationship between the flow of the earth and the flow of the mane and hair of a horse. In those shared rhythms she finds the common bodies of animal and earth.

Today Jagger lives with her three horses on the farm she shares with her wife. The horses lead a natural life, traveling over 10 acres, coming in and out of the barn as they please. She watches them from all the windows in the house: they gallop, roll, sleep flat out, and follow each other as they graze. For Jagger, riding is an immediate connection between her body, the horse, and the landscape. She calls it "predictable joy"—a time when she feels free of all her other pressures. When she is riding, Jagger feels that she and the horse are one, as if her legs were the horse's and all the

Artist Gillian Jagger recalls her earliest memory of a horse: being underneath it and looking up, seeing the fur of its belly above her, like a roof.

"It was as if you were sitting on the horse, looking down, so that the whole thing was blown up in front of you," says Jagger. "That was my way of trying to get close both through memory and touch."

Whorl by Gillian Jagger

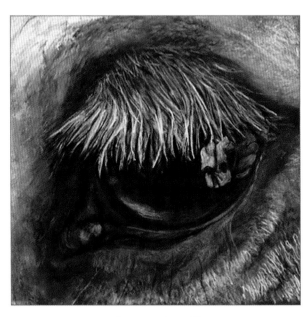

Eye Reflections by Gillian Jagger

separateness between the two bodies melts away as they become part of the terrain they are moving through and over. She says that for her, connection through the body is the clearest, most elemental way of communicating. When riding her favorite horse, she feels she is "speed-reading" with her body. Jagger has always loved that companionable communication with a horse "because the movement is the only language we have, and we feel every motion of the horse transmitting into our bodies. I suppose for me it's an extraordinary communication and at the same time the deepest kind of relaxation."

She explains: "If you are on a horse you are going at the exact pace of the horse, moving together in the landscape. The horse is your connection to everything else. If you go up and down a little hill, or through some woods, a certain effort is taken away from you, and the horse makes all that seem so wonderful without any loss of energy. You begin to absorb the energy of the horse, and it seems to join yours, so your body gets stronger and more able and runs faster and feels the wind better. When you're walking, you're putting the energy into one leg and then the other leg, and there's this ache and that pain, and with the horse all of that is moved along. When you are with your horse in the landscape you really are *in* it instead of outside of it, looking on."

Jagger's art expresses that desire to enter, to get inside: the earth, a horse, or another person. In her paintings and sculptures, she creates openings

Our Horses, Ourselves

and apertures—visual and physical points of entry that allow the viewer a more intimate and immediate access.

"It's that 'going inside' we always want to do—going inside somebody we love," she says. "If you physically hang on to somebody that you love, you still aren't *in them*. We're outside of each other; how do we get in? To go in through the physicality of it seems wildly important to me."

She feels that some artists do not want to deal with the physical—to them it is a barrier—where to her it's the whole business.

In Michael Brenson's essay "The Shock of the Real," he speaks of Jagger's unique ability to draw our attention to the connections between us. He writes: "Responding to the intensity of the call in that horse's eye, in that fallen tree, in those bones and cats, she finds links between their bodies, the human body and the body of nature. Through her sustained attention to those tracks and calls, and to the other in crisis, Jagger proposes an aesthetic space in which human beings can find one another without defenses and communicate without posturing and domination."[100]

Following the Horses *by Gillian Jagger*

When Jagger's best friend of forty years was dying of Lou Gehrig's disease, Jagger created a lead sculpture of a horse, building it around her own body, then encircling it around the body of a tree, leaving it half open. Her friend saw the finished piece in a gallery, taking her wheelchair right inside it, which Jagger hadn't even known someone would be able to do. Watching her friend sitting inside the sculpture, she thought she must have made it with just that in mind.

"She went in there like it was the completion of why that piece was made. It was the best thing I could have done between us, making visible what we shared, because she died shortly after."

THE LAY OF THE LAND

🕐 10 MINUTES

PURPOSE: Letting our bodies be fully supported by the body of the earth is a way to open to the possibility of support in other parts of our lives, including from our horses. Letting ourselves be supported means surrendering control, being willing to be vulnerable, welcoming softness. How often do you allow your horse to truly support you?

1. Stand outside on a grassy area with bare feet. Feel your feet spreading and softening into the grass, and the support of the earth beneath you.

2. Slowly curve your head forward and curl your spine—from the top down—toward the earth. Soften and bend your knees until you can comfortably place your hands on the grass, feeling the earth coming up to meet you

3. Use your arms to bring your whole body onto the grass, feeling each part of that deepening toward the earth. Roll onto your back or side and close your eyes.

4. Let yourself be cradled by the earth, feeling its textures, temperature, shape, and smell. Imagine that you are growing downward, your whole body seeping, pouring into the earth. Feel the layers of skin, muscle, and bone, as well as the weight of your organs, and the fluid within and surrounding each cell. Rest deeply into the feeling of support from the earth. Feel which parts of your body need more support. Shift your position so those places feel fully held.

5. Stay with one position until you feel that you have fully settled into that support. Alternate slowly shifting and resting into the support of the earth until you feel your whole body and mind letting go, deeply present. Trust your body to guide and inform you.

6. Slowly return to standing, pausing along the way and feeling the support of the earth as you come back into the vertical.

7. Stand quietly for a few minutes. Feel how that sense of being supported can move with you into the rest of your life. How much can you allow yourself to be supported? How can you allow your horse support you? How can you support your horse?

THE WHOLE, THE PARTS

Old Mare
Start anywhere
sunburst of whiskers
curve of lip on lip
whorl of small hairs beneath
cavernous nostrils warming air
scatter of freckles, pinkness of nose
bumpy avenue of bone and hair
to soft eyes holding what we see
soft ears cupping sounds we hear,
far and wide, far and wide.

Paula Josa-Jones

What if we experience ourselves as a landscape that is unlovely, old, broken, or flawed? Can we find a way to appreciate that as well? Aren't we more than the sum of our disparate parts? The photograph of Sophie, a former Amish workhorse rescued from a slaughter auction, expresses an unabashed homeliness that is at the same time tender and beautiful.

In "A Hand," poet Jane Hirshfield invites us to see the hand as more than its parts. In her description we can feel both the plain anatomy—"the fat's yellow pillow" and the "meander of veins"—as well as the ephemeral expression of what the hand holds: "a single, transparent question."

Sophie.

A Hand

A hand is not four fingers and a thumb.

Nor is it palm and knuckles,
not ligaments or the fat's yellow pillow,
not tendons, star of the wristbone, meander of veins.

A hand is not the thick thatch of its lines
with their infinite dramas,
nor what it has written,
not on the page,
not on the ecstatic body.

Nor is the hand its meadows of holding, of shaping—
not sponge of rising yeast-bread,
not rotor pin's smoothness,
not ink.

The maple's green hands do not cup
the proliferant rain.
What empties itself falls into the place that is open.

A hand turned upward holds only a single, transparent question.

Unanswerable, humming like bees, it rises, swarms, departs.

Jane Hirshfield
"A Hand," *Given Sugar, Given Salt*
Copyright © 2001 by Jane Hirshfield.
Reprinted by permission of HarperCollins Publishers

Is it possible that in differentiating and deeply *feeling* the separate parts of our bodies, our experience, and our environment, we can discover a greater wholeness? Differentiation is a confluence of perception and awareness. For example, in slowing down, we can more clearly feel the details of how movement passes from one part of the body to another. With attention, we are more aware of our breathing, how our weight is balanced, where there is softening or stiffness, and which parts of the body call to be included. We feel subtle differences in temperature, weight, and texture. We become more like the horse with his precise and specific sensitivity of skin, senses, and nervous system. We sense the subtle orchestration of our body's structures and the distinct phrasing and sequencing in our movement—the way it winds in continuous pathways from one part of the body to another. Each time we move, we have an opportunity to discover more, to enter and explore the body from a different perspective.

AWAKENING THE PARTS

🕐 10–20 MINUTES

PURPOSE: This sequence of exploratory movements can help you to become more refined in your perceiving of the parts and the whole of your body—and your horse's body. We begin with the hands, so fundamental to our lives that there is a specialized part of the brain specific to their functioning. This exercise also reminds us of the reciprocity of touch—that as we touch we are also being touched.

1. Either sitting in a chair or lying on the floor, close your eyes and bring your hands together, letting them gently explore each other, investigating the details of their inner and outer form. Take your time. Then let your hands rest together, just holding one another.

2. Now let that slow, careful exploration move up the wrists, forearms, elbows, upper arms, and shoulders. Notice any places that want more attention and support and stay with those places, then begin to travel back down the arms, re-visiting each place, and ending again with the hands.

3. Let the arms and hands relax by your sides. After a few moments, begin moving the fingers, letting the movement travel from the hands into the wrists, elbows, and up to the shoulders. Go slowly.

4. Be curious about the differences in sensation between the right and left arms and the way each arm moves in space. Which arm do you feel most clearly? After a minute or two, let the arms rest by your sides.

5. Take some time to gently and carefully explore your horse's lower legs, paying particular attention to feeling for subtle differences in shape as you move from each hoof, to the fetlock, cannon bone, and knee. Be aware of when you are using your fingers, your palms, even the backs of your hands. See how much detail you can "read" with your hands. This is not a massage, you are not fixing anything. You are teaching your hands to become more refined and literate about the details of this part (or any other parts) of your horse's body.

6. Now *very* slowly stroke down each leg from knee to hoof. The movement should take about a minute. How carefully can you *just listen* with your hands? Can you let go of needing to figure anything out?

As we grow older, we can become more adept at savoring, more open to relishing our physical experience, even as it becomes more challenging. When I see my hands in the mirror I am startled, momentarily horrified. How did my mother's veined and wiry hands come to be attached to the ends of my arms? I look at the landscape of my body now and wonder what has been lost and what remains to be found. What am I learning in this exact moment from my body? I think it is to feel myself in the interstitial spaces—the unexamined, subtle strata of sensation and movement, always present beneath the more familiar outer form of what I plainly see.

WHAT IS CONCEALED, WHAT IS REVEALED

The body is the bonehouse where all our experiences and history are stored. Like the hidden anatomy of the earth, or the unplumbed depths of the sea, much of the body is unseen, unknown, undiscovered. The body does not give up its answers all at once, but has secret rooms that reveal themselves over time. It is an archive: a breathing reservoir of thought and movement, earth and air, above and below. What I have found in my six decades living in the changing landscape of my body is that listening to the body is a lifelong practice of listening, moving, stillness, being moved. Discovering what is hidden within requires a kind of contemplative echolocation, a rigorous and patient practice of listening and responding.

Many of the artists I interviewed while working on this book spoke of the horse as shelter—a place of refuge and comfort. Shelter holds our vulnerability, protects us from the storms, and allows us to rest. Shelter is improvisational, too: We shape it as we travel, as we move from place to place, continually constructing little yurts, stables, hollows, and quiet corners in which to stay before moving on. We shelter in the companionship of our families and friends, animal and human. If we pay attention, horses help us open the sheltering, hidden rooms to our embodiment and enlightenment. They can show us how to rest in the sanctuary of the moment.

> *"Whenever I quiet the persistent chatter of words within my head, I find this silent or wordless dance always already going on—this improvised duet between my animal body and the fluid breathing landscape that it inhabits."*
>
> David Abram
> *The Spell of the Sensuous* (Vintage Books, 1997)

RESTING IN THE LANDSCAPE

🕐 15 MINUTES

PURPOSE: The practice of *savasana* in yoga is one of deep rest. In savasana, we "come home" to ourselves. Practicing savasana brings balance into the nervous system, helping to unravel and release stresses. In this rebalancing, we gain resilience and greater capacity to handle whatever arises at home, at work, or in the barn.

1. Place a mat or blanket on the floor in a quiet place. You may wish to have a pillow or bolster under your knees, a folded blanket to support your head and another blanket to cover yourself with to prevent becoming chilled.

2. Slowly and gently bring yourself into position for savasana: lie on your back with your eyes closed and your arms resting comfortably at your sides.

3. Let your awareness settle into the body, withdrawing your focus from the external world. Follow the breath with a soft, open awareness. Notice any sensations in the body or thoughts in the mind.

4. Rest. Allow the landscape of your body to be held by all that surrounds you, sinking deep into its support.

5. After about ten minutes, gently open your eyes, gradually bringing yourself into a more external focus.

6. Slowly roll onto your right side. Rest there for several moments, and then use your arms to bring yourself to a sitting position. Take as much time as you need to move from resting into a more active state.

7. Can you allow this rest to continue to support you throughout the day? You may want to introduce small recuperative rests or changes in focus throughout your day. This might be going outside for a few moments, making a cup of tea, lying down to let the body settle into gravity, or putting on some music. What is your body asking for in this moment?

Primary Sources

It was mud season: early spring and Parents' Weekend at the Putney School in Vermont where my daughter was a student. The weather was warm, with hints of green on the trees and crocuses poking out of the soggy mats of last year's fallen leaves. Skin of all shades peeked out from under skirts and shorts as students entered the big auditorium. Emily Jones, the head of school, spoke about the end of the year, and what came next, offering strategies for weathering the change.

"Here is what I want you to do," she said. "See something beautiful every day and let it make you happy."

In an age of digital preoccupation, Jones was suggesting something different: that we learn to experience the earth and our bodies as primary sources, finding happiness in the world outside and connecting it to an inner world of body, mind, perception, and experience. She wanted us to be moved and changed by what we see, hear, touch, smell, taste. She wanted us to *break into blossom*.

When we transform our own bodies through movement or imagination, when we blend our own sensuous physiology with the earth or our horses, we become a feeling, expressive landscape among other feeling, expressive landscapes. This merging and blending is the path to a deep peace and pleasure, where we abandon our separateness and become connected; woven into the fabric of our world. And in that shared terrain we can more easily feel and find each other...and ourselves.

This painting by Franz Marc is how I want to feel with my animal and human friends and family: like an animal among animals—revealed and included, held in the curves and angles of the landscape and its creatures.

"I am trying to intensify my feeling for the organic rhythm of all things, to achieve pantheistic empathy with the throbbing and flowing of nature's bloodstream in trees, in animals, in the air."

Franz Marc
Letters of the Great Artists—From Blake to Pollock
edited by Richard Friedenthal (Thames and Hudson, 1963)

ENDNOTES

1 *Mary Midkiff, She Flies Without Wings: How Horses Touch a Woman's Soul,* (Delta, 2001), 33.

2 Bonnie Bainbridge Cohen, excerpt from 2014 US BMCA (Body-Mind Centering Association) Pre-Conference entitled "New Frontiers in Body-Mind Centering."

3 http://www.intensiveinteraction.co.uk/

4 Phoebe Caldwell, *From Isolation to Intimacy: Making Friends without Words,* (Jessica Kingsley Press, 2007), 35.

5 Ibid. p. 29.

6 Temple Grandin, *Animals in Translation: Using the Mysteries of Autism to Decode Animal Behavior,* (Scribner, 2005), 9.

7 Caldwell, p. 26.

8 Bonnie Bainbridge Cohen, Foreword by Susan Aposhyan, *Sensing Feeling and Action*, (Contact Editions, 1993), vii.

9 Charles Badenhop, *The Language of the Somatic Self* (www.seishindo.org/language.html, http://www.seishindo.org/2009/02/20/the-language-of-the-somatic-self/).

10 Monty Roberts, *Horse Sense for People*, (Viking, 2001), 33.

11 Bonnie Bainbridge Cohen, An Introduction to Body-Mind *Centering* (http://www.bodymindcentering.com/introduction-body-mind-centeringr).

12 http://www.bodymindcentering.com/introduction-body-mind-centeringr

13 The artist (Bruce Nauman) joins composer-performer Meredith Monk for a discussion with the exhibition's co-curators, Walker Director Kathy Halbreich and Hirshhorn Museum of Sculpture Garden Chief Curator Neal Benezra. Walker Art Center Auditorium: "Discussion of Horses." Interview courtesy of Jill Vuletich and the Walker Art Center.

14 Stephan Nachmanovitch, *Free Play: Improvisation in Life and Art*, (Tarcher, 1991), 143.

15 Mary Oliver, *Listening to the World*, *On Being*, an interview with Krista Tippett, (http://www.onbeing.org) February 5, 2015.

16 Nachtmanovitch, 45.

17 Stuart Brown, *Play: How it Shapes the Brain, Opens the Imagination and Invigorates the Soul*, (Avery, Reprint Edition, 2010), 217.

18 Eckhart Tolle, *A New Earth: Awakening to Your Life's Purpose*, (Penguin, 2008), 301.

19 Paul Patton, *Zoontologies: The Question of the Animal*, (The University of Minnesota Press, 2003), 85.

20 Vicki Hearne, *Adam's Task: Calling Animals by Name*, (The Akadine Press, 1982), 110.

21 Ibid, 110.

22 Erik Herbermann, *A Horseman's Notes*, (Core Publishing, 2003), 16.

23 Hearne, 163.

24 http://www.theclickercenter.com

25 The *Tellington Method*® was first created four decades ago as a system of animal training, healing, and communication that allows people to relate to animals in a deeper, more compassionate way—a way that furthers inter-species connection and honors the body, mind, and spirit of both animals and their people. The Tellington Method utilizes a variety of techniques of touch, movement, body language, and visualization to affect behavior, performance, and health, and to increase an animal's willingness and ability to learn in a painless and anxiety-free environment (http://www.ttouch.com/aboutLinda.shtml).

26 Herbermann, 41.

27 David M. Guss, *The Language of Birds: Tales, Texts, & Poems of Interspecies Communication*, (North Point Press, 1985), ix.

28 Ibid, xi.

29 Eckhart Tolle, *A New Earth: Awakening to Your Life's Purpose*, (Plume/Penguin Group 2006), 276.

30 Gillian Jagger, *Gillian Jagger, Elvehjem Museum of Art Exhibition Catalog*, (University of Wisconsin, 2003), 38.

31 David DeSteno, *"The Morality of Meditation,"* The New York Times, July 5, 2013.

32 Equine Advocates is a national non-profit 501(c)(3) equine protection organization founded by Susan Wagner in 1996. Since that time, they have rescued thousands of equines—including horses, ponies, donkeys, and mules—from slaughter, abuse, and neglect. In 2004 they established Equine Advocates Rescue & Sanctuary, a 140-acre facility in upstate New York, and in 2006, they established a Humane Education Center where visitors can learn about equine issues, responsible horse guardianship, and humane horse handling (equineadvocates.org).

33 Greg Levoy, *Callings: Finding and Following an Authentic Life*, (Three Rivers Press, 1997), 65.

34 Ibid. p. 197.

35 Marion Laval-Jeantet, an interview with Aleksandra Hirszfeld for *Art + Science Meeting*, 2012 (http://artandsciencemeeting.pl/?page_id=306&lang=en).

36 Dans les veines del'artiste coule le sang de cheval (In the veins of the artist runs the blood of the horse), Centre Presse, March 2011(http://www.centre-presse.fr/article-145011-dans-les-veines-de-l-artiste-coule-le-sang-de-cheval.html).

37 Carolee Schneemann, a multi-disciplinary artist, transformed the definition of art, especially discourse on the body, sexuality, and gender. Her work is characterized by research into archaic visual traditions, the body of the artist in dynamic relationship with the social body (http://www.caroleeschneemann.com/bio.html).

38 Marina Abramović is a Serbian and former Yugoslavian artist based in New York, a performance artist who began her career in the early 1970s. Her work explores the relationship between performer and audience, the limits of the body, and the possibilities of the mind (http://en.wikipedia.org/wiki/Marina_Abramovi%C4%87).

39 Susan Richards, *Chosen by a Horse: How a broken horse fixed a broken heart,* (Harcourt Inc., 2006), 2.

40 Ibid. p. 3.

41 Marc Bekoff, *The Emotional Lives of Animals*, (New World Library, 2007), 126.

42 David Abram, *Becoming Animal: An Earthly Cosmology,* (Pantheon Books, 2010), 61.

43 David Bohm, *Wholeness and the Implicate Order*, (Routledge, 2002), 190.

44 Anna Wise, *The High Performance Mind*, (Tarcher, 1997).

45 Bonnie Bainbridge Cohen (http://www.bodymindcentering.com).

46 Andrea Olsen and Nancy Stark Smith, *"Mapping Transformation: Talking About Inspiration and Expiration,"* Contact Quarterly, Summer/Fall 2009, Volume 34, Number 2.

47 Bonnie Bainbridge Cohen, ed. Don Hanlon, *Body-Mind Centering, Groundworks: Narratives of Embodiment*, (North Atlantic Books, 1997), 19.

48 Ann Cooper Albright, *Choreographing Difference*, (Wesleyan University Press, 1997).

49 Karen Diego, "Touch Revolution: Giving Dance," *Contact Quarterly*, Winter/Spring 1996, Volume 21, Number 1.

50 Laban Movement Analysis (LMA) is a method and language for describing, visualizing, interpreting, and documenting all varieties of human movement. It is one type of Laban Movement Study, originating from the work of Rudolf Laban and developed and extended by Lisa Ullmann, Irmgard Bartenieff, Warren Lamb, and many others. Also known as Laban/Bartenieff Movement Analysis, it uses a multidisciplinary approach, incorporating contributions from anatomy, kinesiology, psychology, Labanotation, and many other fields. It is used as a tool by dancers, actors, musicians, athletes, physical and occupational therapists, psychotherapy, peace studies, anthropology, business consulting, leadership development, health and wellness, and is one of the most widely used systems of human movement analysis today (http://en.wikipedia.org/wiki/Laban_Movement_Analysis).

51 The Polyvagal Theory links the evolution of the vertebrate autonomic nervous system to the emergence of social behavior. According to Dr. Stephen Porges, "It is the contradiction between conceptualizing the components of the autonomic nervous system either as a "balance" or "hierarchical" system that served to motivate me to develop the polyvagal theory. In the traditional view of the autonomic nervous system, the sympathetic nervous system is involved in fight and flight

Our Horses, Ourselves

responses, while the parasympathetic nervous system is involved in health, growth, and restoration. However, the polyvagal theory actually describes two defensive systems. In addition to the defensive system of fight-flight, which everyone is familiar with, that requires sympathetic and adrenal responses, the theory identifies a second defensive system. The second system is linked not to mobilized fight-flight behaviors, but to immobilization, shutting down, fainting, and dissociating." Dr. Stephen Porges, interviewed by Serge Prengle, Somatic Perspectives on Psychotherapy, November 2011.

[52] Stephen W. Porges, *Neuroception: A Subconscious System for Detecting Threats and Safety*, (Zero to Three, 2004), 20.

[53] In mammals this system, when triggered as a defense system, inhibits breathing, slows heart rate, and promotes defecation. However, in safe contexts, this system supports the subdiaphragmatic organs to promote health, growth, and restoration. The sympathetic nervous system when triggered as a defense system functionally inhibits the old vagus and stops digestion and diverts energy resources from visceral support, such as digestion, to mobilization (http://stephenporges.com/index.php/ scientific-articles/publicationss/28-somatic-perspectives-on-psychotherapy-interview).

[54] Somatic Experiencing is a form of alternative therapy aimed at relieving the symptoms of post-traumatic stress disorder (PTSD) and other mental and physical trauma-related health problems by focusing on the client's perceived body sensations or somatic experiences (https://en.wikipedia.org/ wiki/Somatic_experiencing).

[55] Peter Levine, *Freedom from Pain: Discover Your Body's Power to Overcome Physical Pain,* (Sounds True, 2012), 1.

[56] Temple Grandin, "Thinking the Way Animals Do: Unique Insights from a Person with a Singular Understanding," (Western Horseman, November 1997), 140-145.

[57] http://tintageltalent.com/training.html

[58] *Authentic Movement* is a meditative, intuitive improvisational movement practice involving a mover and a witness. With eyes closed, maintaining a focus on bodily sensation and the flow of consciousness, the mover allows herself to be moved by whatever impulse is arising in the body.

[59] https://grabcad.com/library/cube-with-diagonals

[60] Deep Listening® is a philosophy and practice developed by Pauline Oliveros that distinguishes the difference between the involuntary nature of hearing and the voluntary selective nature of listening. The result of the practice cultivates appreciation of sounds on a heightened level, expanding the potential for connection and interaction with one's environment, technology, and performance with others in music and related arts.

[61] Pauline Oliveros, *Roots of the Moment*, (Drogue Press, 1998), 86.

[62] Pauline Oliveros, *Software for People: Collected Writings 1963-80, (*Smith Publications, 1984), 139.

[63] *Teach Yourself To Fly*, the first of Pauline Oliveros's many "Sonic Meditations," shows just what it is that sets Oliveros apart from dozens of superficially related American composers. The Sonic Meditations were largely developed in the early 1970s and explored many times in real musical situations before ever being written down. Some are simpler than others, such as *Re Cognition*, which reads only: *"Listen to a sound until you no longer recognize it."*

[64] Porges, p. 12.

[65] In the *levade*, the horse raises its forehand off the ground and tucks the forelegs evenly, carrying all weight on the hindquarters, to form a 30–35° angle with the ground. This angle makes the *levade* an extremely strenuous position to hold, and requires a great effort from the horse.

[66] Flying by Foy is the most prolific and widely respected theatrical flying service in the world. The company was established in 1957 by Peter Foy, whose innovative techniques and patented mechanical inventions revolutionized theatrical flight in the second half of the twentieth century, elevating the ancient practice of stage flying to a modern art form. Foy provides flying effects, Aereography®, and state-of-the-art automation for Broadway shows, London's West End, ballet and opera companies, concert tours, industrial events, feature films, and television productions worldwide (http://www. flybyfoy.com/).

[67] Karen Pryor, *Don't Shoot the Dog: The New Art of Teaching and Training*, (Bantam Revised edition, 1999).

[68] The piaffe is a dressage movement where the horse is in a highly collected and cadenced trot, in place or nearly in place. Collection is when the horse carries more weight on the hind legs. The horse's body is drawn into itself so that it is like a giant spring (http://en.wikipedia.org).

69 Natalie Goldberg, The *Long Quiet Highway*, (Bantam, 1994), 148.

70 Sonja Swenson, *Choreographer, performer and conceptual artist, Ann Carlson – Borrowing their breath*, Gender News, June, 6, 2011 (http://gender.stanford.edu/news/2011/choreographer-performer-and-conceptual-artist-ann-carlson-borrowing-their-breath).

71 Anat Baniel, *Move into Life*, (Crown Archetype, 2009), 20.

72 http://en.wikipedia.org/wiki/Robert_Ellis_Dunn

73 http://www.ted.com/talks/vs_ramachandran_the_neurons_that_shaped_civilization.html - 277000

74 Meg Daley Omert, *Made for Each Other:The Biology of the Human-Animal Bond*, (Da Capo Press, 2009), 94.

75 Eckhart Tolle, *A New Earth: Awakening to Your Life's Purpose*, (Penguin, 2004), 233.

76 John Berger, "Why Look at Animals," *About Looking*, (Pantheon 1980), 11.

77 Ibid, 6.

78 Bonnie Bainbridge Cohen, *Sensing, Feeling and Action*, (Contact Editions, 1993).

79 http://www.bodymindcentering.com/course/fluid-system

80 Ibid.

81 Linda Tellington-Jones with Rebecca M. Didier, *Dressage with Mind, Body and Soul: A 21st Century Approach to the Science and spirituality of Riding and Horse-and-Rider Well-Being*, (Trafalgar Square Books, 2013), 251.

82 Andy Merrifield, *The Wisdom of Donkeys: Finding Tranquility in a Chaotic World*, (Walker & Company, 2010), 4.

83 http://www.sedona.com/What-Is-The-Sedona-Method.asp?aff=SHWFM1

84 Anna Halprin, dancer, PhD (with permission).

85 Stephen Nachmanovitch, *Free Play: Improvisation in Life and Art*, (Penguin Group, 1991), 79.

86 Vicki Hearne, *Adam's Task: Calling Animals by Name*, (The Akadine Press, 2000), 110.

87 Pauline Oliveros, *Software for People*, (Smith Publications, 1984).

88 Since 1972, Japanese-born choreographer/dancers Eiko and Koma have created a unique and riveting theater of movement out of stillness, shape, light, and sound (http://www.eikoandkoma.org).

89 Maggie Stiefvater, *The Scorpio Races*, (Scholastic Press, 2011).

90 Eckhart Tolle, *The Power of Now: A Guide to Spiritual Enlightenment*, (New World Library, 1997), 43.

91 This exercise is based on the "Segment Intending" exercise in *Ask and it is Given: Learning to Manifest your Desires* by Esther and Jerry Hicks, (Hay House,2004), 217.

92 Robert Pinsky and Maggie Dietz, *Americans' Favorite Poems*, (W.W. Norton and Company, 2000), 302.

93 Ibid, 302.

94 Jalal Al-Din Rumi, *A Year with Rumi*, Edited and Translated by Coleman Barks, (Harper One, 2006), 5.

95 Ibid, 6.

96 Alice Walker, *Horses Make the Landscape More Beautiful*, (Harcourt Brace and Company, 1984), xiii.

97 Joy Harjo, *She Had Some Horses*, (Thunder's Mouth Press 1983).

98 http://www.bodymindcentering.com/blogs/the-role-of-the-organs-in-movement

99 http://www.bodymindcentering.com/blogs/fluidity-of-movement-in-health-and-vitality

100 Michael Brenson, "The Shock of the Real" in *The Art of Gillian Jagger*, (Elvehjem Museum of Art, University of Wisconsin-Madison, 2003).

BIBLIOGRAPHY

Abrams, David. *Becoming Animal: An Earthly Cosmology.* New York: Pantheon Books, 2010.

Abram, David. *The Spell of the Sensuous,* New York: Vintage Books, 1997.

Bainbridge Cohen, Bonnie. *New Frontiers in Body-Mind Centering®.* Excerpt from 2014 Body-Mind Centering Association Pre-Conference.

Bainbridge Cohen, Bonnie. *Sensing Feeling and Action.* Contact Editions, 1993.

Bainbridge Cohen, Bonnie. Ed. Don Hanlon, *"Body-Mind Centering, Groundworks: Narratives of Embodiment.* Berkeley: North Atlantic Books, 1997.

Baniel, Anat. *Move Into Life.* New York: Crown Archetype, 2009.

Bekoff, Marc. *The Emotional Lives of Animals.* Novato, CA: New World Library, 2007.

Berger, John. *"Why Look at Animals," About Looking.* New York: Pantheon, 1980.

David Bohm, *Wholeness and the Implicate Order.* London: Routledge, 2002.

Brown, Stuart. *Play: How it Shapes the Brain, Opens the Imagination and Invigorates the Soul.* New York: Avery, 2010.

Caldwell, Phoebe. *Delicious Conversations: Reflections on autism, intimacy and communication.* East Sussex, UK: Pavilion Publishing, 2012.

Caldwell, Phoebe. *From Isolation to Intimacy: Making Friends without Words.* Philadelphia: Jessica Kingsley Press, 2007.

Coetzee, J.M. *The Lives of Animals,* Princeton, NJ: Princeton University Press, 1999.

Cooper Albright, Ann. *Choreographing Difference.* Fishers, IN: Wesleyan University Press, 1997.

DeSteno, David. "The Morality of Meditation," *The New York Times.* July 5, 2013.

Diego, Karen. "Touch Revolution: Giving Dance," *Contact Quarterly,* Winter/Spring 1996, Volume 21, Number 1.

Eddy, Martha, RSMT, CMA, Ed.D. *Somatic Inquiry and the Socially Conscious Body,* Hampshire College, October 15, 2012. <https://youtu.be/mVwJg1quwpk>

Natalie Goldberg. *Long Quiet Highway.* New York: Bantam, 1994.

Grandin, Temple. *Animals in Translation: Using the Mysteries of Autism to Decode Animal Behavior.* New York: Scribner, 2005.

Grandin, Temple. "Thinking the Way Animals Do: Unique insights from a person with a singular understanding." *Western Horseman,* November 1997.

Guss, David M. *The Language of Birds: Tales, Texts, & Poems of Interspecies Communication.* New York: North Point Press, 1985.

Hearne, Vicki. *Adam's Task: Calling Animals by Name.* New York: The Akadine Press, 1982.

Hearne, Vicki. *Nervous Horses.* Austin: University of Texas Press, 1980.

Herbermann, Eric. *A Horseman's Notes.* London: J.A. Allen & Company Ltd., 1999.

Jagger, Gillian. *Gillian Jagger: Elvehjem Museum of Art Exhibition Catalog.* Madison: University of Wisconsin, 2003.

Harjo, Joy. *She Had Some Horses* New York: Thunder's Mouth Press, 1983,1997.

Hicks, Esther and Jerry. *Ask and it is Given: Learning to Manifest your Desires* Carlsbad, CA: Hay House, 2004.

Hirshfield, Jane. *Given Sugar, Given Salt.* New York: Harper Collins, 2001.

Hirshfield, Jane. *Lives of the Heart.* New York: Harper Perennial, 1997.

Hirshfield, Jane. "Thoreau's Hound: On Hiddeness." *Brick, A Literary Journal,* (Issue 68, Fall 2001), 18.

Horowitz, Alexandra. *On Looking: Eleven Walks with Expert Eyes.* New York: Scribner, 2013.

Katz, Jon. *Rose in a Storm.* New York: Random House, 2011.

Laval-Jeantet, Marion. Interview with Aleksandra Hirszfeld for *Art + Science Meeting,* 2012. <http://artandsciencemeeting.pl/?page_id=306&lang=en>

Lee, Li-Young. *Book of my Nights.* Rochester, NY: BOA Editions, 2001.

Lepkoff, Daniel. "Contact Improvisation or What happens when I focus my attention on the sensation of gravity, the earth and my partner," *Contact Improvisation,* Nouvelles de Danse, No 38/39. <http://www.daniellepkoff.com>

Levoy, Greg. *Callings: Finding and Following an Authentic Life.* Steelville, MO: Three Rivers Press, 1997.

Levine, Peter. *Freedom from Pain: Discover Your Body's Power to Overcome Physical Pain.* Sounds True, 2012.

Marc, Franz. *Letters of the great artists – from Blake to Pollock*. Ed. Richard Friedenthal. London: Thames and Hudson, 1963.

Matt, Daniel C. *The Essential Kabbalah: the Heart of Jewish Mysticism*. New York: HarperOne, 1996.

Merrifield, Andy. *The Wisdom of Donkeys: Finding Tranquility in a Chaotic World*. New York: Walker & Company, 2010.

Midkiff, Mary. *She Flies Without Wings: How Horses Touch a Woman's Soul*. Guildford, UK: Delta, 2001.

Nachmanovitch, Stephen. *Free Play: Improvisation in Life and Art*. Los Angeles: Tarcher, 1991.

Oliveros, Pauline. *Deep Listening: A Composer's Sound Practice*. iUniverse, 2005.

Oliveros, Pauline. *Quantum Improvisation: The Cybernetic Presence*. Deep Listening Publications, 1999.

Oliveros, Pauline. *Roots of the Moment*. Drogue Press, 1998.

Oliveros, Pauline. *Software for People: Collected Writings 1963-80*. Smith Publications, 1984.

Oliveros, Pauline. *Sonic Meditations*. Smith Publications, 1974.

Olsen, Andrea and Nancy Stark Smith, Nancy. "Mapping Transformation: Talking About Inspiration and Expiration," *Contact Quarterly*, Summer/Fall 2009, Volume 34, Number 2.

Omert, Meg Daley. *Made for Each Other: The Biology of the Human-Animal Bond*. Boston: Da Capo Press, 2009.

Patton, Paul. *Zoontologies: The Question of the Animal*. Minneapolis: The University of Minnesota Press, 2003.

Pert, Candace. *Your Body is Your Subconscious Mind* (audiobook). Sounds True Incorporated, 2004.

Peterson, Allan. *All the Lavish in Common*. Amherst: University of Massachusetts Press 2006.

Pinsky, Robert and Maggie Dietz, Maggie. *Americans' Favorite Poems*, New York: W.W. Norton and Company, 2000.

The Poetry of Horses. Collection by Olwen Way. London: J.A. Allen, 1995.

Porges, Stephen W. *Neuroception: A Subconscious System for Detecting Threats and Safety*. Zero to Three, 2004. <http://www.frzee.com/neuroception.pdf>

Porges, Stephen W. <http://stephenporges.com/index.php/scientific-articles/publicationss/28-somatic-perspectives-on-psychotherapy-interview>

Pryor, Karen. *Don't Shoot the Dog: The New Art of Teaching and Training*, New York: Bantam Revised edition, 1999.

Ramachandran, V.S. <http://www.ted.com/talks/vs_ramachandran_the_neurons_that_shaped_civilization.html - 277000>

Richards, Susan. *Chosen by a Horse: How a Broken Horse Fixed a Broken Heart*. New York: Harcourt Inc., 2006.

Roberts, Monty. *Horse Sense for People*, New York: Viking, 2001.

Rumi, Jalal al-Din. Translated by Coleman Barks, *The Essential Rumi*, New York: HarperOne, 2004.

Rumi, Jalal Al-Din. Translated by Coleman Barks, *The Illuminated Rumi*. New York: Broadway Books,1997.

Rumi, Jalal Al-Din. *A Year with Rumi,* Edited and Translated by Coleman Barks, New York: Harper One, 2006.

Ryan, Kay. *Say Uncle: Poems*. New York: Grove Press, 2007.

Stiefvater, Maggie. *The Scorpio Races*. Danbury, CT: Scholastic Press, 2011.

Swenson, Sonja. "Choreographer, performer and conceptual artist, Ann Carlson—Borrowing their breath." *Gender News*, June, 6, 2011.

<http://gender.stanford.edu/news/2011/choreographer-performer-and-conceptual-artist-ann-carlson-borrowing-their-breath>

Sze, Arthur. *The Redshifting Web*. Port Townsend, WA: Copper Canyon Press, 1998.

Taylor, Alan. *The Murmurations of Starlings*, The Atlantic, February 28, 2014.

Tellington-Jones, Linda with Didier, Rebecca M. *Dressage with Mind, Body and Soul: A 21st Century Approach to the Science and Spirituality of Riding and Horse-and-Rider Well-Being*. North Pomfret, VT: Trafalgar Square Books, 2013.

Tolle, Eckhart. *A New Earth: Awakening to Your Life's Purpose*. New York: Penguin, 2008.

Tolle, Eckhart. *The Power of Now: A Guide to Spiritual Enlightenment*. Novato, CA: New World Library, 1997.

Walker, Alice. *Horses Make the Landscape More Beautiful*. New York: Harcourt Brace and Company, 1984.

Walker, Alice. *Shambala Sun*. January 1997.

Williams, Margary. *The Velveteen Rabbit*. New York: Harper Festival, 2006.

Wise, Anna. *The High Performance Mind*. Los Angeles: Tarcher, 1997.

Wright, James. *Above the River: The Complete Poems*. New York: Farrar, Strauss & Giroux, 1990.

Xenophon, *The Art of Horsemanship*. New York: Dover Publications, 2006.

SPECIAL THANKS

I thank my life partner and wife, Pam White, who is a brilliant inspiration and artist, and the one who illuminates every part of my life. Her beautiful photographs and paintings and her deep critical wisdom are woven into every part of this book. Thanks to my daughters, Bimala and Chandrika, who remind me daily why I was put on this earth, and who teach me about the resilience and tenacity of love. A very special thanks to my godson Jacob and his parents, Jo-Ann Eccher and Derrill Bazzy, for their kindness and grace of spirit, which inspire me daily.

I am deeply grateful to each of the horses I have loved, touched, ridden, and danced with: Djuma, Deborah, Tilly, Mia, Goliath, Tsjalling, Judge, Roy Wind, Bijli, Nelson, Sanne, Capprichio, Amadeo, and Escorial. I thank all of the horses that I have touched and who have touched me.

Thank you Jeffrey Anderson for your stunning photographs of our work with Sarah Hollis and Pony; for capturing the heart of "horse dancing" with DeAnna and Ingrid. Thanks to Sarah Hollis of Tintagel Talent, who taught us how to dance with Pony. Your work is an indelible part of our work. Thank you to my beautiful, valiant horse dancers: DeAnna Pellecchia, Ingrid Schatz, Alissa Cardone, Harriett Jastremsky, Mia Keinanen, Dillon Paul, and aerialist-dancer Paola Styron. These women are possessed of wild, inquisitive minds and bodies that give their dancing a gorgeous, fierce, and always unpredictable edge. Working with them has been and is a privilege and joy.

Thanks to all of my horse dancing friends: Annie Hale Long, Sally Apy, Francesca Kelly, Megan Perley Graham, Lindsay Garcia, Jessica Benjamin, and Lauren Withers, all of whom became essential and elegant parts of RIDE. Special thanks to my videographer and friend Ellen Sebring, and to our always steady and supportive stage manager, Jayne Murphy. Thanks to Flying by Foy and Jamie Leonard for their generous support of our aerial work. Thank you to Bill Hamilton and Peter Kross of Kross Creek Farm for your beautiful and kind care of my horses for the past ten years. And thank you to Susan Fieldsmith, for hearing my horse dreams and helping me realize them.

A very deep thanks to my friends and mentors Bonnie Bainbridge Cohen and Pauline Oliveros, whose work continues to profoundly inspire and shape my dancing, writing and investigation. Thanks also to my teachers and trainers, Linda Tellington-Jones, Alexandra Kurland, Mark Rashid, Ellie Coletti, Brandi Rivera, and Tom Davis.

Thank you to all of the artists and practitioners that I interviewed for this book including Jeffrey Anderson, Ann Carlson, Eiko and Koma, Joy Harjo, Jane Hirshfield, Gillian Jagger, Marion Laval-Jeantet, Jon Katz, John Killacky, Maria Wulf,

Mariah MacGregor, Pauline Oliveros, Allan Peterson, Susan Richards, Sheila Ryan, Allen Schoen, Paola Styron, Linda Tellington-Jones, Pam White, Meredith Monk and Robert Wrigley. My deep thanks to Henri Ton for his beautiful photographs of Mustangs in the wild.

Thanks to the many wise voices who have inspired me, including David Abram, Michael Brenson, Alexandra Horowitz, David Guss, Candace Pert, Stephen Nachtmanovitch, Dr. Peter Levine, Dr. Stephen Porges, Andy Merrifield, Charlie Badenhop, Paul Patton, Vicki Hearne, Meg Daley Omert, Temple Grandin, Phoebe Caldwell, and Eckhart Tolle.

A special thanks to Karen Magid for her generosity in inviting us to create and perform RIDE at the Red Pony Farm in West Tisbury, Massachusetts. Thanks to Carol Paterno and Mistover Farm in Pawling, New York, for allowing us to use their arena and install a gigantic truss to fly Ms. Styron and create FLIGHT. Thank you to Susan and Karen Wagner at Equine Advocates in Chatham, New York, for the privilege of working with Nelson, and to Lynn Cross of Little Brook Farm in Old Chatham, New York, for her enthusiastic support of our creation of *All the Pretty Horses* with her students and valiant rescued horses.

Thanks to Michael and Patricia Snell and Libby Kaponen for their early help in finding the heart of this book, and to the Bogliasco Foundation and the Corporation of Yaddo for the invaluable gift of time and space to write and dance.

Finally, my very deepest thanks to Trafalgar Square Books, and Martha Cook and Caroline Robbins, for shepherding this book to completion, and to my extraordinary editor, Rebecca Didier, who has winnowed my writing into something far finer than I could have managed without her patience, wisdom, and guidance.

INDEX

275

Our Horses, Ourselves